IMAGES
of America

ARDEN

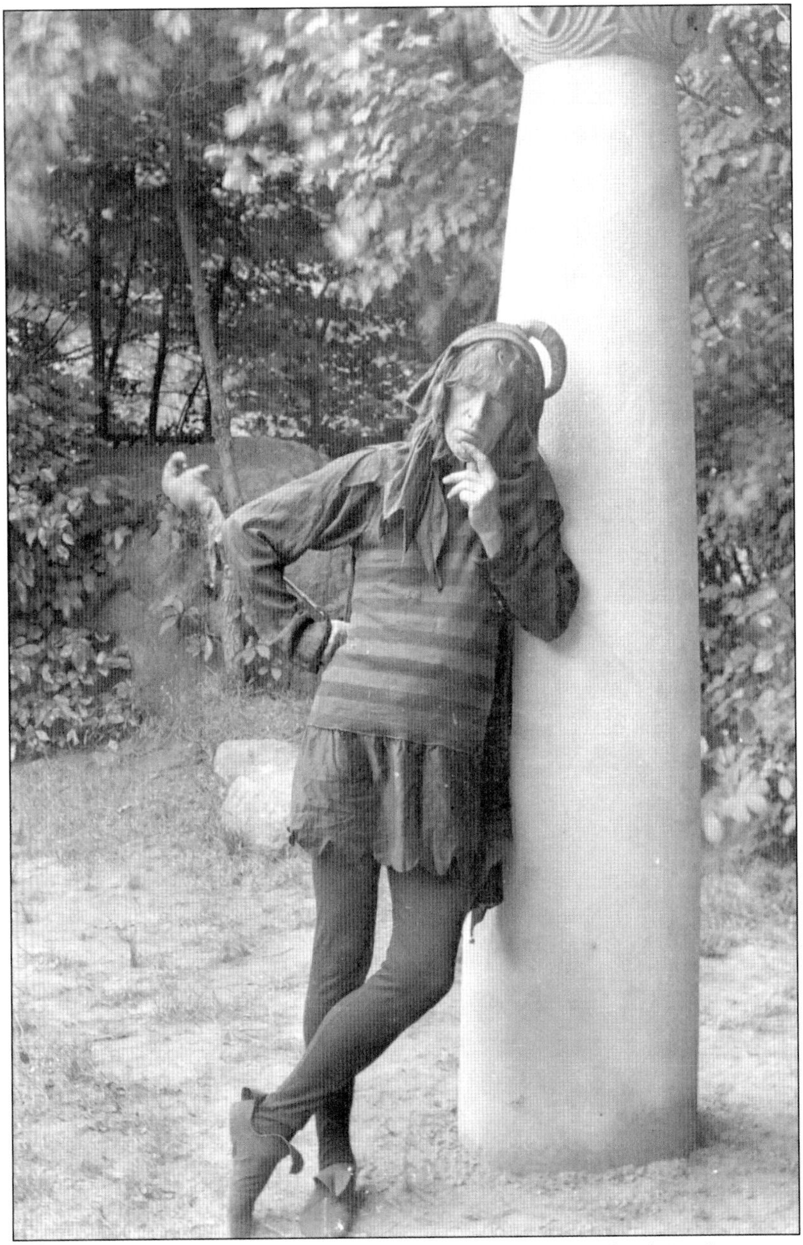

Frank Stephens is seen here in 1915 at Arden's Field Theater in the role of Touchstone, a character from William Shakespeare's play *As You Like It*. In the mid-1890s, Frank Stephens and Will Price were members of a Shakespearean club that met Monday evenings at Stephens's Filbert Street home in Philadelphia. Other Arden residents known to have been members were Carson Davenport, Haines Albright, and Ella Reeve Ware. The village of Arden is named in tribute to that acting club.

ON THE COVER: Pete Helbrun takes his turn at the anvil in this Arden Forge publicity photograph taken around 1928 by Earl Brooks. Both residents and non-residents worked in the forge through the years, but the exact number is undocumented. The candleholder to the left can also be seen on page 99. (Courtesy of the Arden Craft Shop Museum.)

IMAGES
of America

ARDEN

Mark Taylor

ARCADIA
PUBLISHING

ISBN 978-0-7385-8559-8

Published by Arcadia Publishing
Charleston, South Carolina

Printed in the United States of America

Library of Congress Control Number: 2009938008

For all general information contact Arcadia Publishing at:
Telephone 843-853-2070
Fax 843-853-0044
E-mail sales@arcadiapublishing.com
For customer service and orders:
Toll-Free 1-888-313-2665

Visit us on the Internet at www.arcadiapublishing.com

This book is dedicated to three extraordinary people that I've met along the way, Caroline Stephens Holt, Alex Roberts, and the late Peggy Stephens Aumack. The hours I've spent in your company sifting through photographs and listening to your stories of early Arden are some of the most enjoyable I've ever known.

About the Organization

The Arden Craft Shop Museum, to which all proceeds from the sale of this book are directed, is a not for profit 501 C-3 dedicated to preserving the history of the three villages of Arden, Ardentown, and Ardencroft. Established in 2004, the museum is located in Arden's historic Red House. For further information on the museum and the Ardens, please visit our website at www.arden.delaware.gov. Unless otherwise credited, all images appear courtesy of the Arden Craft Shop Museum.

Contents

ACKNOWLEDGMENTS

Whether it is for a well-timed word of encouragement or a critical bit of information, my debts for this book are many. First and foremost, my thanks to Betty Elzea and her husband, the late Rowland Elzea, whose 1976 Delaware Art Museum exhibition, "The Pre-Raphaelite Era 1848–1914," started me on this path many years ago. In Arden, thanks are due to all past and current members of both the Arden Craft Shop Museum board of directors and the Archives Committee. Specific thanks are due to Lew Aumack, Maria Burslem, Orlando Cole, Terry Colgan, Mike Curtis, Rick Darke, Linda Eaton, Heidi Nasstrom EvansRobert and Joyce Foote, Miriam Gerstine and her husband the late Milton Gerstine, Sally and Aaron Hamburger, Bob Helms, Hardy Hoegger, Carolyn Lewis, Herbert Mason, Lisa Mullinax, Morris Potter, Hugh Roberts, John Saltmarsh, Bernie Schwab, Sonia Sloan, Bruce Smith, Annde Solway, Sadie Somerville, and Catherine Talley. And finally, a shout from the rooftops to my partner Michele McCandless, who somehow in these past three months cheerfully managed to keep the home fires burning.

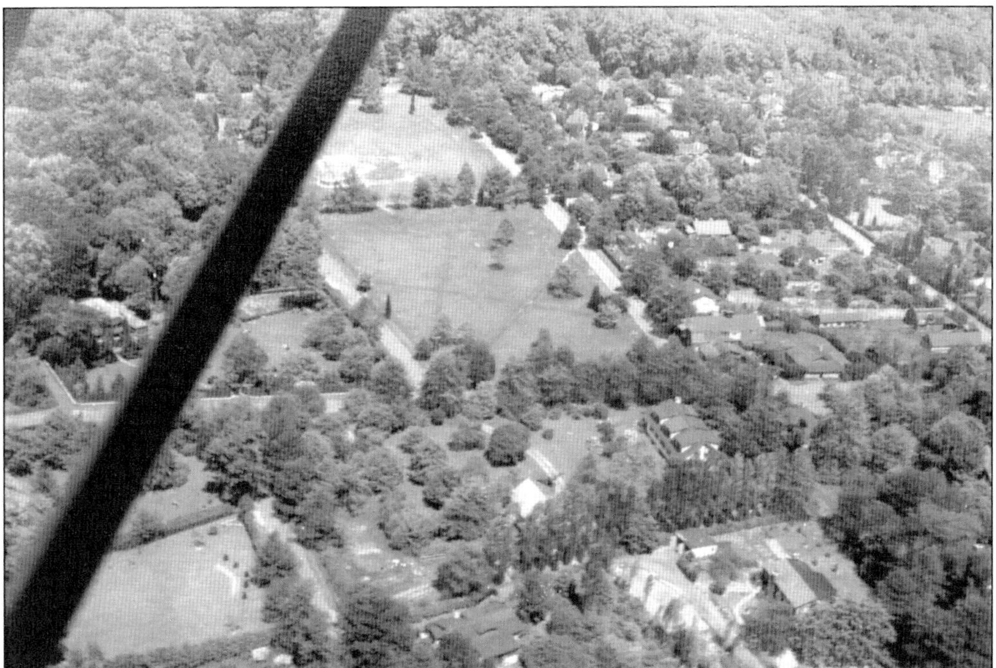

Considerably more wooded in 1936 than it was in 1900, this aerial view of Arden shows the layout of the Village Green on the Woodland side of the community.

INTRODUCTION

On Saturday, June 15, 1895, a group of 13 men crossed the Delaware border by train from Philadelphia's Broad Street Station to begin one of the most unusual and colorful campaigns in the state's history. For those who happened to be on the streets of Wilmington, Hockessin, or Newark on that particular day, the group would have been hard to miss; all were conspicuously dressed in blue flannel shirts and ties, brown canvas leggings, and military style hats. Many of the men also carried knapsacks stuffed with campaign literature. And if that wasn't enough to draw attention to themselves, their leader, a 36-year-old sculptor by the name of George Frank Stephens, or Frank as he was known, was likely strumming a banjo and singing campaign songs he had written for the occasion, songs with lyrics like:

> Oh! We want the earth again,
> For the landless sons of men,
> We know how to get it back and keep it there.
> Get the landlords off your backs,
> With our little single tax,
> And there's lots of fun ahead for Delaware.

The group that day, which also included Frank Stephens's 8-year-old son, Don, was the advance guard for what would become known as the Delaware Invasion. All of the men were disciples of the American economist Henry George. Their objective was to convince Delawareans to support candidates in the 1896 election who were sympathetic to George's philosophy of the single tax, which George defined in his book *Progress and Poverty* (1879) as a tax on the value of land, exclusive of improvements. Reminiscent of Englishman Gerrard Winstanley's 17th century Diggers, Georgists, as they were known, asserted as their fundamental principle that "all men are equally entitled to the use of the earth." They proposed therefore, that "no one should be permitted to hold land without paying to the community the value of the privilege thus accorded, and from the fund so raised, all expenses of government should be paid."

The Delaware Invasion quickly became a national campaign. Henry George declared himself "heartily in favor of the Delaware campaign," and traveled to Wilmington several times to speak, as did such single tax luminaries as Louis Post and Edward McGlynn. Foot soldiers came from across the country, living for weeks at a time at campaign headquarters in Wilmington's McVey Building at Eighth and Market Streets while they made their way across the state. By one account, in the first four months of campaigning, single taxers held 469 meetings, with 1,060 addresses by 76 speakers, before an estimated audience of more than 90,000. They were "aflame with enthusiasm" according to Stephens, and indeed, from the writings that have come down to us, many seem almost religious in their zeal. "If it wins," proclaimed one campaigner, "it will mark the greatest turning point in the political, industrial, and economic development of this country, perhaps of the civilized world." Delaware authorities apparently, however, felt otherwise. As in the battles over free speech and the right to assembly simultaneously being waged in Philadelphia, many campaigners, including Frank Stephens, were sentenced to time in the Dover jail. In Stephens's case, he received a pardon from the governor before serving out his full sentence of 30 days.

After a year of educational effort and campaigning, in September 1896, Georgists finally announced their slate of candidates, standing behind the candidate for governor, Dr. Lewis Slaughter, and others who had pledged themselves sympathetic to their cause. In the end, however, Delawareans appear to have agreed with the editor of the *Delaware Daily Republican*, who declared single tax "the greatest humbug of the day." Of the 38,000 votes cast that year, little more than 3 percent voted Single Tax. Although *Justice* (the single tax newspaper) tried to portray the results in a positive light, it is hard not to view the election as a resounding defeat for the Single Tax Party. It is here, however, in the wake of that defeat, that the story of Arden begins.

According to an unpublished lecture by Frank Stephens, he and Will Price met through one of Stephens's Philadelphia decorative arts firms. Most likely it was through his architectural terra cotta business, Stephens, Armstrong, and Conkling, which was located at 46th Street and Gerard Avenue in Philadelphia, and whose products were used by architects nationwide. Price was an early convert of Stephens to "the great gospel of the land for the people," and a participant in the Delaware Invasion. Now it was he, in turn, who came to Stephens and proposed "an arts and crafts colony that should let us work out the truths of both Henry George and William Morris." After looking at a property in New Jersey, which they ironically lost to a land speculator, the two men decided upon a 162-acre farm outside of Wilmington, Delaware, 2 miles east of the Delaware River near the crossroads of the village of Grubb's Corner. The farm was owned by David Derrickson and it was purchased by Frank Stephens on June 12, 1900, for $9,000, $2,500 paid in cash and the remainder held in mortgage, which was later acquired by Joseph Fels, heir to the Fels–Naptha soap fortune and a passionate crusader for social justice. On October 17, 1901, Stephens conveyed the land under trusteeship to Will Price (who also that year founded the Rose Valley community), Frank Martin, a member of Price's architectural firm, and himself. Will Price designed the land plan for the village, much of it inspired by the English Garden Cities movement, and leaseholds were rented by the three trustees for a period of 99 years to "whomever applies for it." From this land rent, all taxes levied by the state and county were to be paid with the remainder turned over to the town to be spent for communal purposes. Village government was by a monthly town meeting in which all residents shared an equal vote, men, women, and children, regardless of age.

Although Will Price and Frank Stephens's experiment was designed to prove the "truths of Henry George and William Morris," ultimately it became much more. As Frank Stephens described it "we are making in Arden, slowly and thoroughly a working model of a civilization which shall know more of the beauty of life and art than we have found in the world outside." Arden's early pioneers truly believed they were participants in the creation of a new society. Hopefully some of their vision and passion is portrayed within the pages of this book.

One

Arden's Founders

The problem of the arts and crafts and the problem of the land are complementary to each other.

—C. R. Ashbee

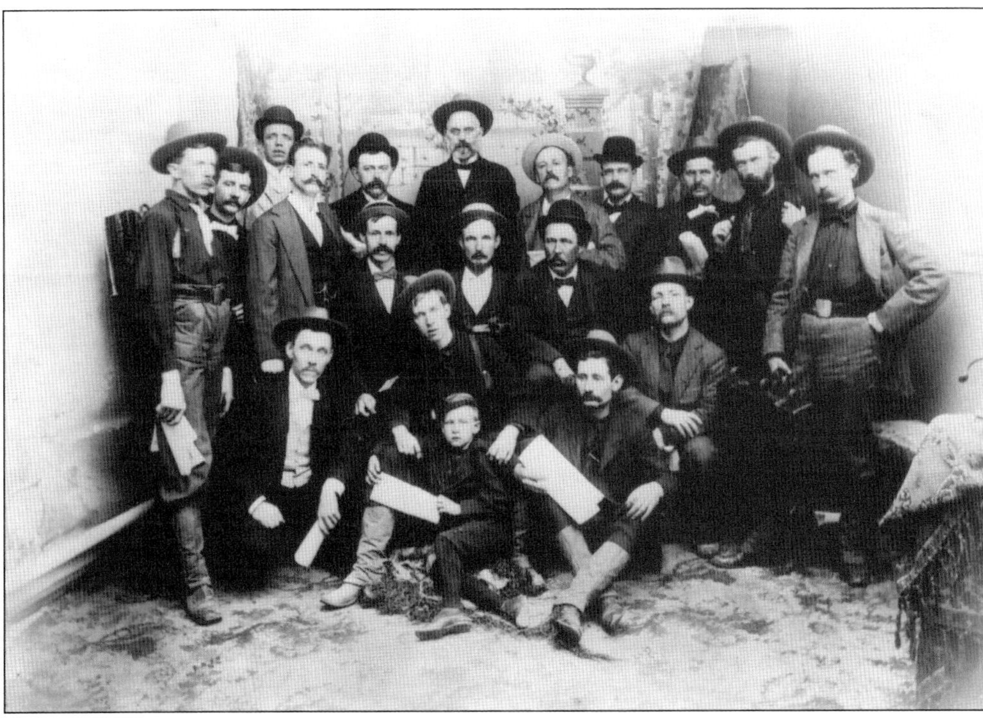

Members of the Delaware Single Tax Campaign pose here on June 16, 1895, for a photograph to commemorate the first weekend of the Delaware Invasion. Frank Stephens is in the first row, center, with his son, Don, seated in front of him. Although Will Price is absent from the photograph, according to the single tax newspaper *Justice*, he participated in the first weekend's campaign as well.

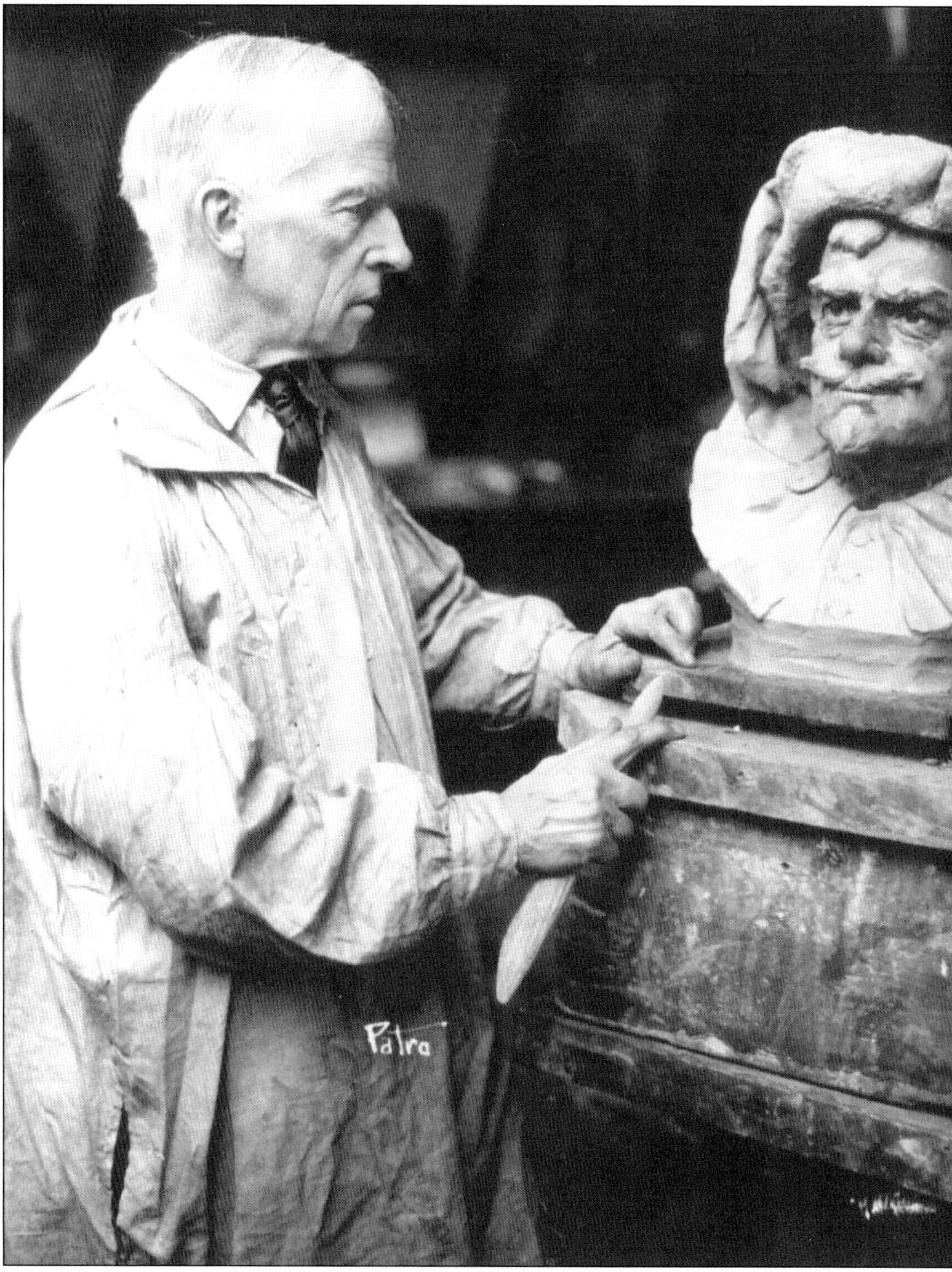

Frank Stephens is shown here around 1925 putting the finishing touches to his sculpture of Haines Albright as Sir Toby Belch, a character from Shakespeare's *Twelfth Night, or What You Will*. Frank Stephens studied sculpture at the Pennsylvania Academy of Fine Arts under Thomas Eakins. Shortly after leaving the Academy, he worked with Alexander Milne Calder on the statues for Philadelphia's City Hall, as well as a number of private commissions. He founded the architectural terra cotta company Stephens, Armstrong, and Conkling, and the decorative arts firm Stephens, Cooper, and Company. It was through his work at these decorative arts firms that he met the architect Will Price.

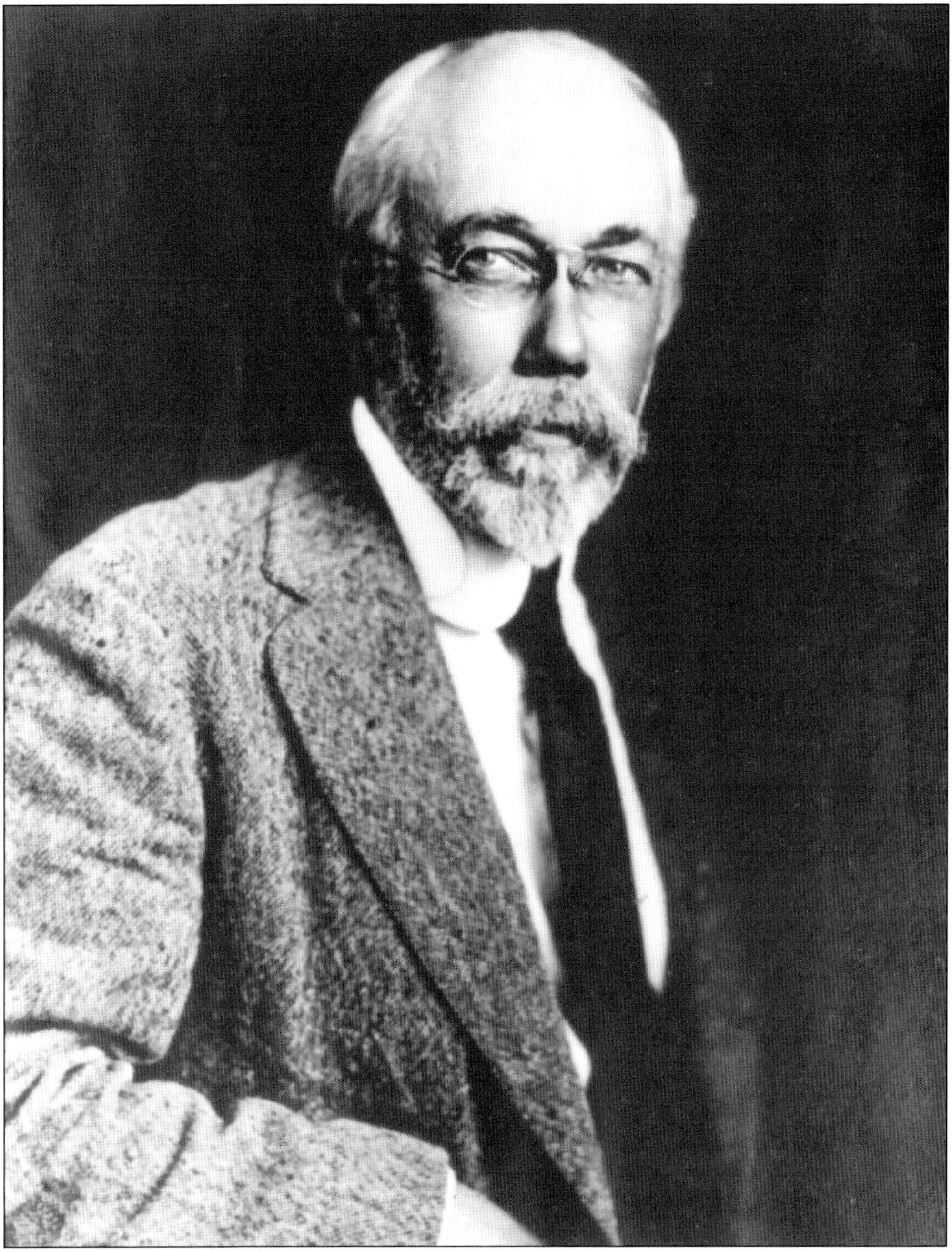

Architect William Lightfoot Price received his training in the offices of one of the giants of Philadelphia architecture, Frank Furness. He was employed by Furness from 1878 to 1881, when he left to start an architectural practice with his brother Frank. While there is little to distinguish Will Price's work at the turn of the century from the historicism that then prevailed in American architecture, many regard his Atlantic City hotels, the Blenheim (1905) and the Traymore (1912) as landmarks on the road to the modernist style. In addition to Arden, Will Price also founded the Rose Valley community in Moylan, Pennsylvania, which is where he made his home, and the single tax enclave of Halidon, Maine, the latter with Frank Stephens.

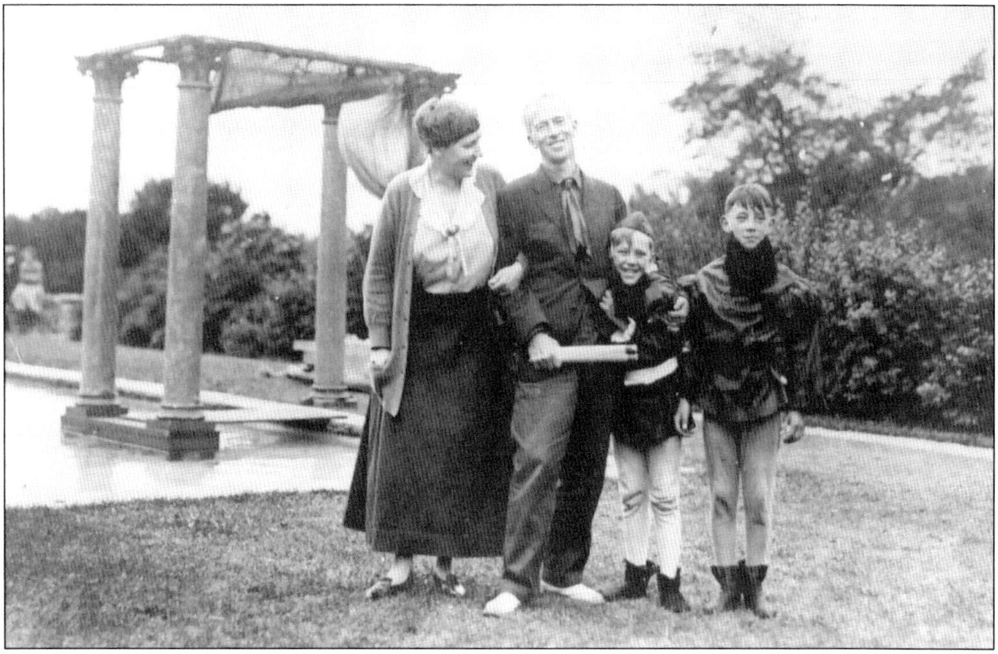

Frank Stephens was in great demand as a speaker and lectured frequently on art as well as economics. This photograph was taken around 1907 in Wyoming, New York. The location is likely Hillside, the Greek Revival mansion built by Dr. Pliny Hayes that served as a forum for many notable speakers.

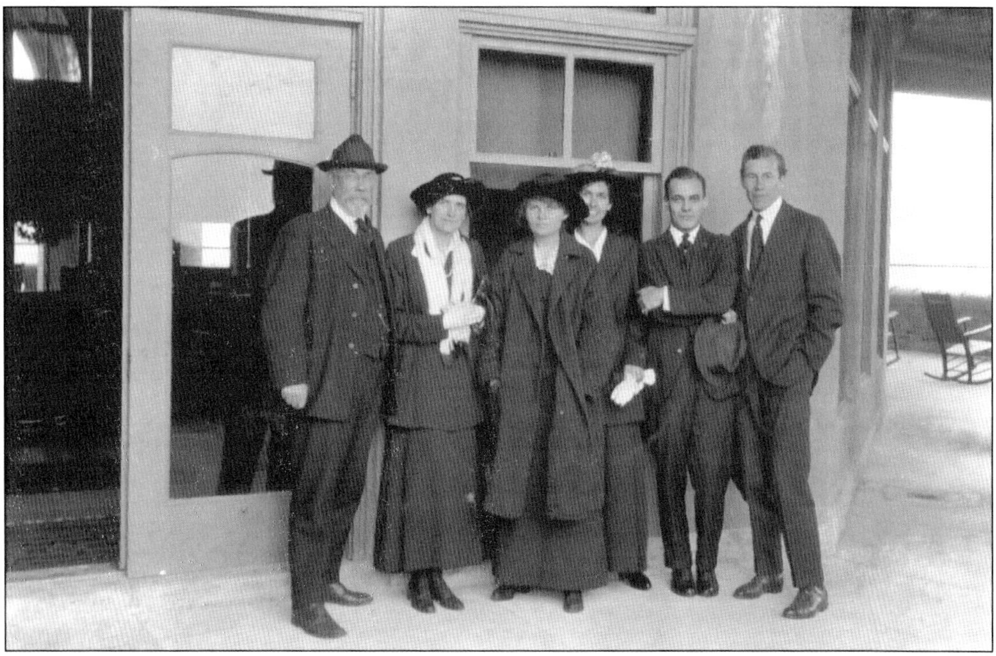

In 1915, Will Price welcomed a group of Arden visitors to the Traymore Hotel in Atlantic City, one of the architect's most celebrated commissions. Pictured from left to right are Will Price, Edith "Jimmie" Ware, Ingeborg "Inky" Stephens, Margaret Stephens, Hamilton "Buzz" Ware, and Harold "Hal" Ware.

Two

HUMBLE BEGINNINGS

We were so disgusted with civilization that we determined then and there to go out into the open and make a better one.

—Frank Stephens, 1923

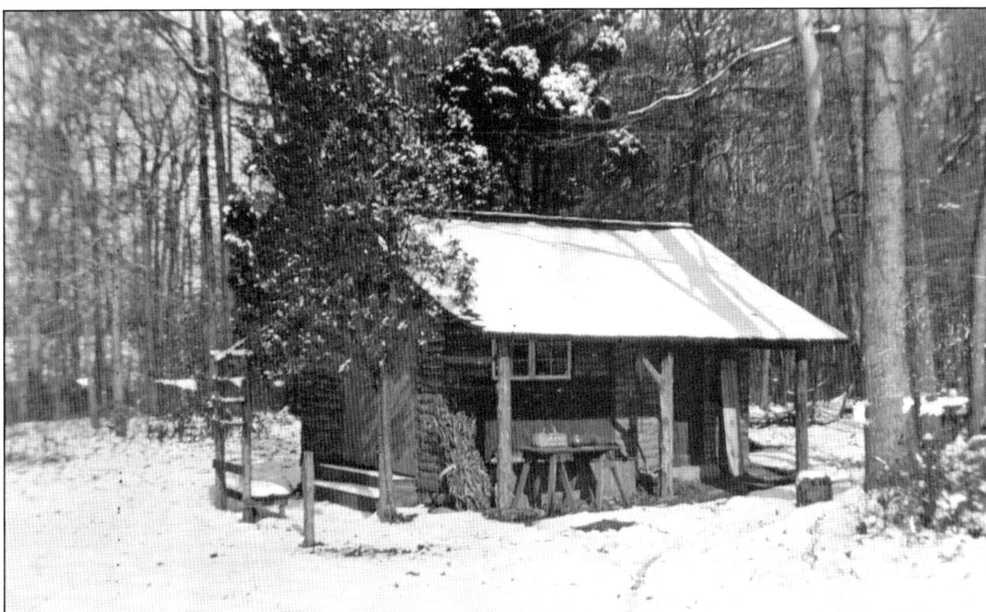

The first house constructed in the new community was the Homestead, seen here in the winter of 1909. Built by Frank Stephens and a group of friends in 1900, the Homestead served as a weekend and summer cottage for the Stephens family.

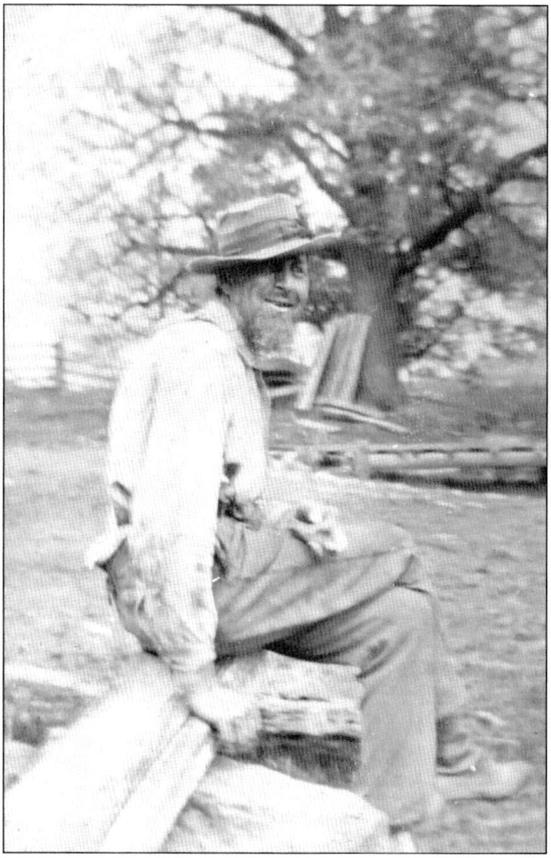

Jerry Harvey owned the farm bordering Arden to the southeast. When Frank Stephens began looking for land for the new community, it was Jerry Harvey who pointed out the Derrickson property to him.

Taken just on the outskirts of Arden, this 1906 photograph of Veale Road from its intersection with Grubb's Road captures the rural character of the new community. (Photograph by L. A. MacDonnald of Harvey, Delaware.)

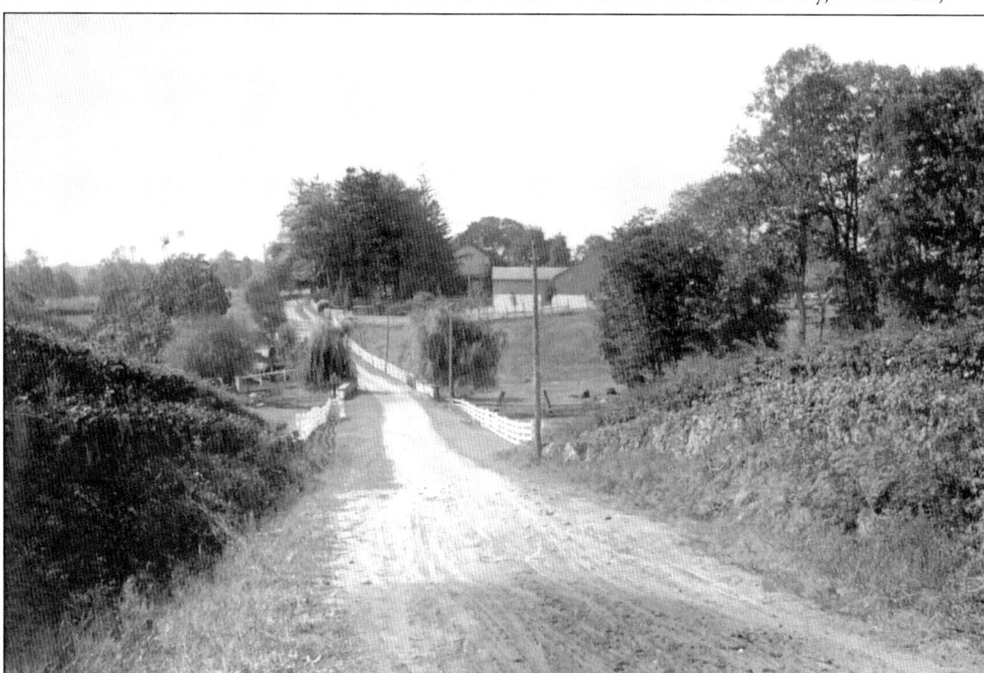

The trip from center city Philadelphia to the Harvey Station took 30 minutes; giving, as one resident wryly noted, barely enough time to crack the cover of the Esperanto textbook. Most of Arden's early settlers were commuters who used the community as a weekend or summer retreat. In this 1906 photograph, a commuter waits patiently for the southbound train. The station cat, however, appears more interested in the photographer.

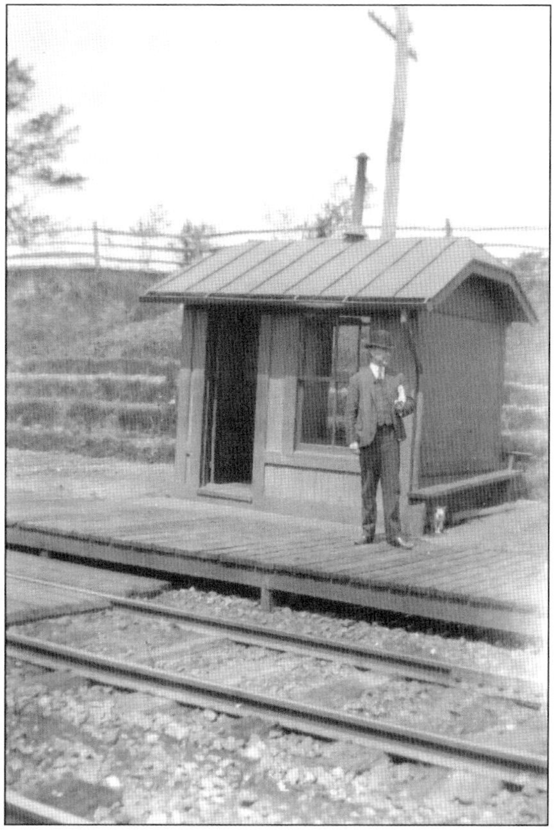

Frank Cole, Tom Bird, and Tony (from left to right) await the northbound train to transport Tom Bird's milk cans to Philadelphia. Tony, the station master, was known for his terraced garden, which is visible here in 1906 on the hillside behind the group.

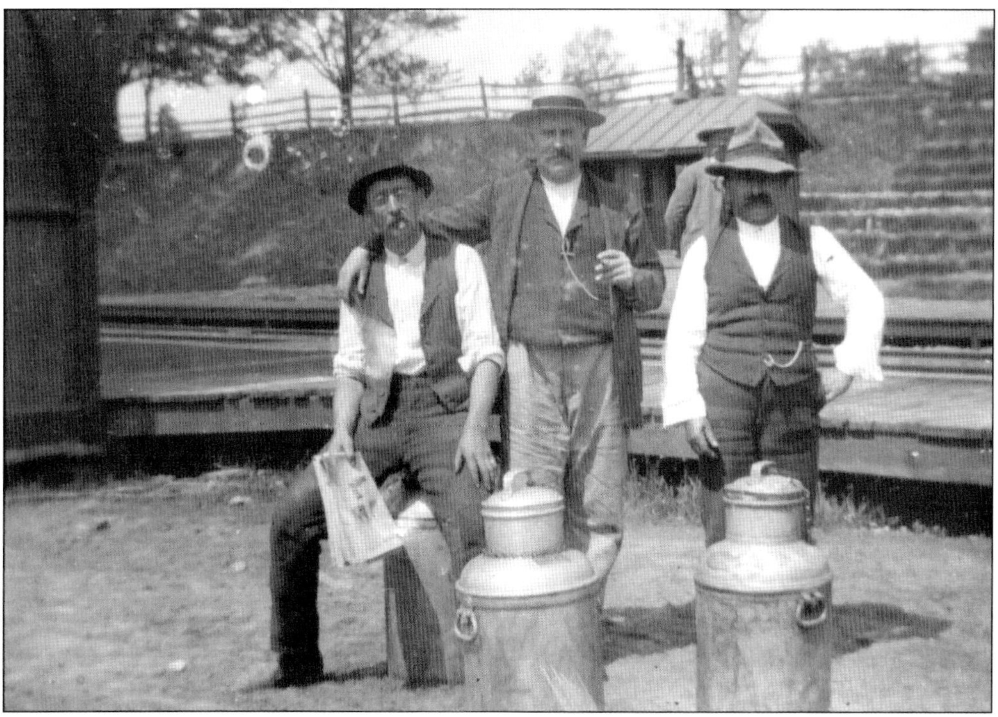

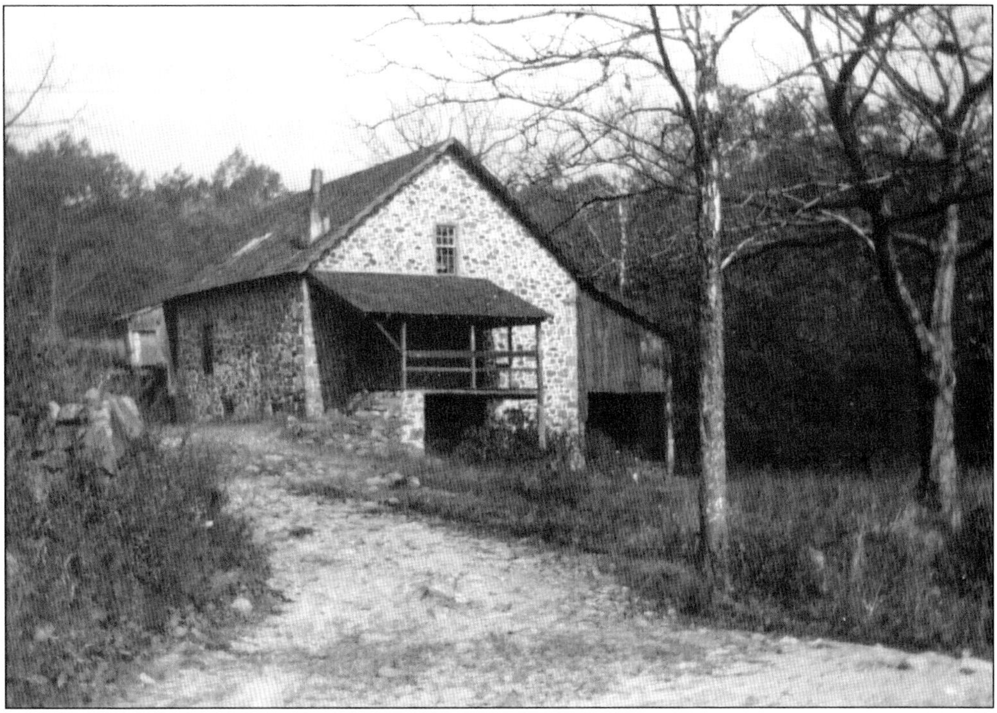

The old Grubb family grist mill on Marsh Road dates to the early 1700s and reputedly supplied grain to Gen. George Washington's troops during the Revolutionary War. It was later taken over by the Harvey family, from whom the Arden Water Company purchased the property in 1924.

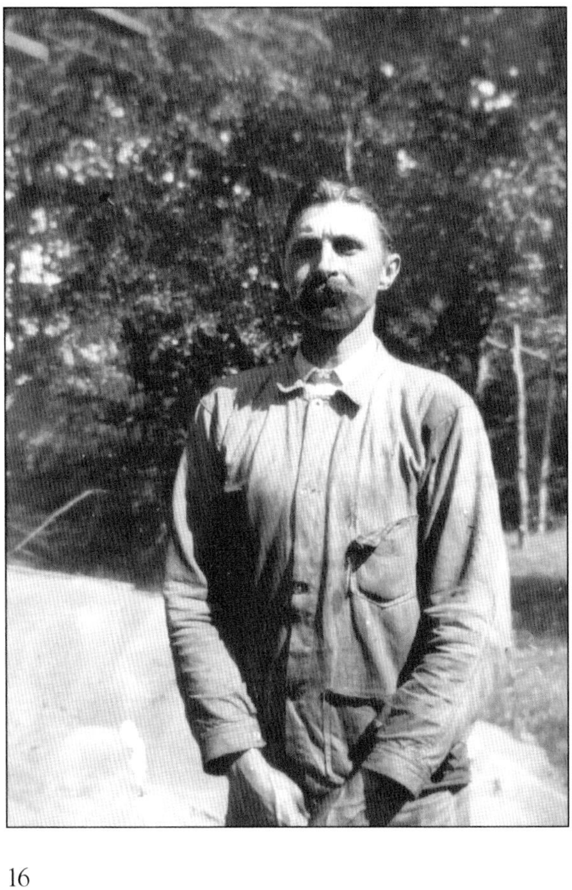

Jerry Harvey's son, Al, is seen here at the grist mill in 1906. Like many of the local farmers, Al was very active in the community. At various times he operated the mill, worked the forge, and helped with construction projects throughout the village.

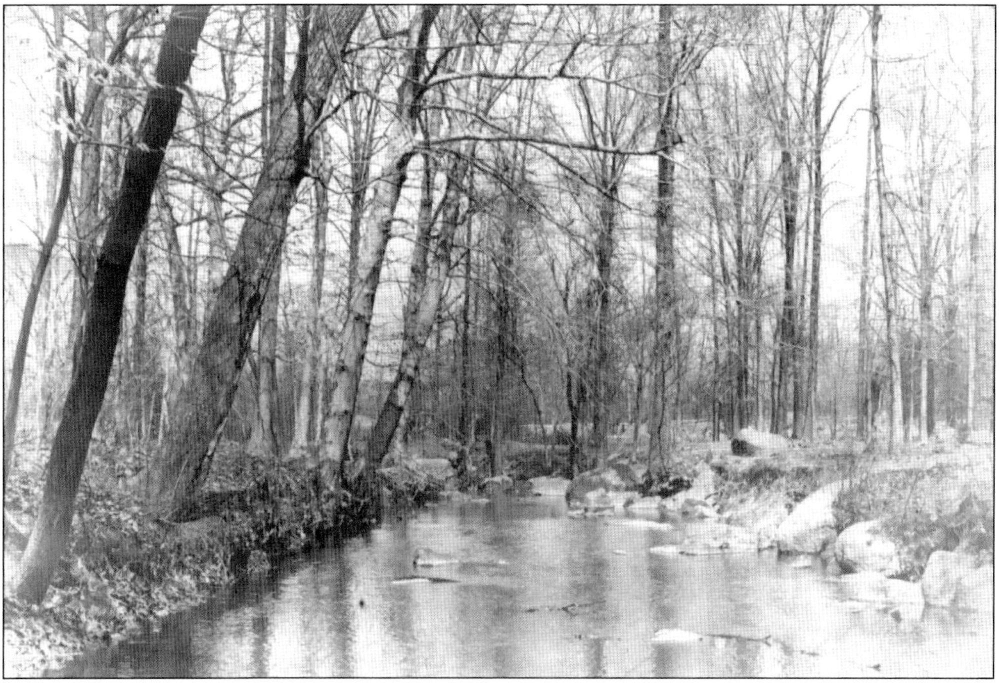

Arden's boundaries to the southwest and north are defined by two creeks, the largest being Naaman's to the north, which is shown here in 1906. Naaman's Creek is a six-mile-long tributary of the Delaware River, and it provided the water to power the Grubb Grist Mill. The creek was named for a Minqua Indian chief who befriended the area's Swedish settlers, and over the years, many Native American artifacts have been found along its banks.

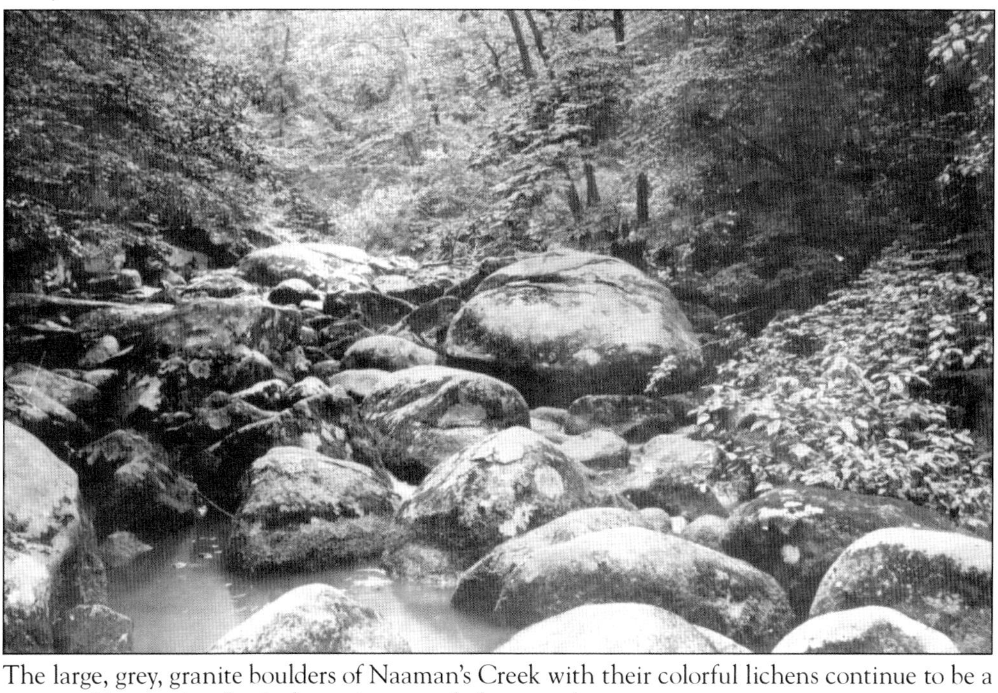

The large, grey, granite boulders of Naaman's Creek with their colorful lichens continue to be a source of inspiration for Arden painters and photographers.

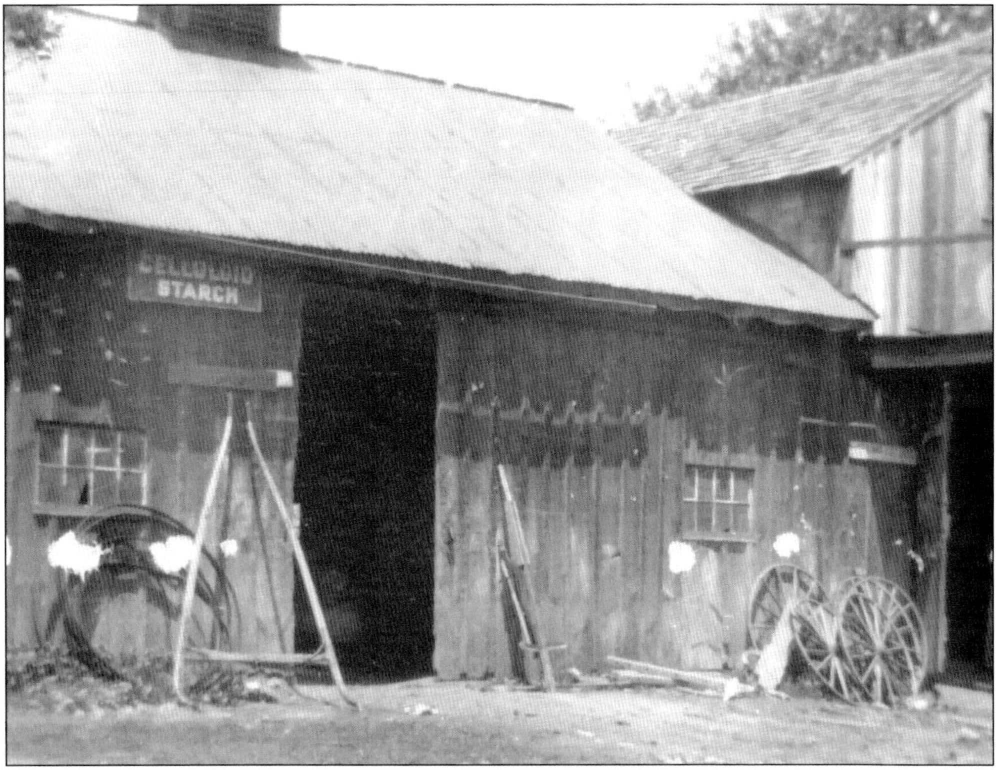

The small village of Grubb's Corner at the western edge of Arden included this blacksmith shop that stood at the intersection of Grubb's Road and Marsh Road.

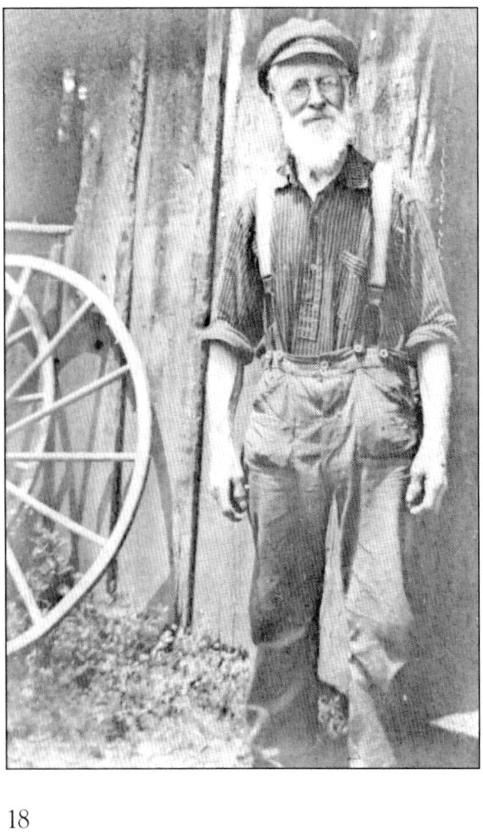

The Grubb's Corner blacksmith is seen here in this faded photograph taken around 1906. His name is unfortunately unknown.

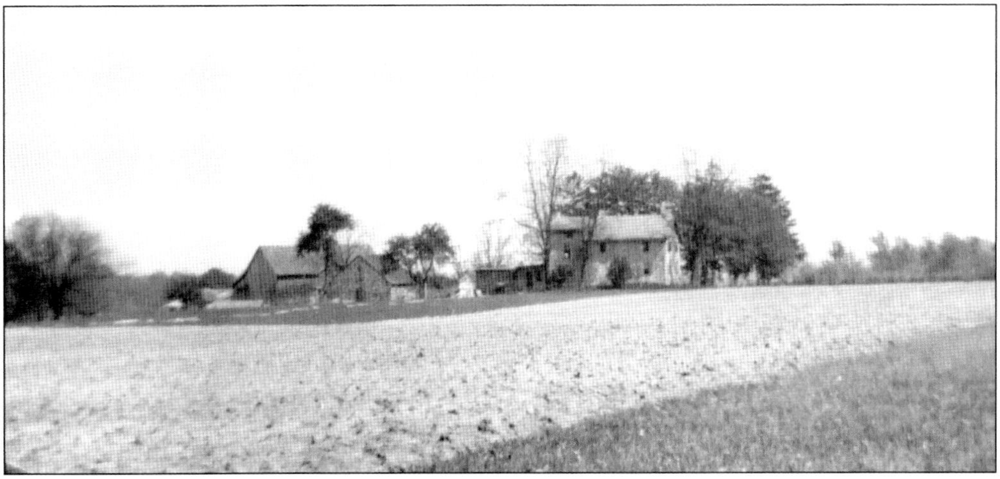

Jerry Harvey's farmhouse and barn are seen in this 1906 photograph taken from Grubb's Road. The 110-acre farm would later become the single tax village of Ardentown, which was founded December 23, 1922.

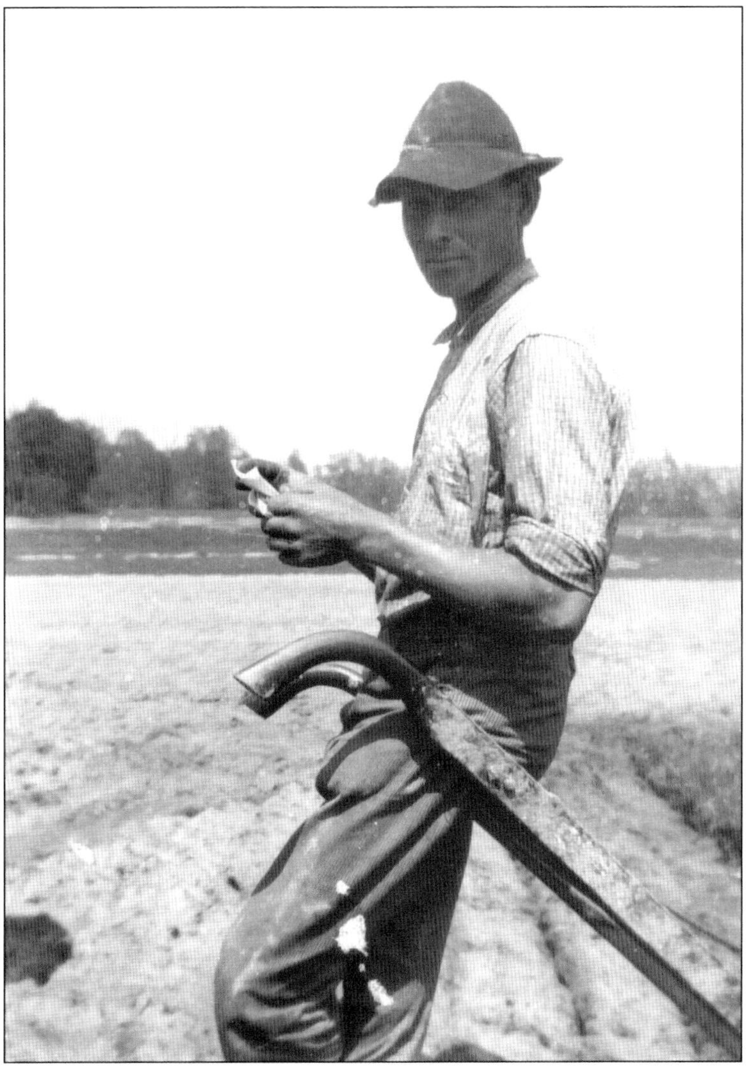

In this 1906 photograph, Harry Vandever takes a break from his job plowing Jerry Harvey's farm.

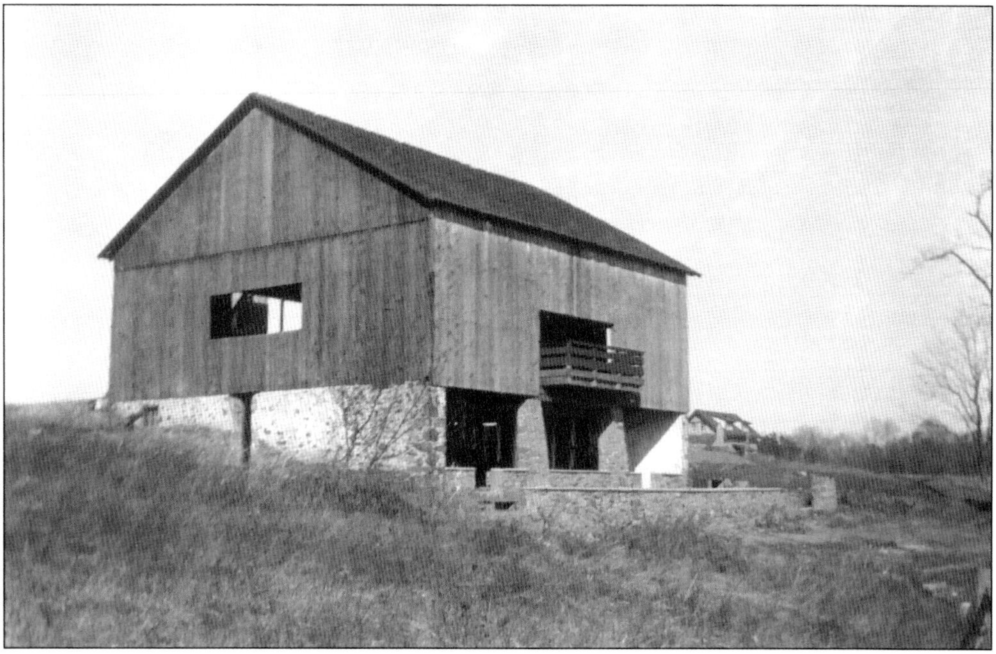

The Derrickson barn was considerably more dilapidated when Frank Stephens and Will Price purchased the property in 1900. According to Stephens, "the farm was paying neither the owner nor tenant anything except the little they could steal from each other, the landlord by levying on the tenants' belongings and the tenant by defaulting on the rent and burning the lower portion of the house and barn for fuel." This photograph dates from the barn's renovation in 1910.

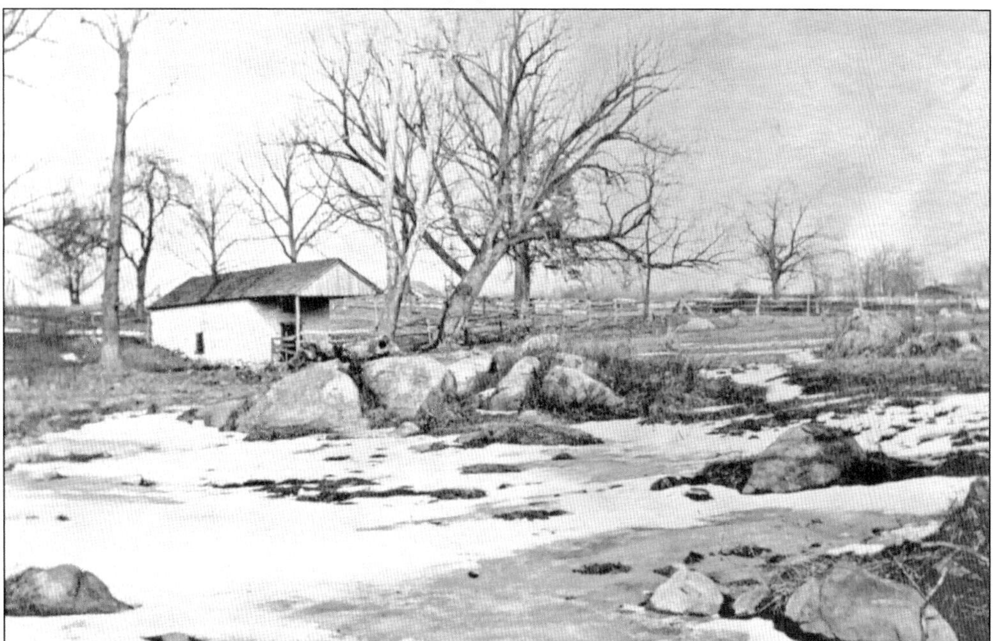

The sparseness of the early Arden landscape is evoked in this 1907 winter photograph of the Derrickson springhouse. Still standing today, the springhouse is located in the meadow just below the barn and the Grubb family cemetery.

Cows were often seen grazing the neighboring meadows along Veale Road in 1906.

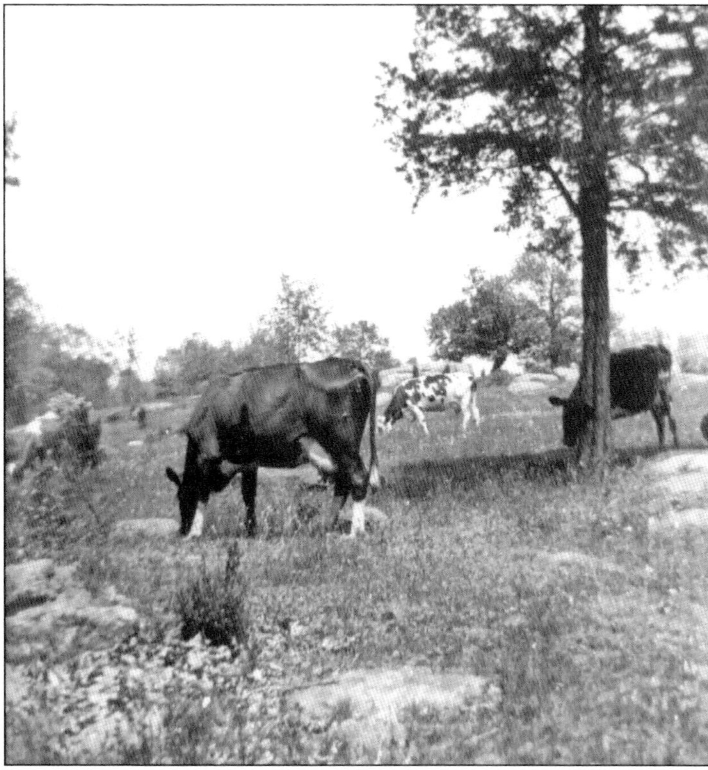

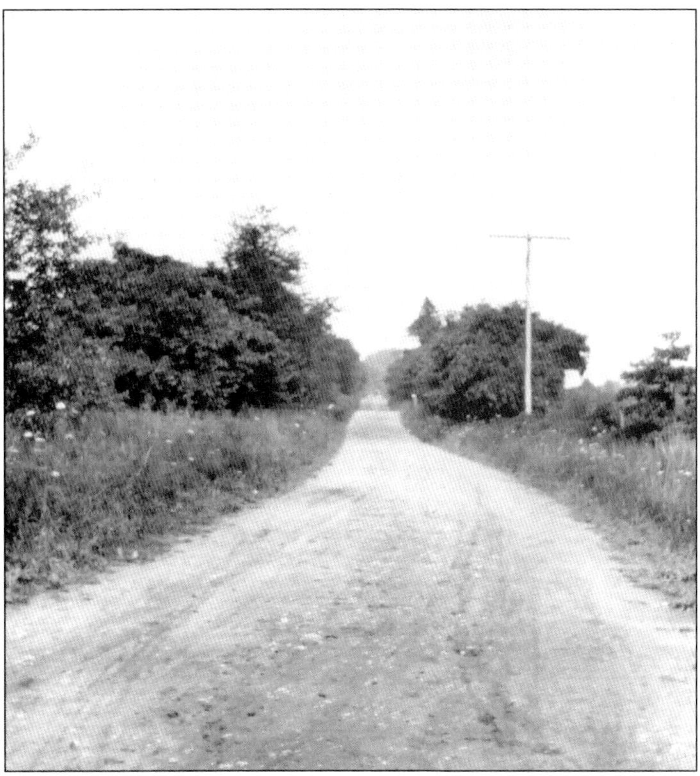

The entrance to Arden and its stile path gateway was five-eighths of a mile from the Harvey Station, up what was originally known as Grubb's Lane. When automobiles first appeared in town, several residents ran shuttle services to the station.

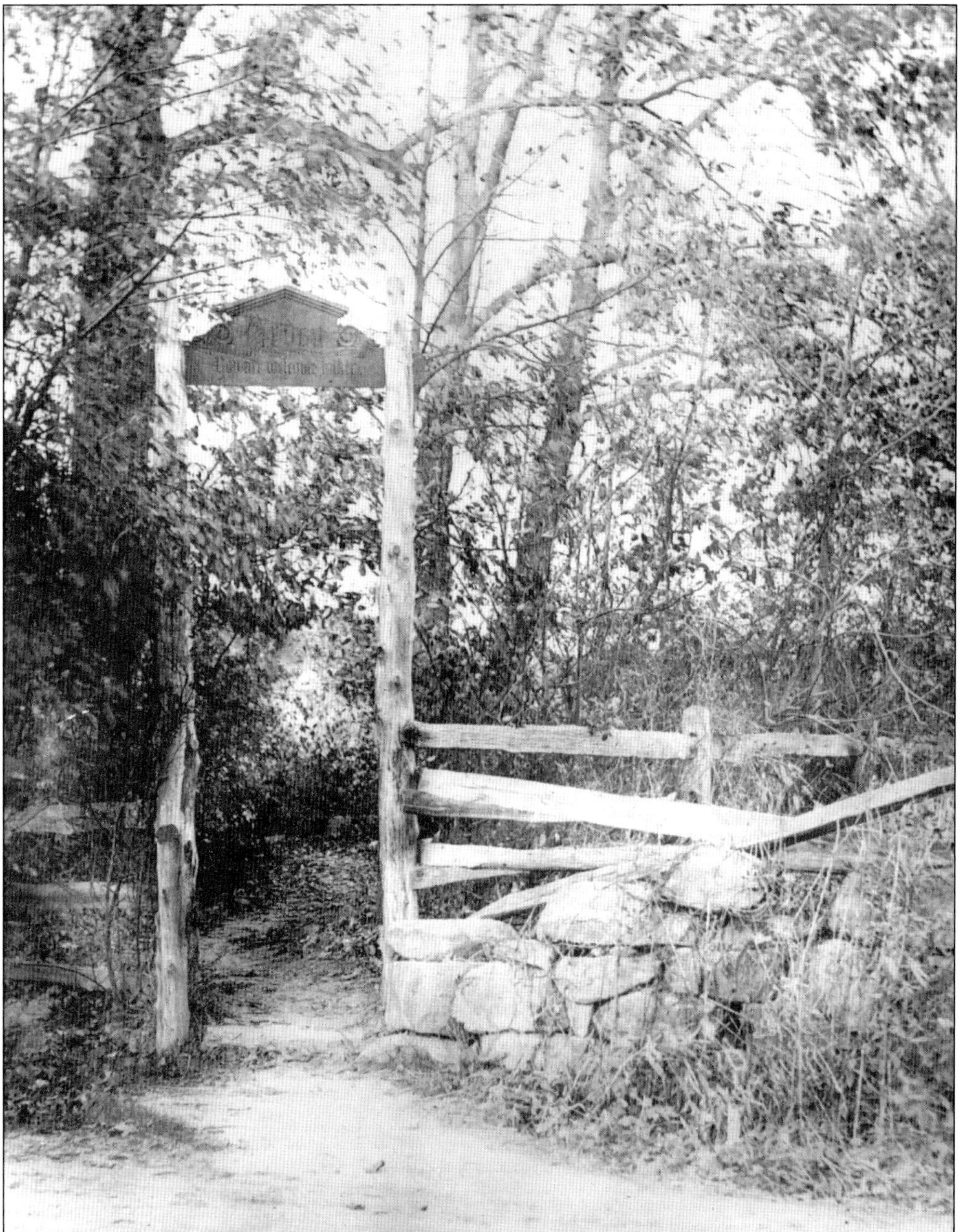

The Arden stile is seen here as it appeared in 1906. Inspired by the stile steps of the English countryside, the stile marked the formal entrance to the community. Carved across the front in medieval lettering was the greeting "You Are Welcome Hither," taken from the last act of William Shakespeare's *King Lear*. The reverse, meant to be read as one leaves the village, reads "If we do meet again, why we shall smile," and is taken from Act V of *Julius Caesar*. Regardless of one's beliefs, in Arden you were welcome.

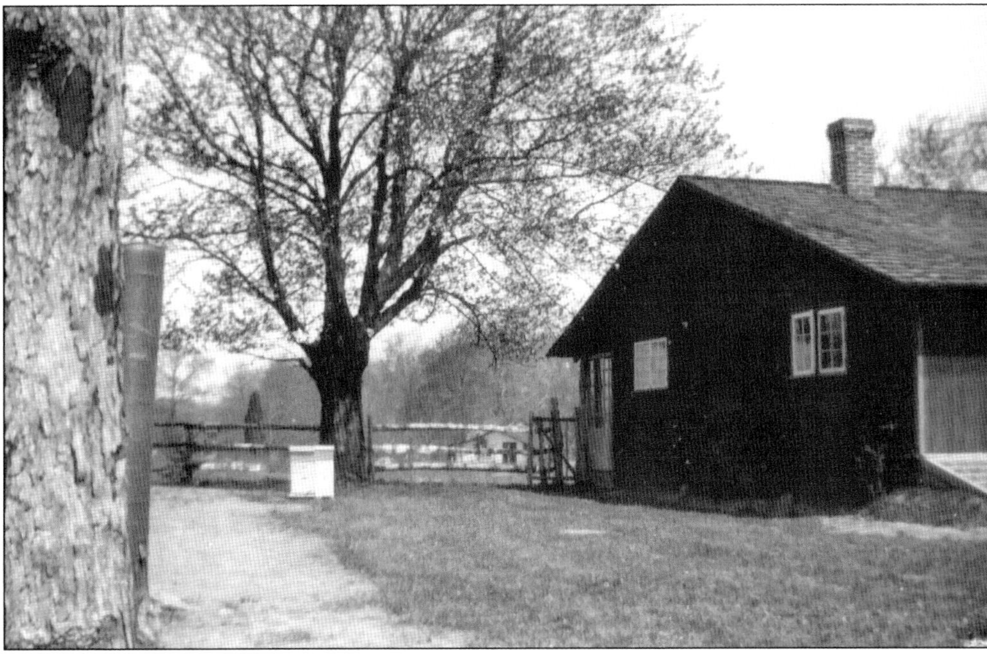

As one walked Arden's stile path in 1907, the first building one encountered was the Red House, located at the corner of Cherry Lane and Miller's Road. The cottage visible in the distance (through the fence) is the Admiral Benbow. Also noteworthy in this photograph is the beehive, which was tended by Elena Darling.

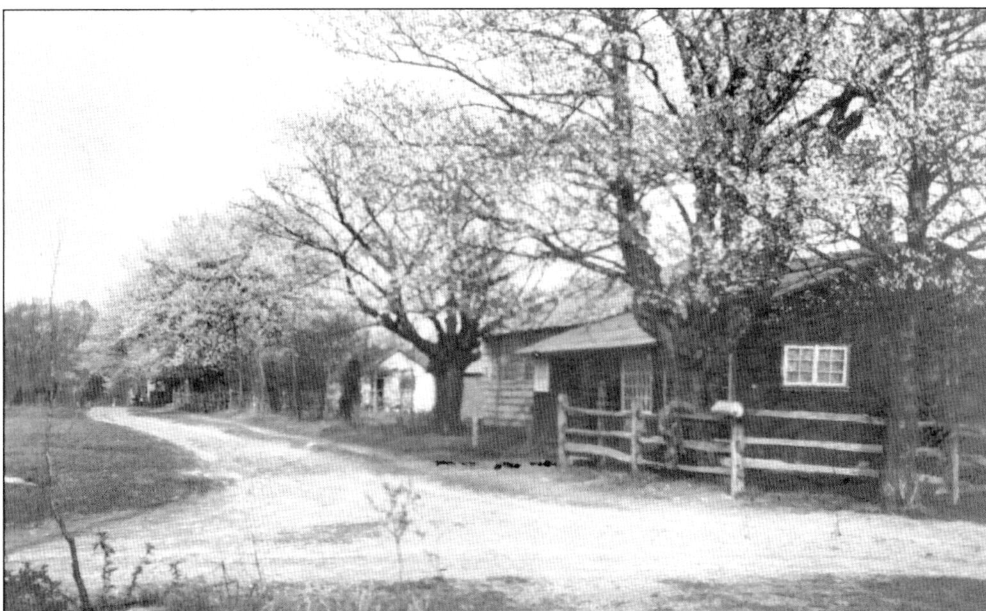

During Arden's first decade, the Red House, seen here from Cherry Lane in 1910, was the social and artistic center of the village, serving as library, music room, art studio, furniture shop, weaving studio, and greenhouse. The first addition to the one-room farm building was an open-air dance floor, bringing to mind American anarchist Emma Goldman's often quoted declaration, "If I can't dance, I won't be part of the revolution." The Red House grew by need rather than design.

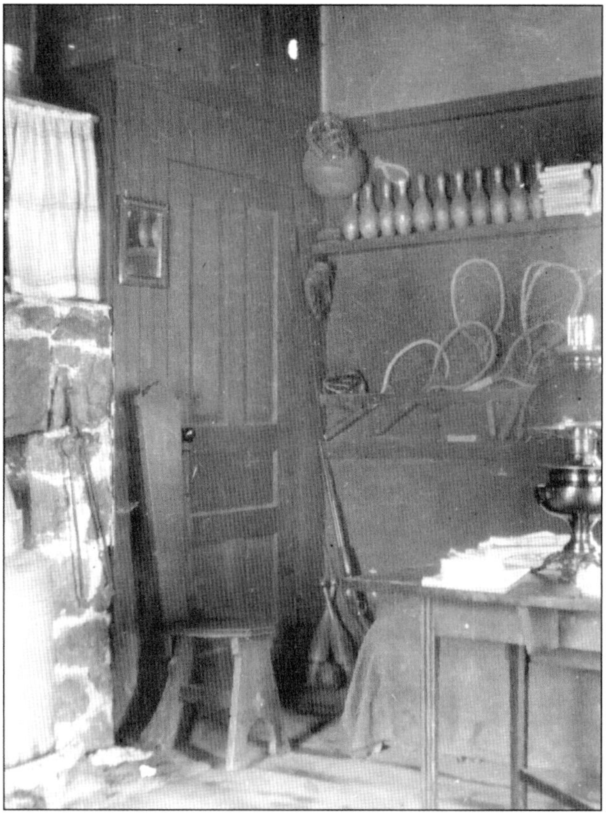

In addition to being the industrial center of Arden, the Red House served as the first home of the Arden Club, which was established on July 16, 1908, "to promote the social and educational interests of Arden." Frank Stephens's son, Don, who did much of the photography used in this book, labeled this 1908 photograph the *Sporting Corner*, and it tells us much about early activities in town.

Ardenite Elena Darling was an apiculturist in addition to fabricating stained and leaded glass for many of Arden's early homes. Under construction behind her in this 1906 photograph is the Red House. The barn to the left is an old wagon house of the Derricksons'.

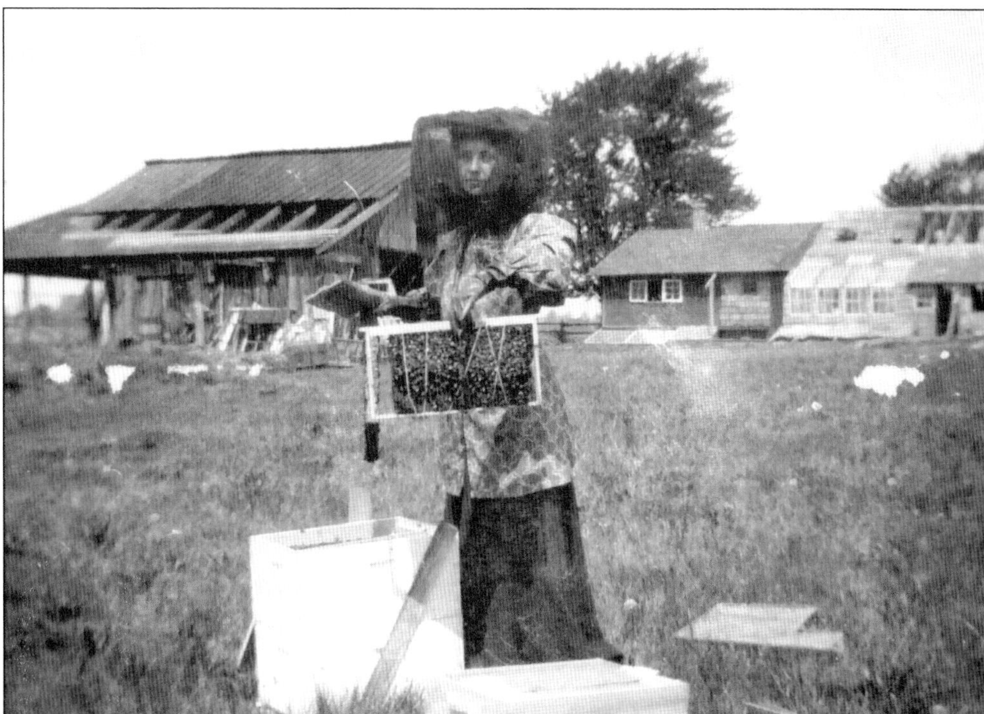

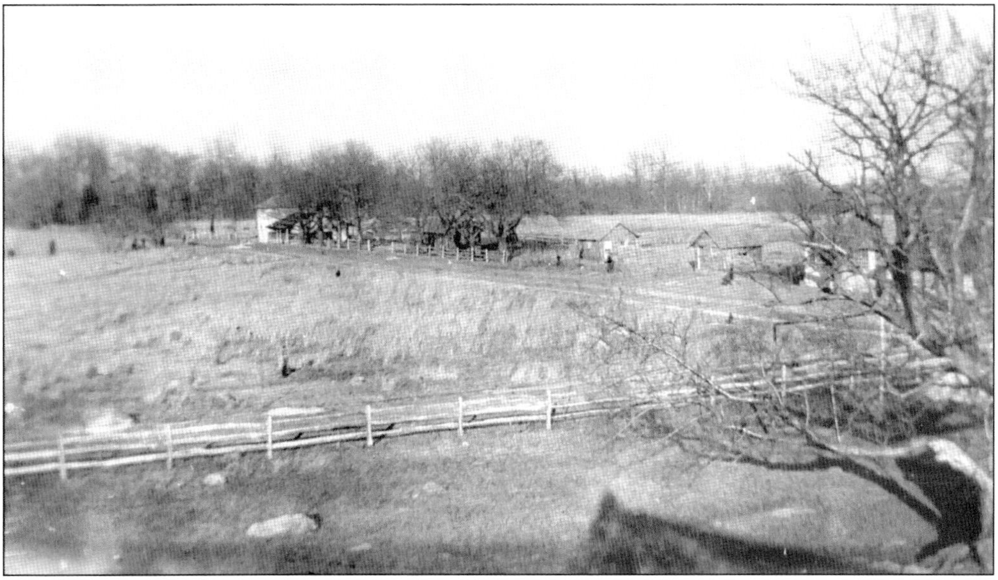

The Village Green was little more than pasture land in 1907. Visible in this photograph are the Arden Inn, Cherry Lodge, and two rustic guest cabins that were built to house the community's frequent visitors. Both photographs on this page were taken by Don Stephens from the roof of the Nesbitt house, which sits at the intersection of Orleans Road and Miller's Road.

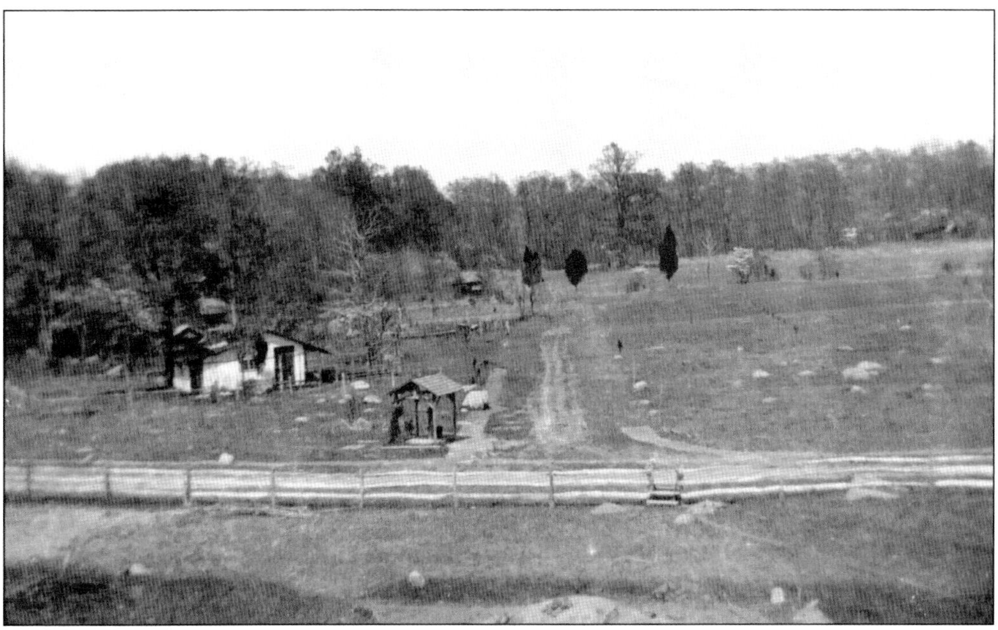

In the second photograph of our series, Don looks directly at his home, the Admiral Benbow. Visible just beyond the Benbow is the Field Theater. The rustic structure in the foreground is a water pump.

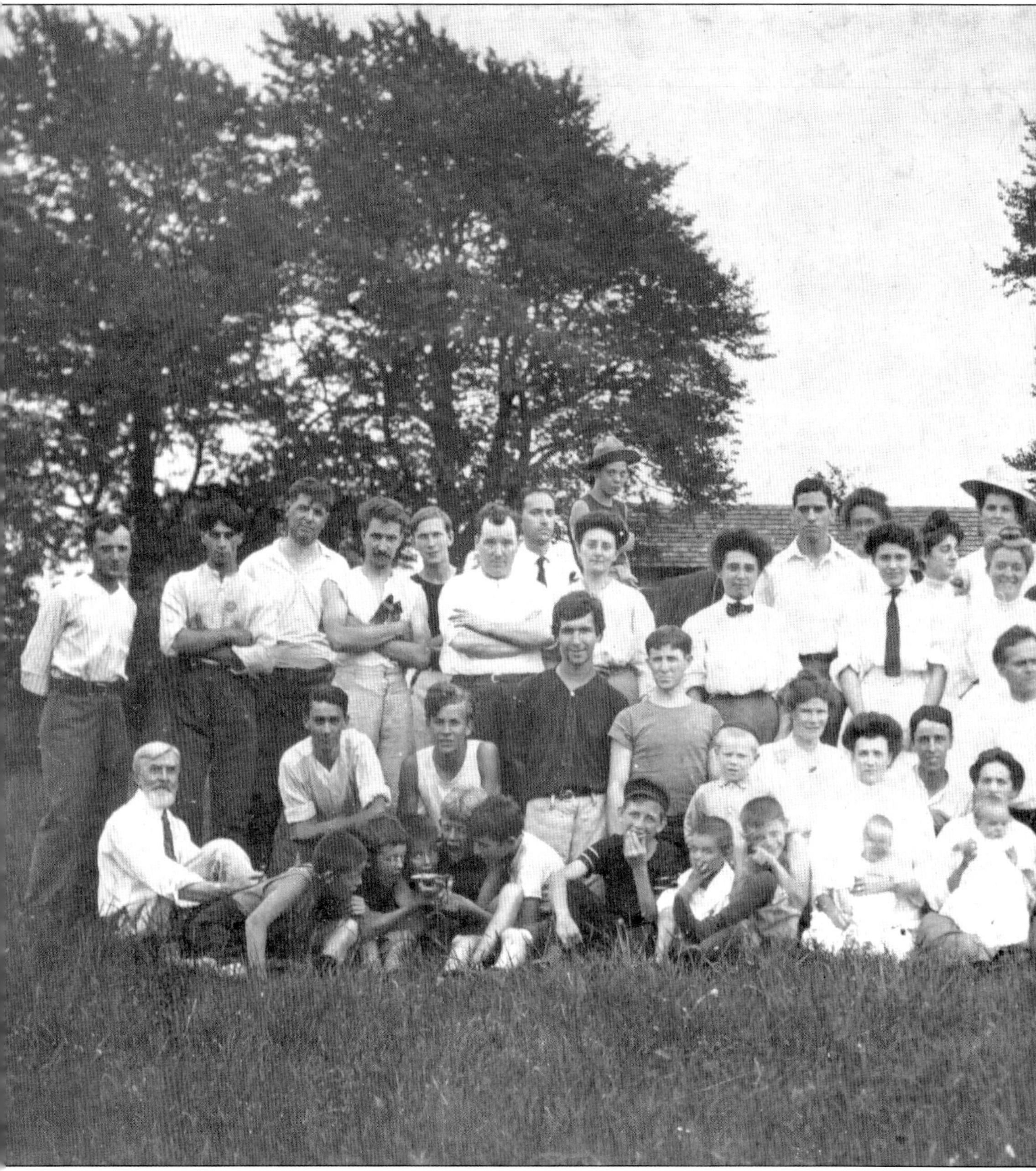

Single taxers, socialists, communists, and anarchists stand shoulder to shoulder in this 1908 Arden family portrait. The photograph was taken on the Village Green in front of Cherry Lodge

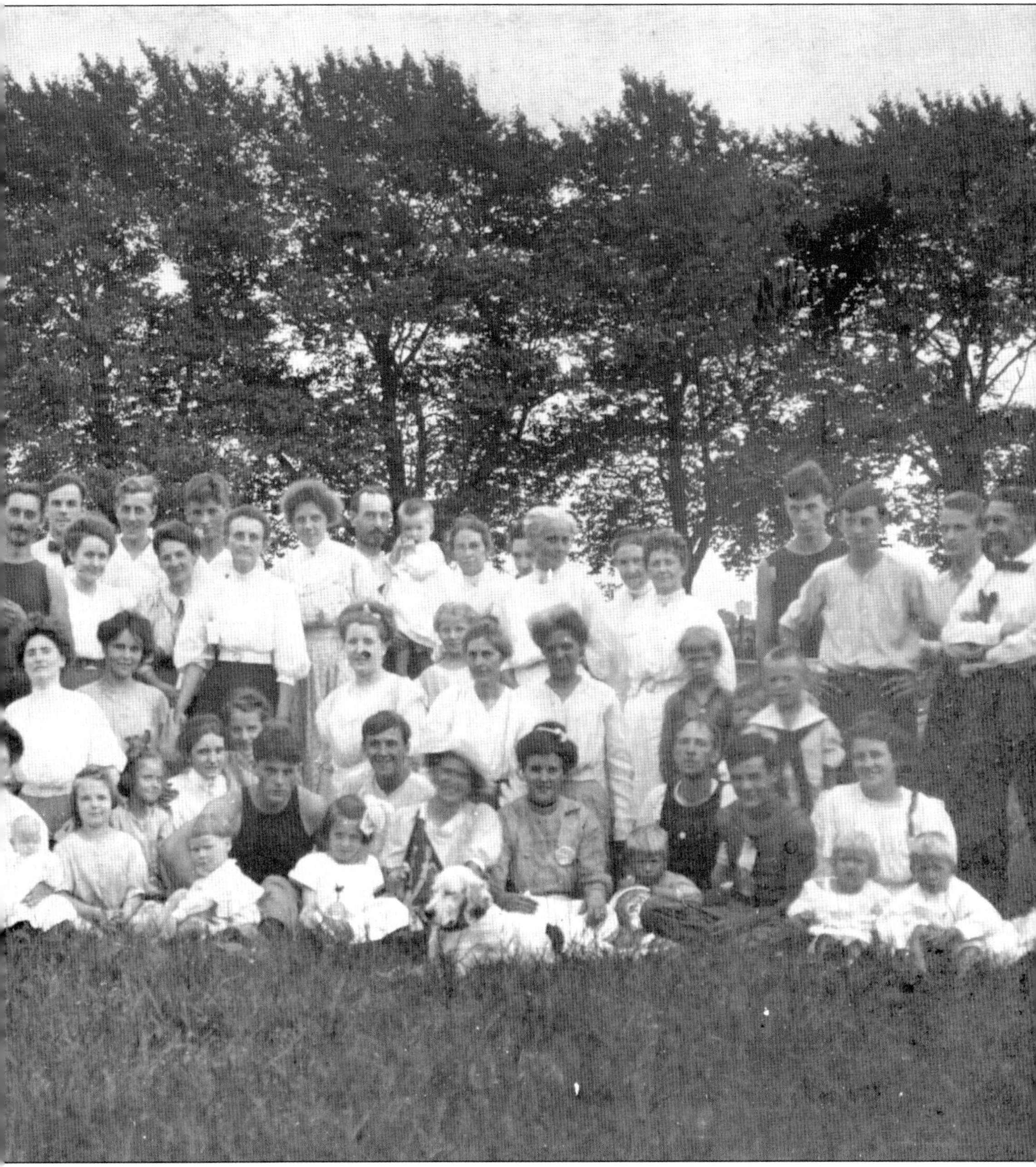

and was published in the *Philadelphia North American* in the winter of 1909. Frank Stephens is seated third from right.

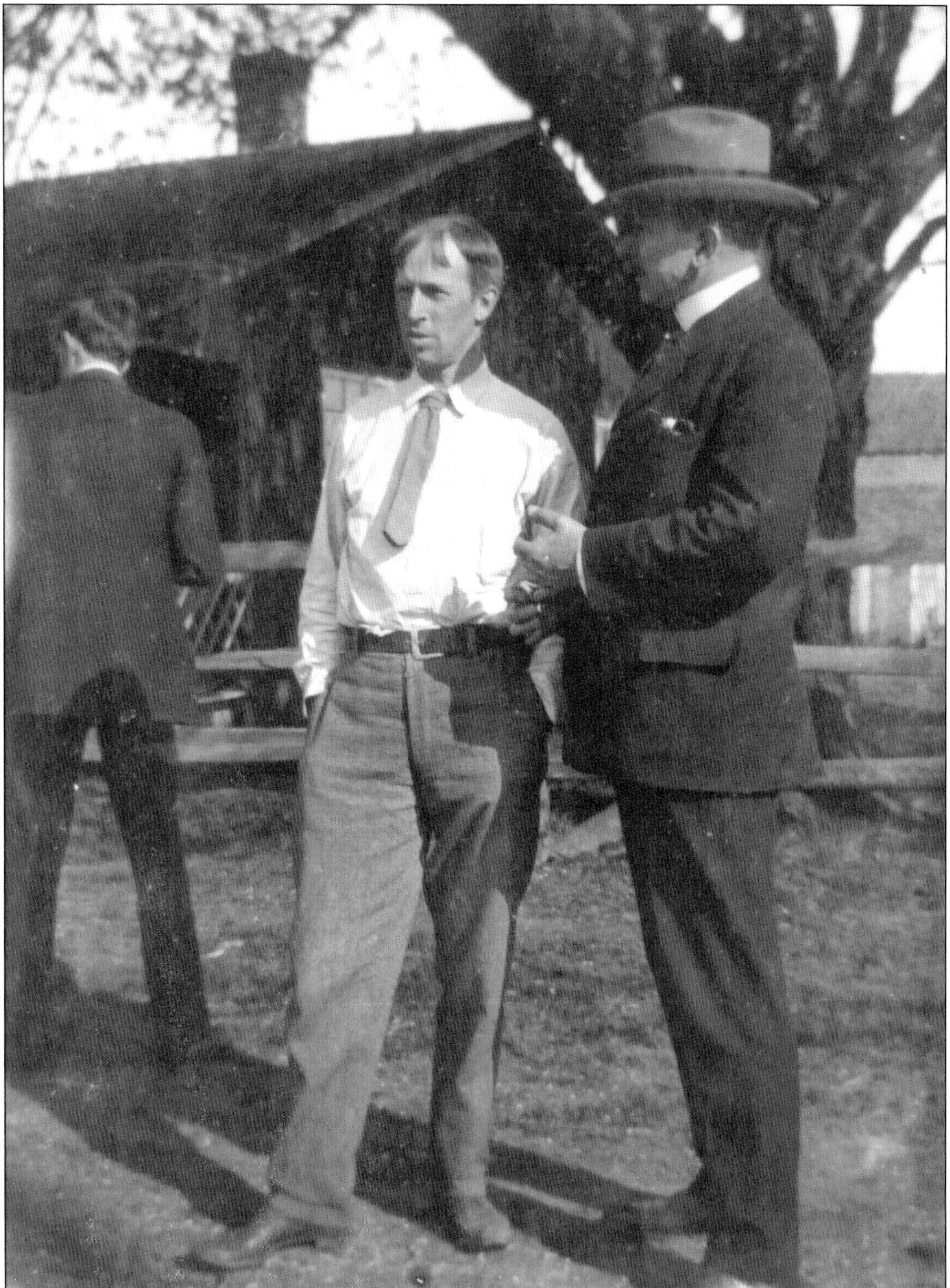

One of the first artists to settle in the community was Frank F. English, seen here outside the Red House conversing with Frank Stephens in 1907. Frank English and his wife, Anna, built a home in Arden in March of that year, although they appear to have spent much of 1906 in the community as well. Two of the activities Frank was known to have enjoyed during his Arden years were dancing and boating on the Delaware River. This photograph is one of only two known of the artist who was widely recognized for his pastoral scenes of rural life.

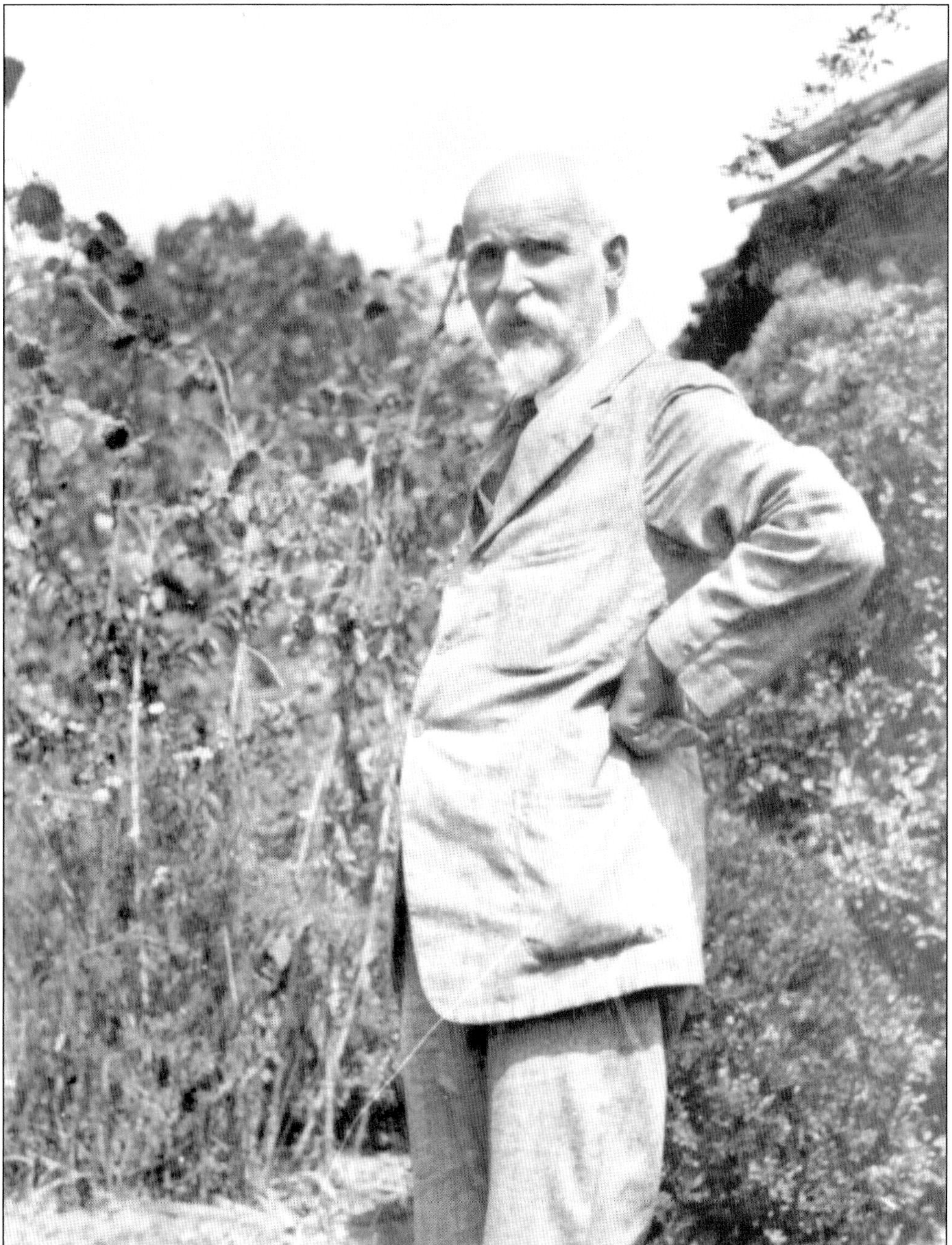

Canadian born sculptor Fredrick Dunbar was active in the Detroit, Michigan, area before moving to Wilmington in 1906. Commissions that he received in Wilmington included a Civil War memorial to Gen. Thomas Smyth of Delaware, which was to be erected on the triangle just beyond Washington Street Bridge. Although his model was accepted, the memorial does not seem to have been completed, most likely due to lack of funds. According to an article published in the *Sunday Morning Star*, Dunbar spent summers with his family in Arden. He is listed as a leaseholder until 1913 when he reputedly returned to Canada. He is seen here in 1909.

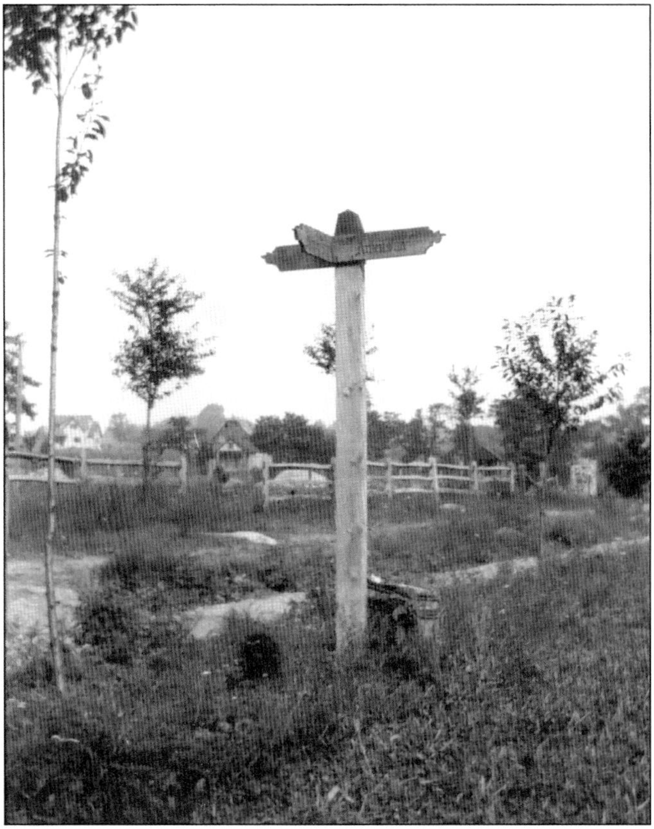

In 1906, this Arden signpost pointed the way, quite literally, to the Arden Inn. In Arden's earliest years, posts along Arden lanes were decorated with sculptures by Frank Stephens of Br'er Rabbit, Br'er Fox, and other animals from the Uncle Remus stories.

Located along the Village Green, the two-story Arden Inn was a prominent landmark in the community. Open seasonally, many residents took their meals there as well as their baths, since it was the first building in town with a tub. The three men relaxing on the bench by the front door in this 1907 photograph are, from left to right, Fred Whiteside, Frank Stephens, and Charles Ervin.

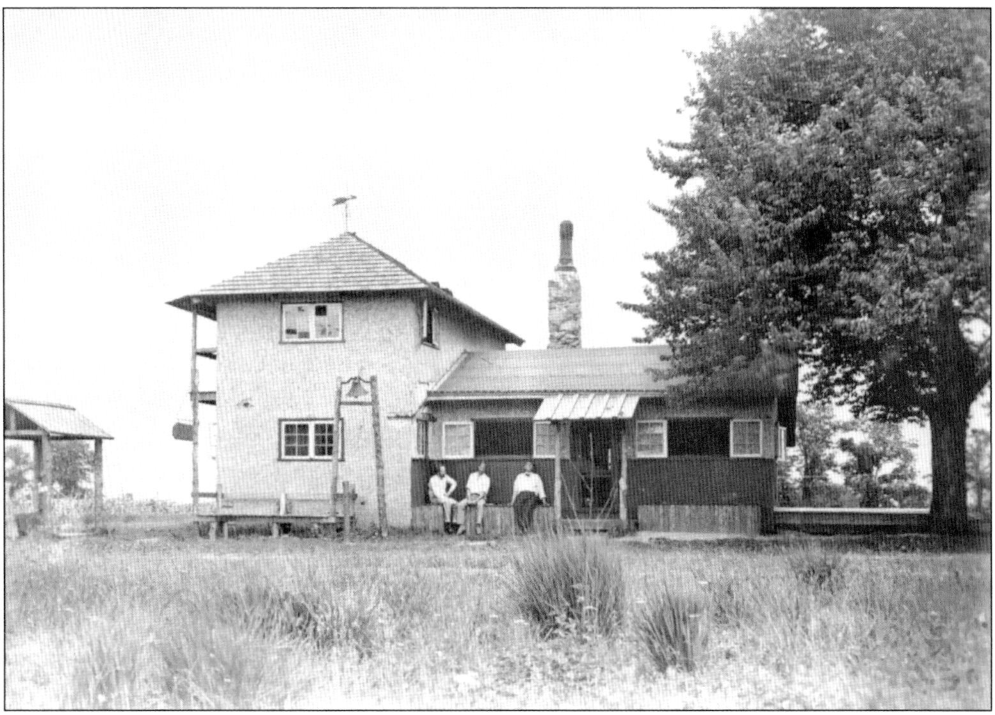

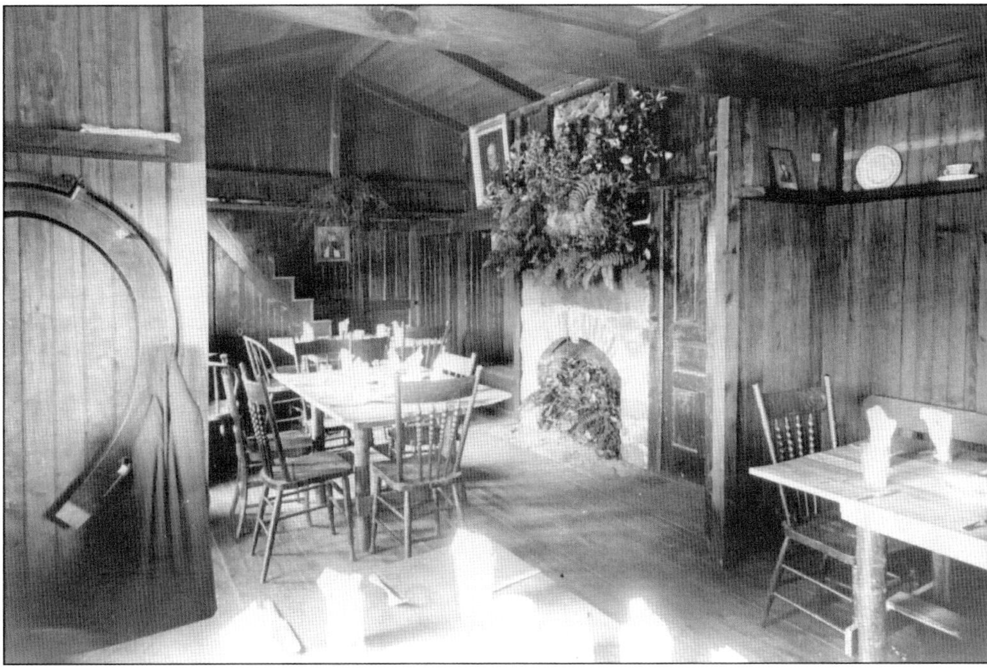

The Arden Inn was operated for many years by communists George and Minnie Newcomb. Meals were served family-style at large rustic tables and were mainly vegetarian. The staircase to the guest rooms can be seen at the far end of the room.

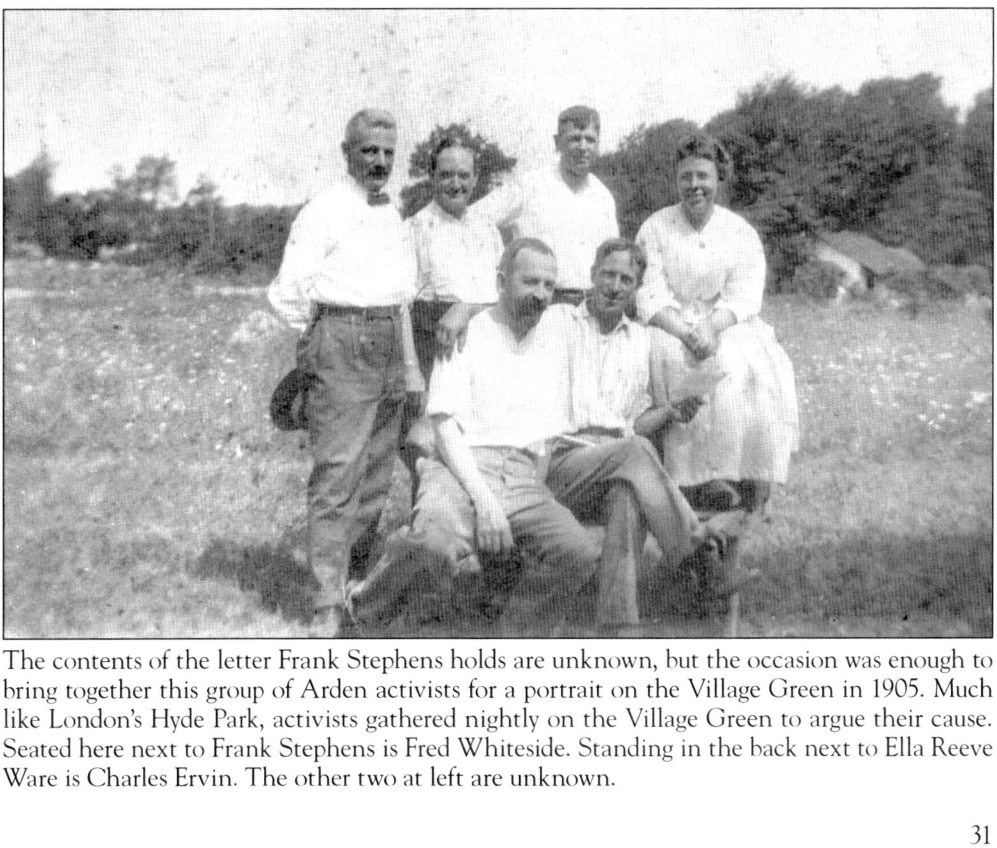

The contents of the letter Frank Stephens holds are unknown, but the occasion was enough to bring together this group of Arden activists for a portrait on the Village Green in 1905. Much like London's Hyde Park, activists gathered nightly on the Village Green to argue their cause. Seated here next to Frank Stephens is Fred Whiteside. Standing in the back next to Ella Reeve Ware is Charles Ervin. The other two at left are unknown.

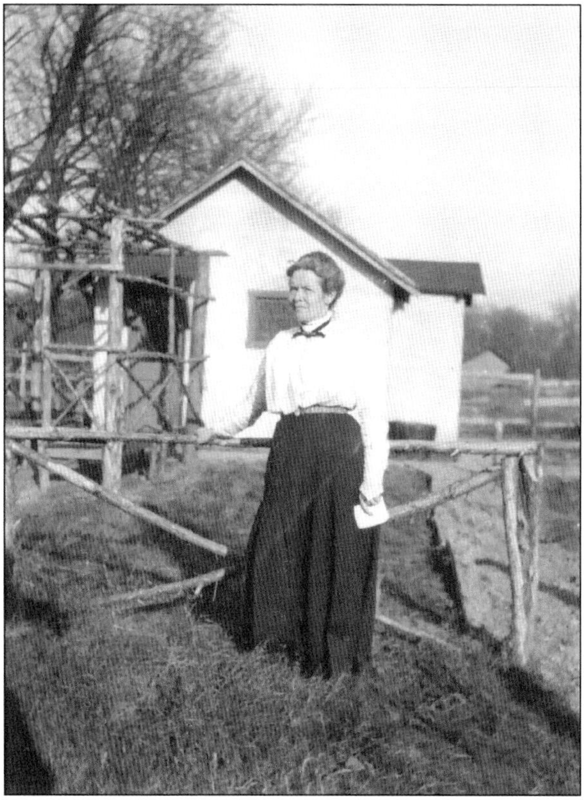

Ella Reeve Ware, also known as Mother Bloor, started her activist career in the 1890s as a member of the Knights of Labor, and went on to become active in the Socialist Party as a state organizer in Delaware. Later associated with this party's militant left wing, she was part of the leftist walkout that subsequently formed the Communist Party USA. Throughout her life she was a tireless activist for workers' rights, particularly those affecting women and children. She is pictured here in Arden around 1910 standing outside her first husband Lucian Ware's cottage on Cherry Lane.

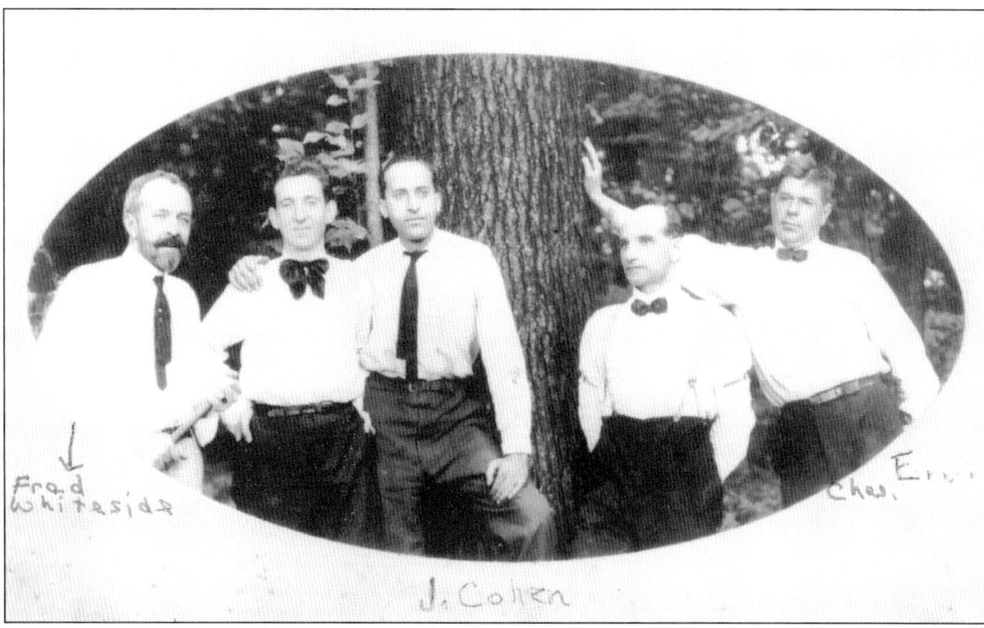

Seen here, from left to right, are socialists Fred Whiteside, Simon Lebros, Joe Cohen, Phillip Marassian, and Charles Ervin, who posed for an Arden portrait in 1907. According to Scott Nearing's autobiography, as early as 1905, single tax was on the wane in Arden and socialism on the rise. Eventually socialists far outnumbered the single taxers in the community.

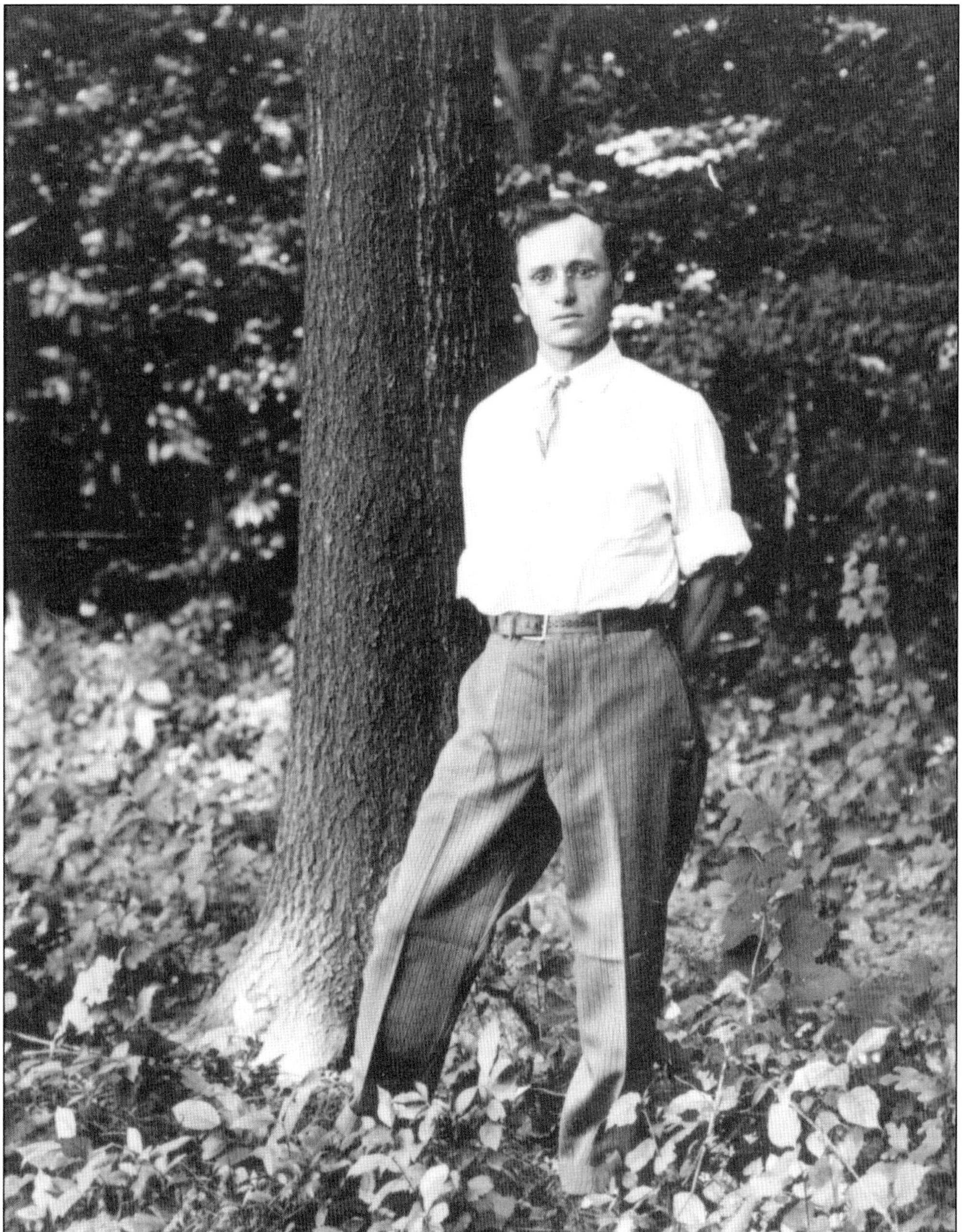

Emmanuel Gerstine, seen here in 1908, and his Russian-born first wife, Laura, spent summers in Arden. They were active members of the Philadelphia anarchist community and like Arden resident Mary Hansen, were close friends with Voltairine de Cleyre, the influential Philadelphia anarchist who is known to have visited Arden on several occasions. Because the philosophy of anarchism has much to do with early Arden, it is important to note that, although anarchism is equated in the popular vocabulary with violence, nothing could be further from the truth. To quote Emma Goldman, it is rather "the philosophy of a new social order based on liberty unrestricted by man-made laws."

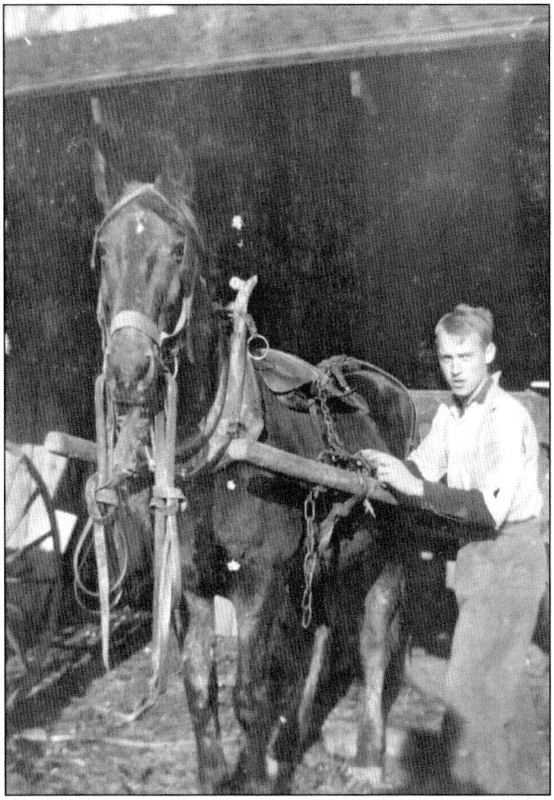

One of Arden's most famous residents, Scott Nearing, spent weekends and summers in the community from 1905 to 1915 while teaching at the Wharton School of Economics in Philadelphia. He was introduced to Arden by Fred Whiteside, a fellow member of the Philadelphia Ethical Society, who had asked for Scott's help surveying his Arden leasehold. Scott is seen here in 1907 with Bill, one of the horses from Frank Stephens's Philadelphia decorative arts firm, Stephens, Cooper, and Company.

When Scott arrived in Arden, his leasehold was the last plot of land available fronting the Village Green. The land rent on the low lying, swampy parcel was $13 a year, and Scott took it immediately. He is seen standing on the porch of his Arden cottage in 1914 with his first wife Nellie Seeds and Prof. Frank Watson of the University of Pennsylvania, with whom Scott coauthored a book on economics.

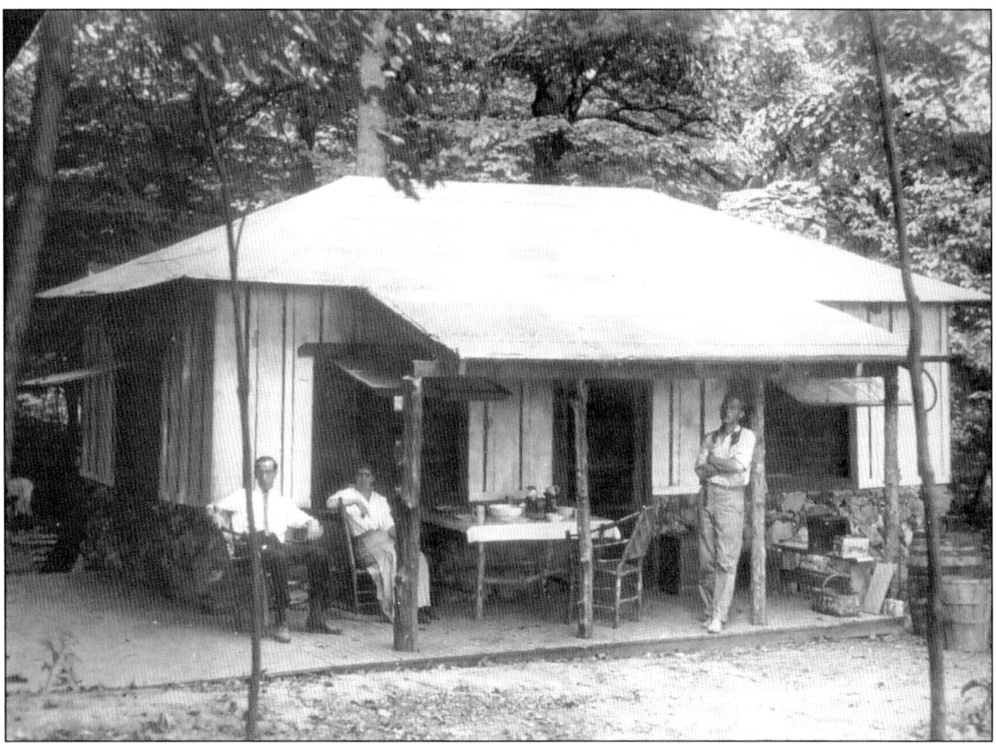

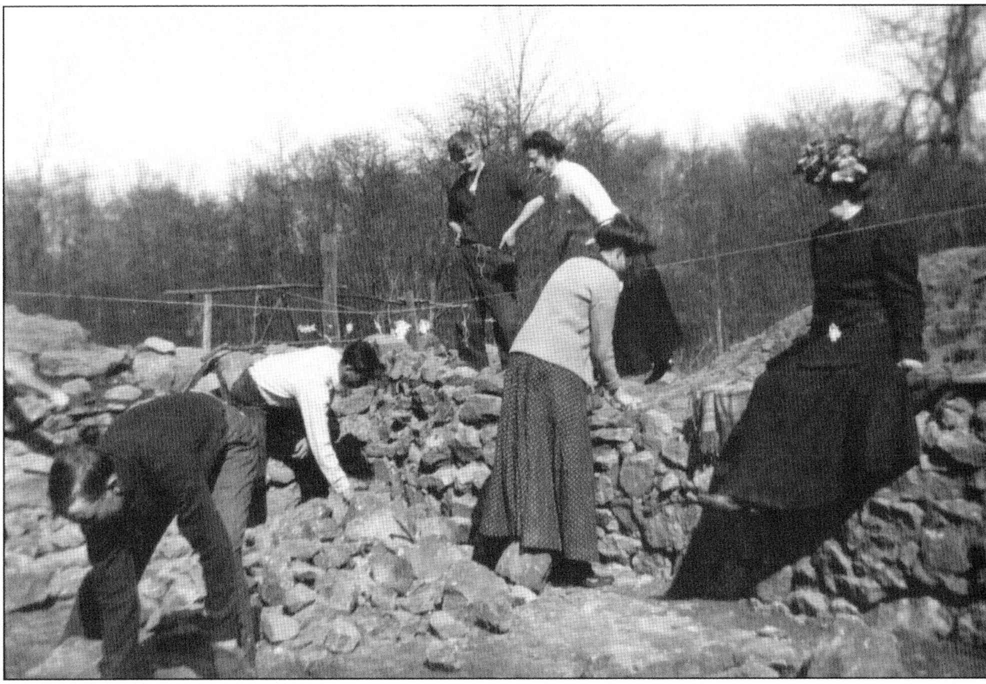

With supervision and help from neighboring farmers, many of Arden's first houses were built by the leaseholders themselves. In this 1910 photograph, a crew sorts stone for the foundation of a new home. The woman to the far right, however, appears to have other plans for the day.

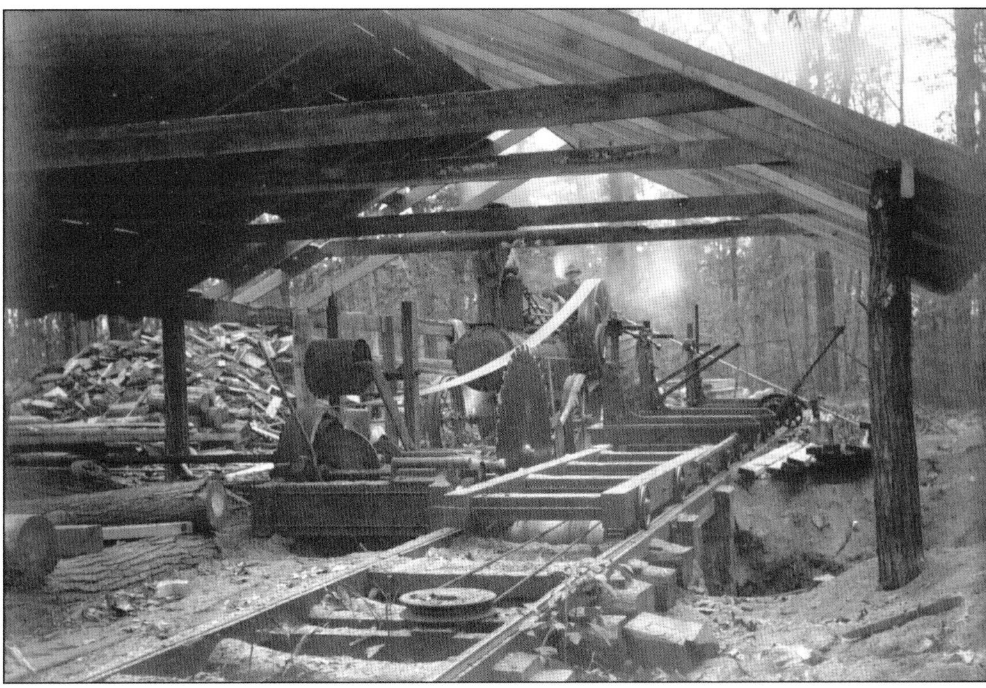

In 1906, the Arden sawmill was located in the meadow just below the Derrickson barn. It was operated by Jerry Harvey, and was a source of lumber for many early cottages. (Photograph by L. A. MacDonnald of Harvey, Delaware.)

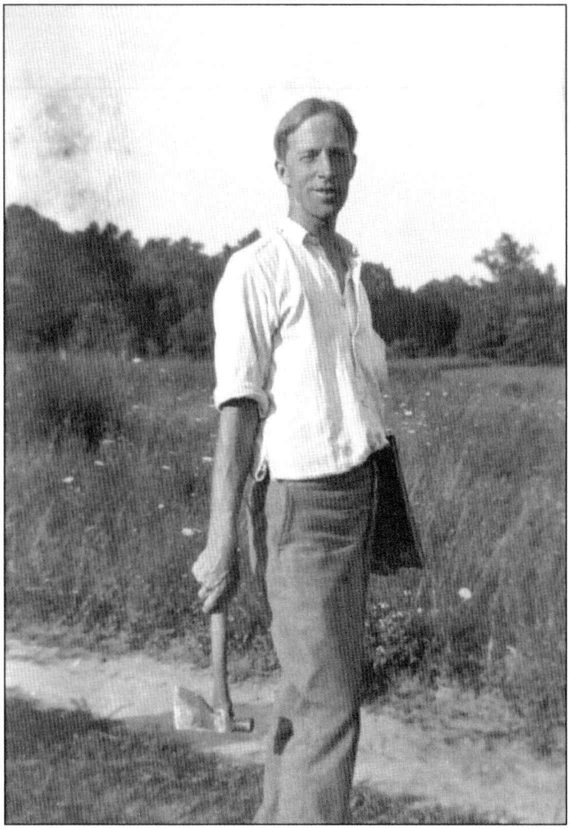

Frank Stephens took an active role in both the construction and design of many early cottages. He is seen here in 1907 returning from a building project at the Clement property.

One of the most photographed cottages in early Arden, the Admiral Benbow was a gift from Frank Stephens to his children Don and Margaret when they were in their early teens. The name is taken from Robert Louis Stephenson's book *Treasure Island,* which the family had been reading that year. This photograph of the cottage dates to 1908. No longer standing, it was originally located at the corner of Miller's Road and Woodland Lane.

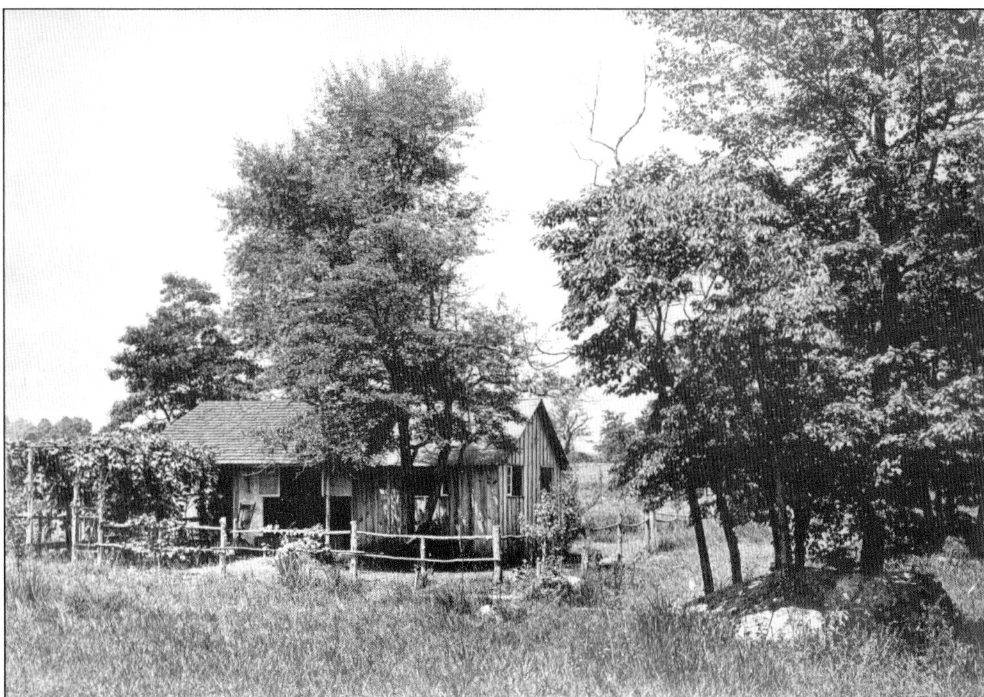

The Admiral Benbow was first known as Saint's Rest. It was built by Frank Martin, a member of Will Price's architectural firm, who along with Stephens and Price was one of the original trustees of Arden. According to Don Stephens, Martin sold Saint's Rest in 1902, which is when this photograph was taken, saying that he felt the Village Green had become overcrowded.

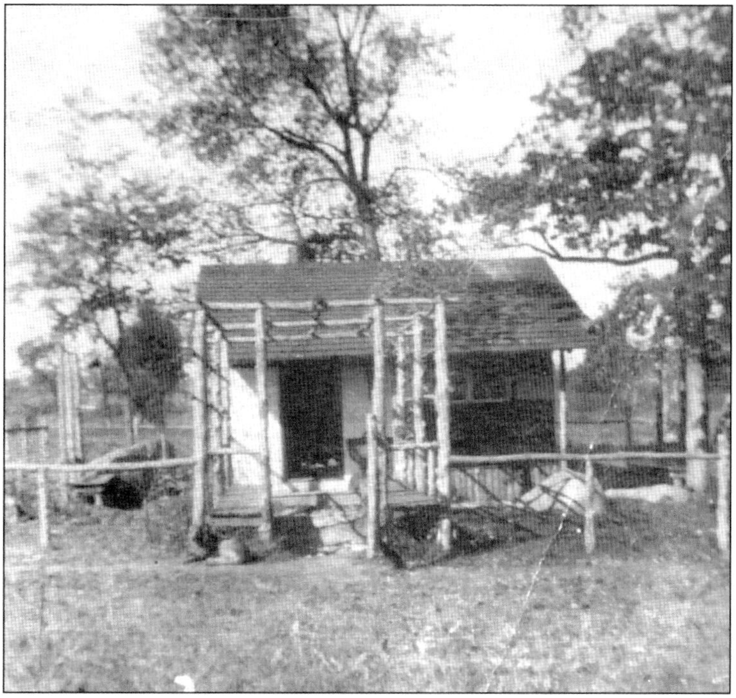

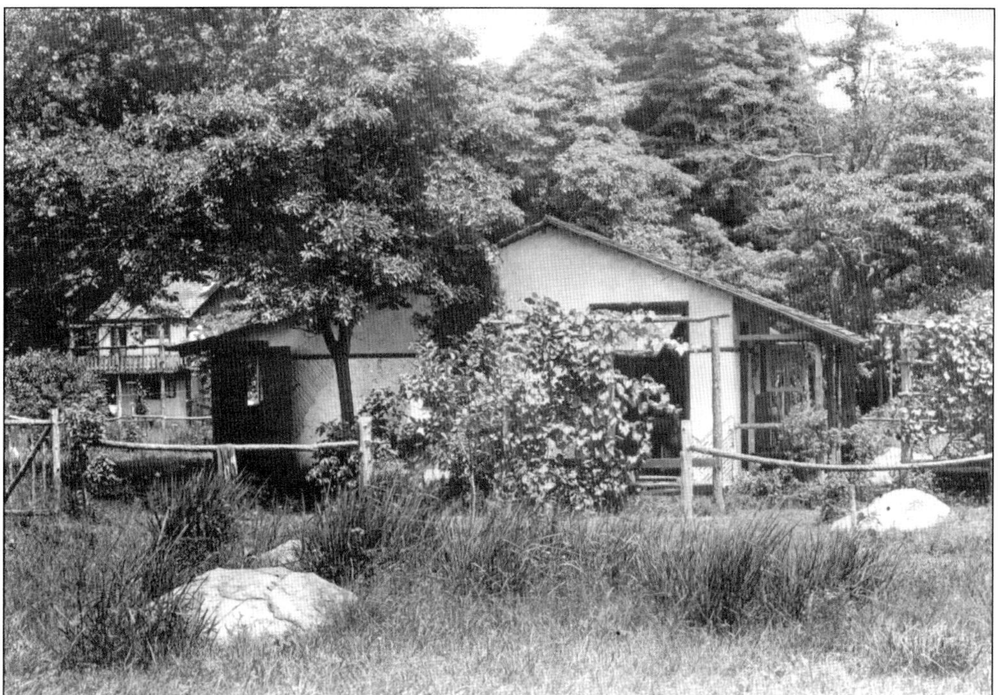

The Admiral Benbow is seen here again in 1908, but this time from Woodland Lane. Behind it can be seen the Brambles, which was built sometime prior to 1902 by George Leach, Harry Vandever, and Frank Stephens. In 1902, the Brambles was the summer home of Mother Bloor and her second husband, Dick Cohen.

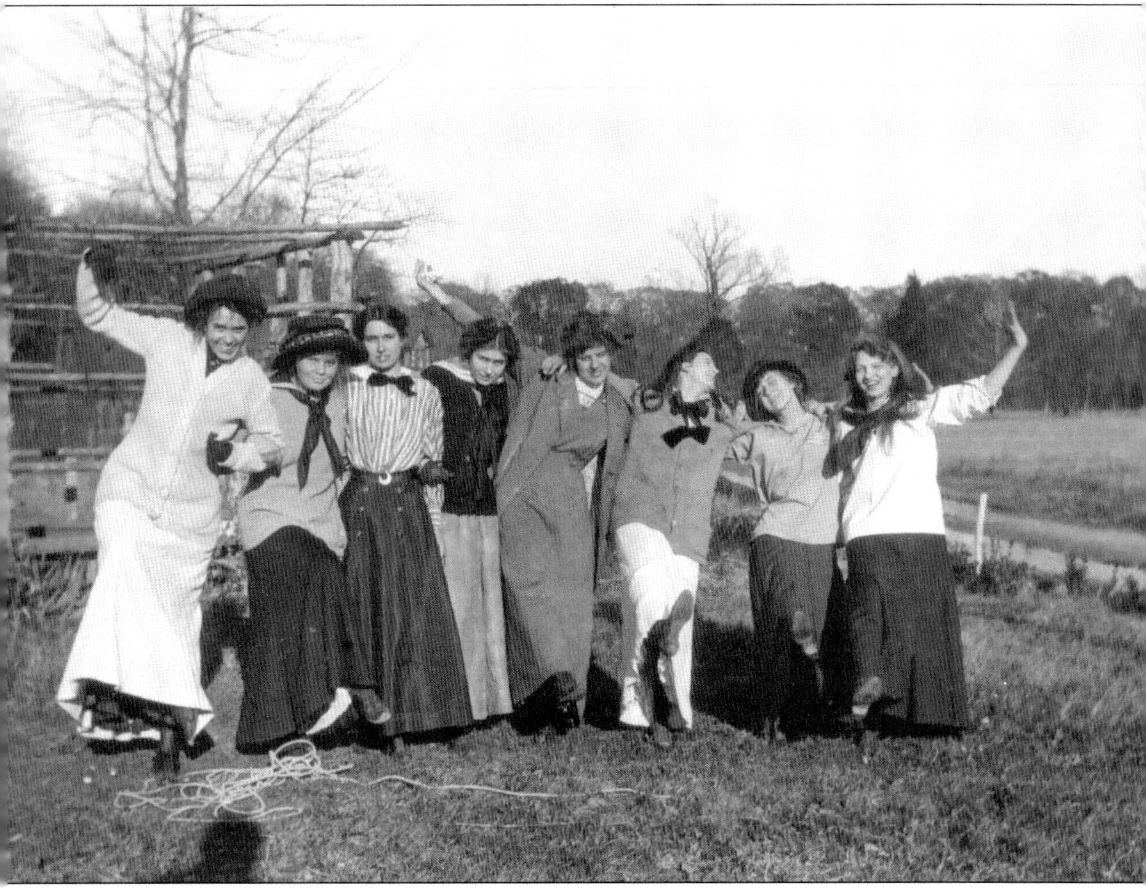

The Admiral Benbow was the place where Margaret Stephens and her friends could literally and figuratively "kick up their heels," as they are seen doing here in 1908. Arden young people were given an unprecedented amount of freedom in the community, but were expected in turn to take an active role in town affairs. From the beginning, children as well as women were afforded voting rights. In the case of the former however, it was much abused and stories abound of babes in arms being poked and prodded to vote their parents' wishes. In a raucous town meeting in August 1916, children's suffrage was rescinded and the voting age set at 18, which is where it stands today.

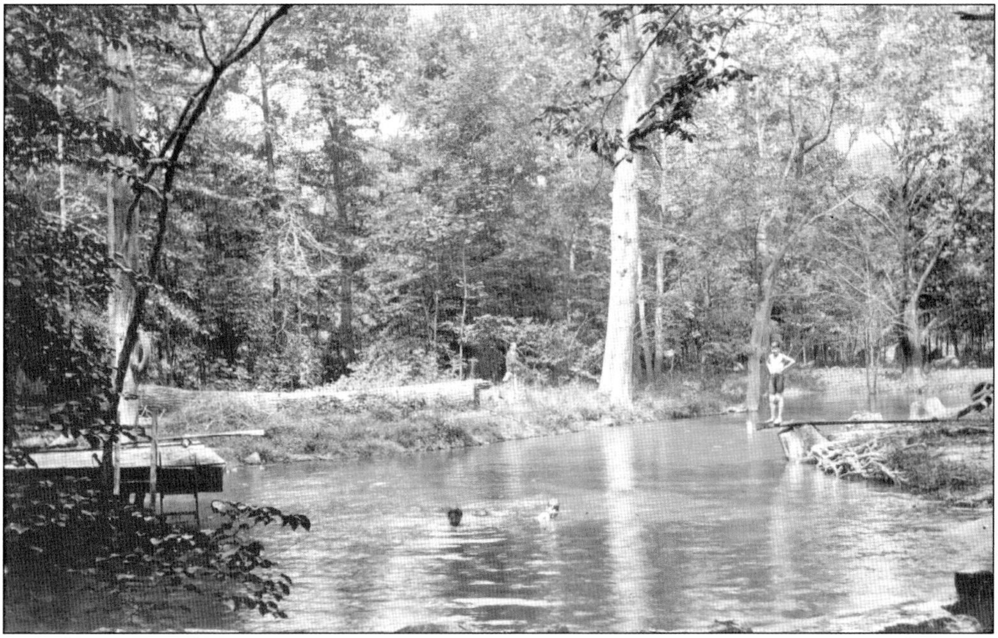

The Arden swimming pool on Naaman's Creek, seen here in 1908, was a popular gathering spot for young and old alike. On summer's hottest days children generally spent as much time there as their parents would allow. Night bathing was a much loved activity.

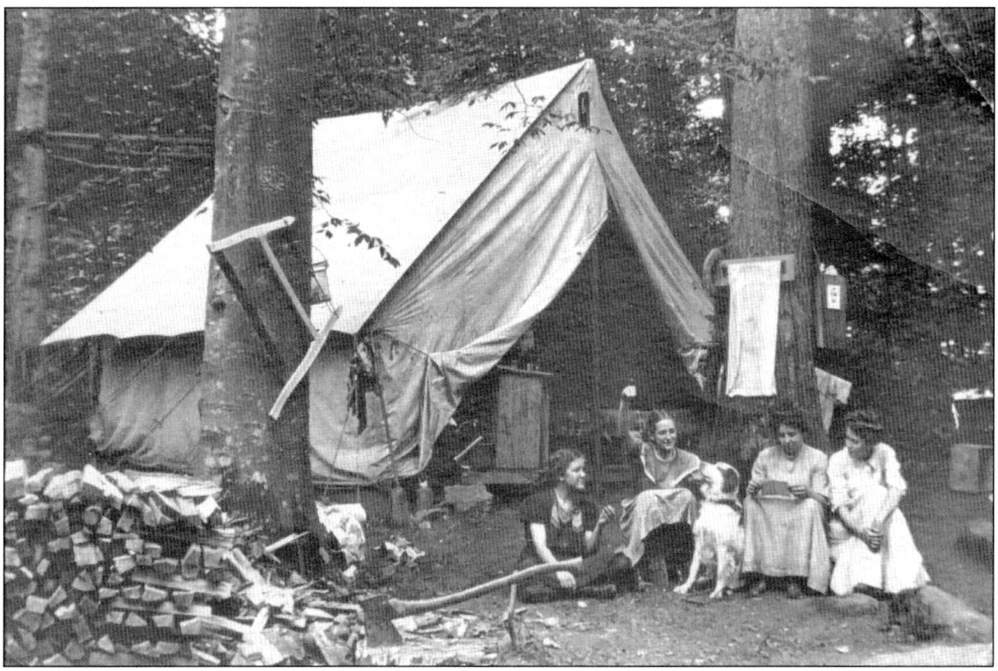

Camp Shankwood, near the site of the swimming pool on Naaman's Creek, was a gathering spot for Arden's young people. It was presided over by Marguerite Shanklin, affectionately known as "Shanks," who is shown here around 1907 seated with her back to the tree. Seen from left to right are Rachael Shanklin (Marguerite's sister), Jimmie Ware, Marguerite, and possibly Margaret Stephens.

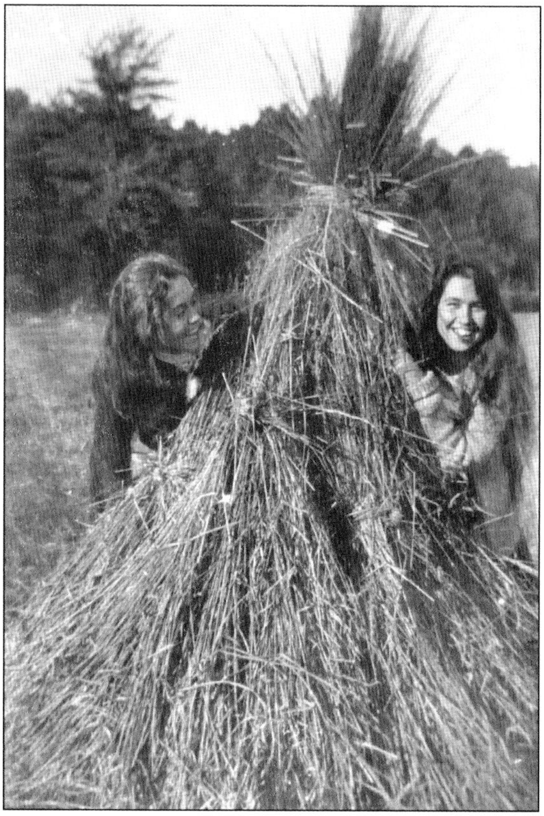

Margaret Stephens (right) and Margaret Wood play "Indians" on the Village Green in this 1908 photograph. "Indians" and "Lay, Sheepy, Lay" were much enjoyed games among Arden young people.

To children from the city, country life was quite exciting. The boy with the grin on his face atop the hay wagon on the Village Green in 1901 appears to be Roger Stephens, Frank Stephens's third child. Roger was raised by an aunt in New Jersey, but spent a great deal of time in Arden as well.

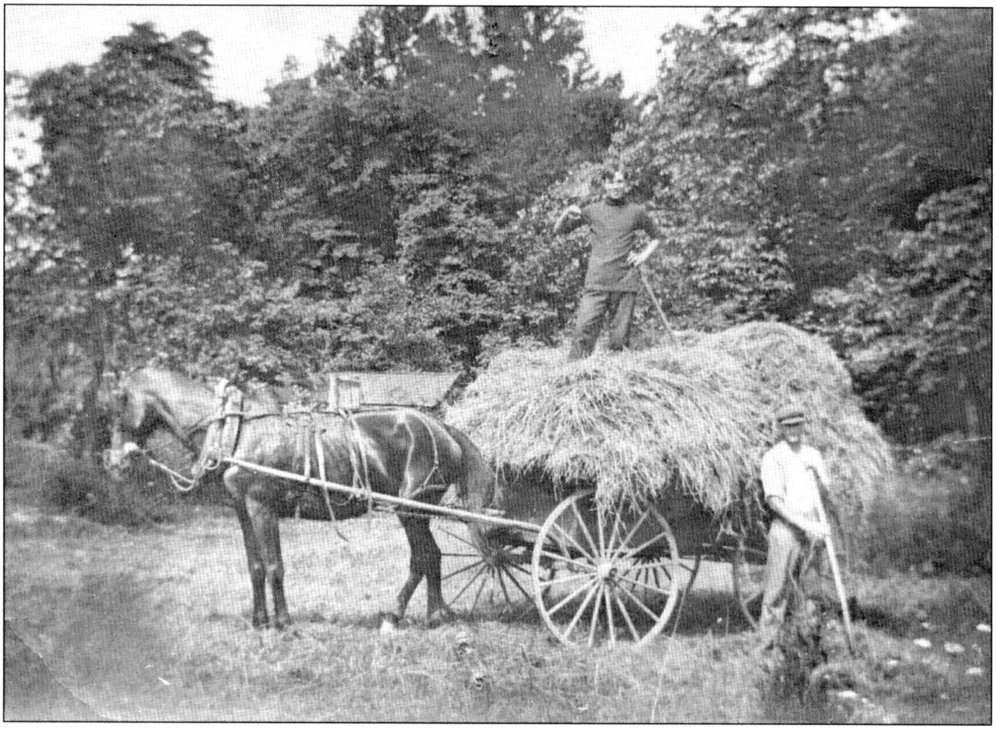

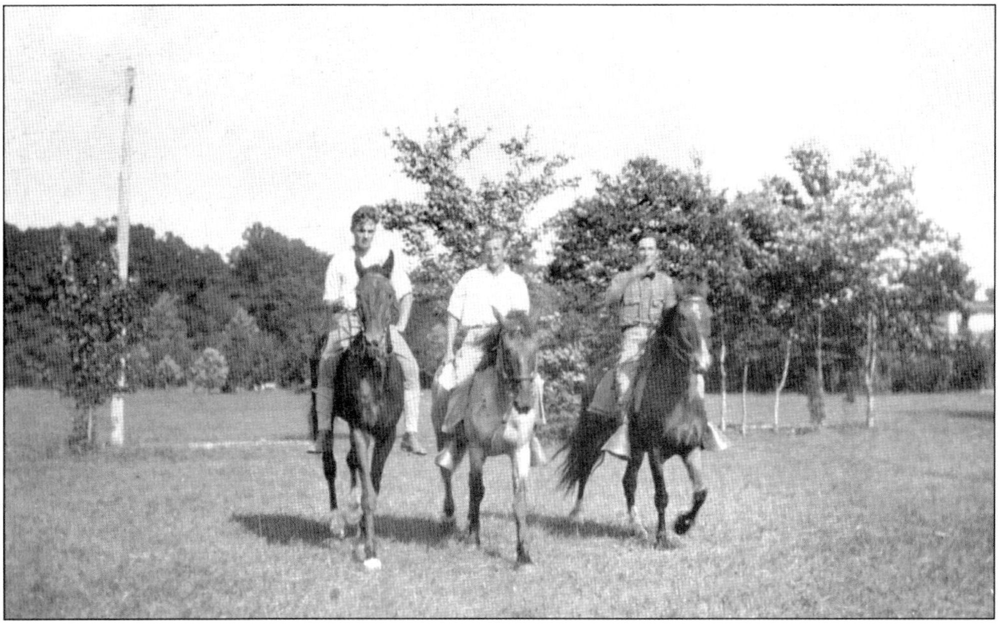

Horseback riding was another favorite pastime. While horses were most certainly borrowed from neighboring farmers, many residents stabled horses as well. In this 1909 photograph, Roger Stephens (right), Hal Ware (center), and an unidentified rider cantor past the flagpole on the Village Green.

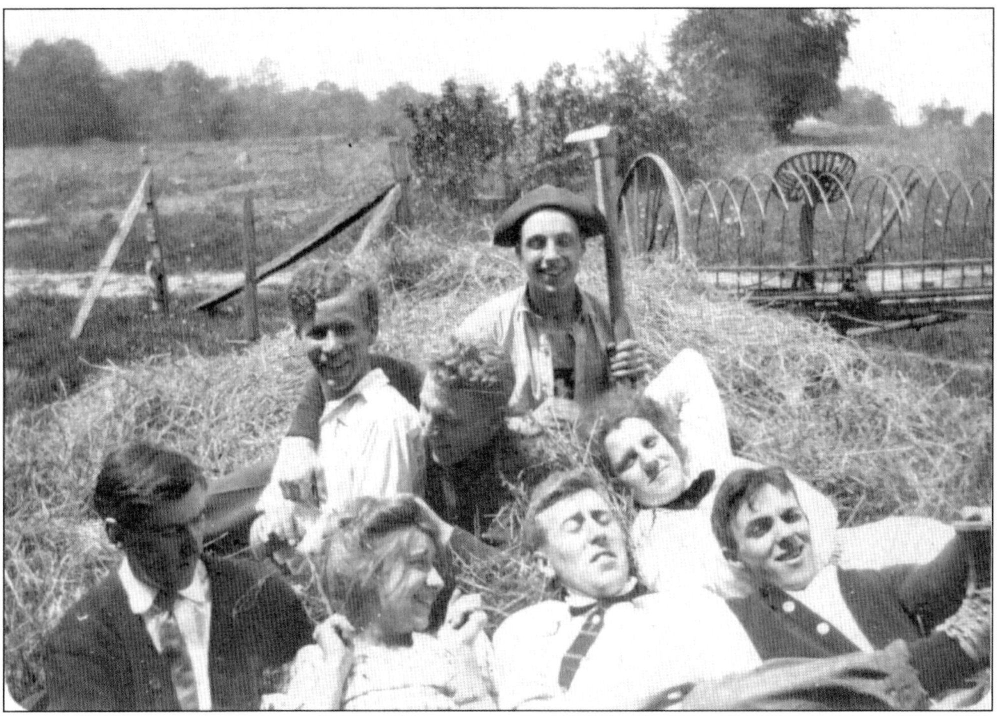

One can almost hear the laughter in this 1908 photograph of an early Arden hayride. Hal Ware is to the back left. Bonnie and John Terrace are in the front row center. The others are unfortunately unknown.

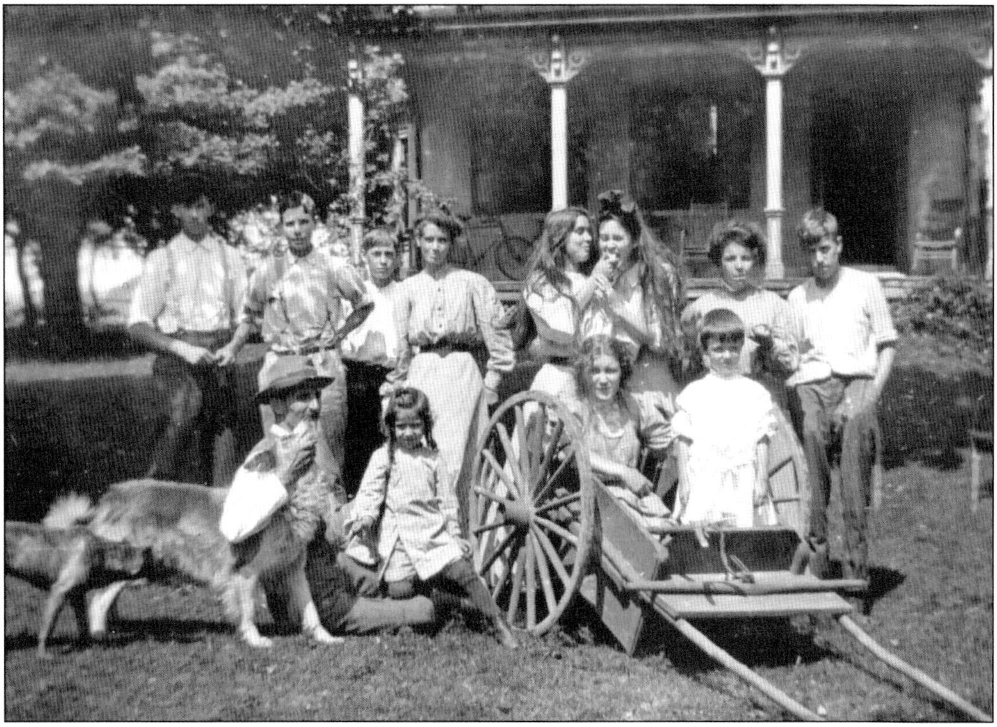

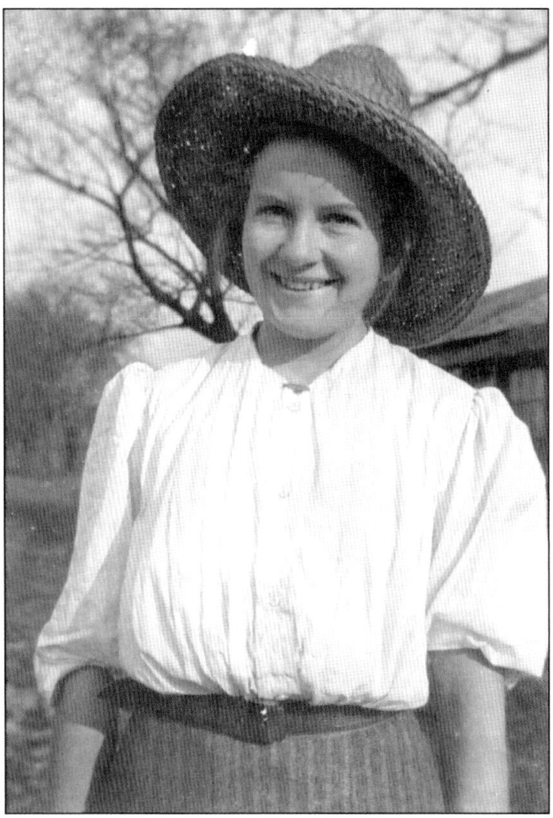

The children of Arden's first settlers were a close-knit group and were known collectively as "the Bunch." Several of them pose here in 1907 with farmer Jack Veale (seated far left) and his family after a wagon ride to the Veale farmhouse, a popular destination for ice cream. Behind the wagon, from right to left, are Dick ?, Marguerite Shanklin, Margaret Stephens, and Margaret Wood. Seated in the wagon is Rachael Shanklin. The names of Jack Veale's family members are unknown.

Helen Ware's smile in this 1907 photograph illustrates why she was such a favorite in Arden. The second of Mother Bloor's six children, she developed a love of the violin at an early age, becoming a much sought-after performance and recording artist. She was known particularly for her interpretations of Hungarian gypsy music.

For the Arden pioneers, Naaman's Creek offered opportunities for more than just swimming, as Jimmie Ware demonstrates in 1907.

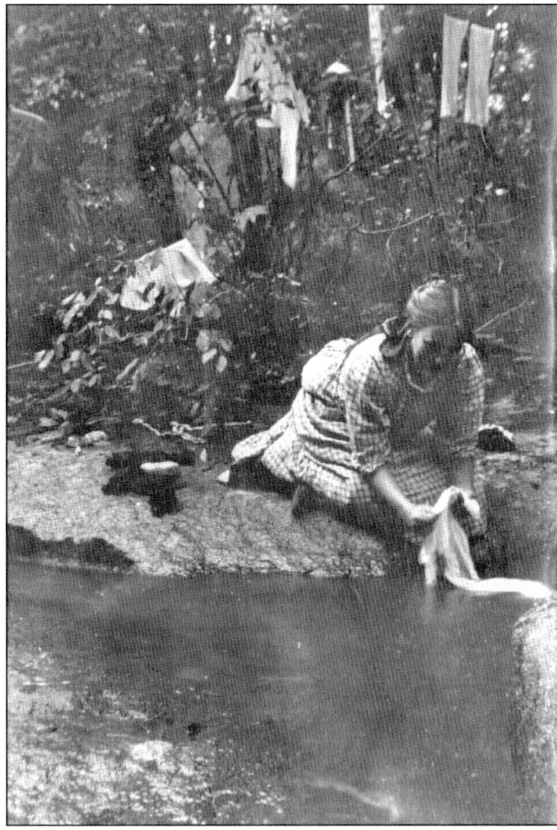

Jimmie Ware stands here beside the Roserie around 1912. The Roserie, another much photographed early cottage, was one of five Arden cottages featured in the November 1909 issue of Gustav Stickley's *Craftsman Magazine*. The uncredited writer thought the chimney top "an interesting variation in chimney building," likening it to a crow's nest. (Courtesy of Terry Colgan.)

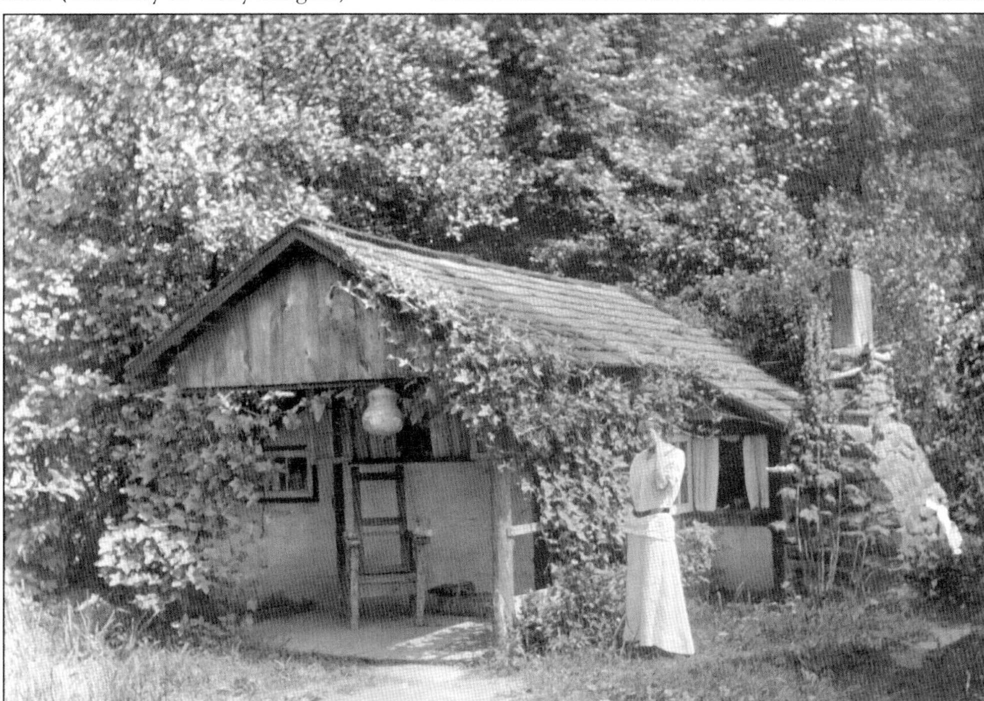

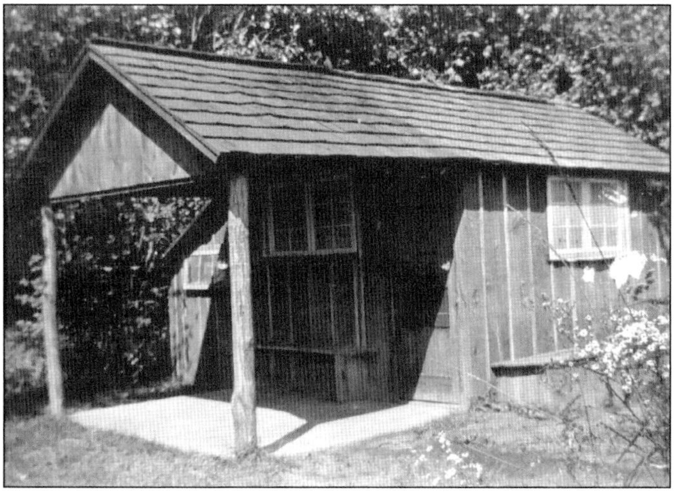

Oral tradition has it that the Roserie was named in honor of two of the cottage's earliest residents, both named Rose. Oral tradition is not so forthcoming, however, for the reason behind the name the Bug House, which is how the cottage was known in 1902 when this photograph was taken. As with most Arden cottages, the Roserie evolved through the years to reflect its current owners' needs and tastes.

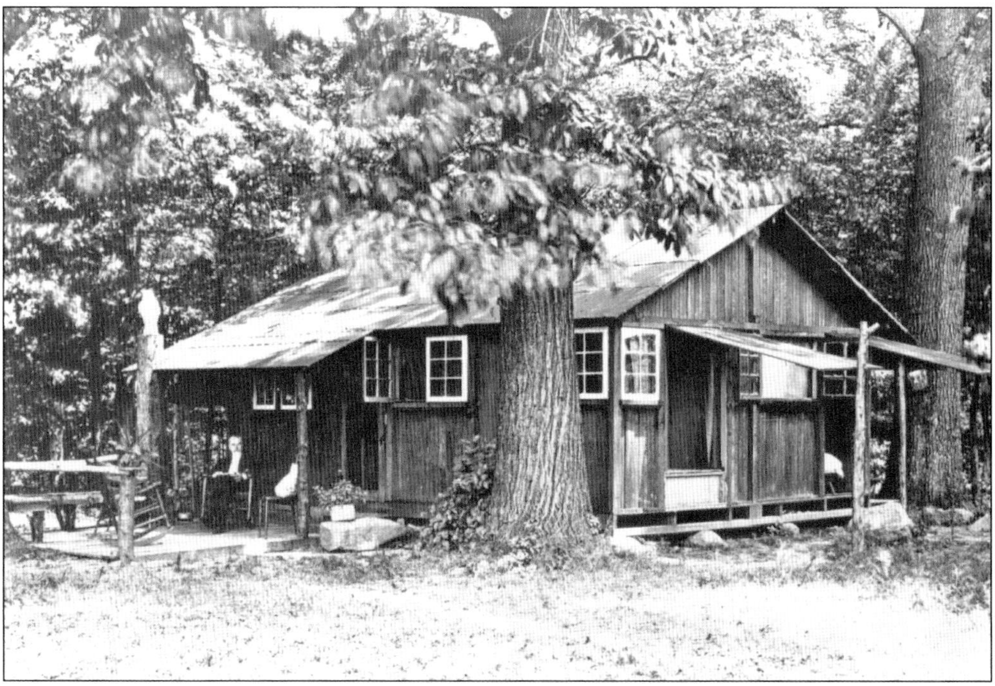

When the writer and tastemaker Mabel Tuke Priestman visited Arden in 1908 on assignment for *American Homes and Gardens*, Williams Irwin's bungalow the Owls Nest was one of several cottages that caught her eye. Ms. Priestman thought the cottage "Japanese" in taste, and with its green paint, touches of peacock blue and white windows, somewhat "unusual" in appearance. The cottage took its name from a family of owls that nested nearby. Ironically, when a sculpture of an owl was mounted beside the cottage in tribute, the original inhabitants decamped, never to be seen again.

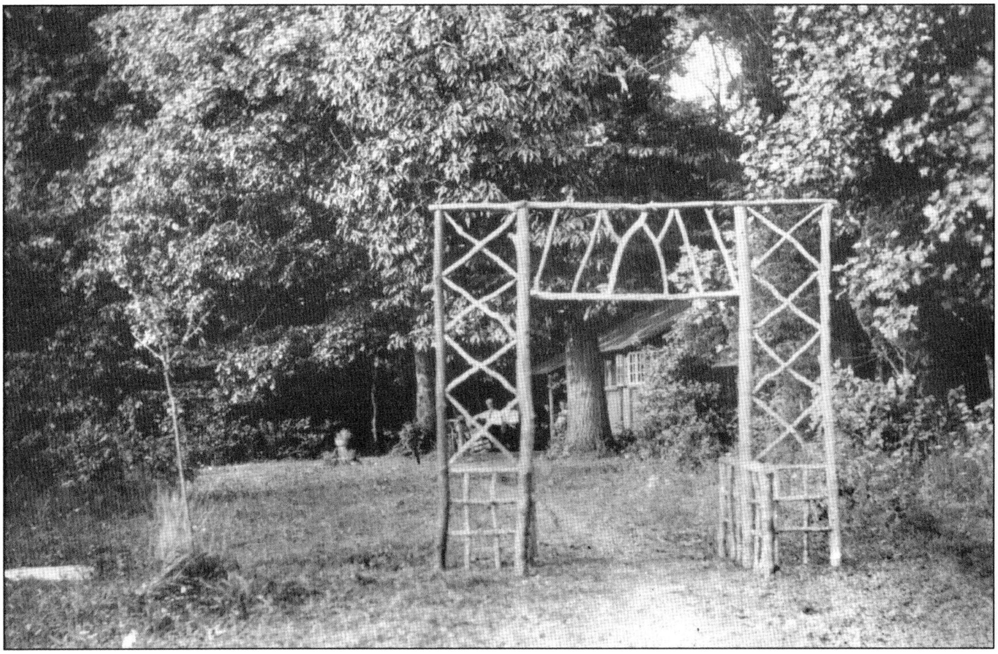

This rustic arch, photographed in 1908, made for a very artistic entryway to the Owls Nest. In the early Arden landscape, rustic touches such as this served to blur the distinction between the architecture and the surrounding environment.

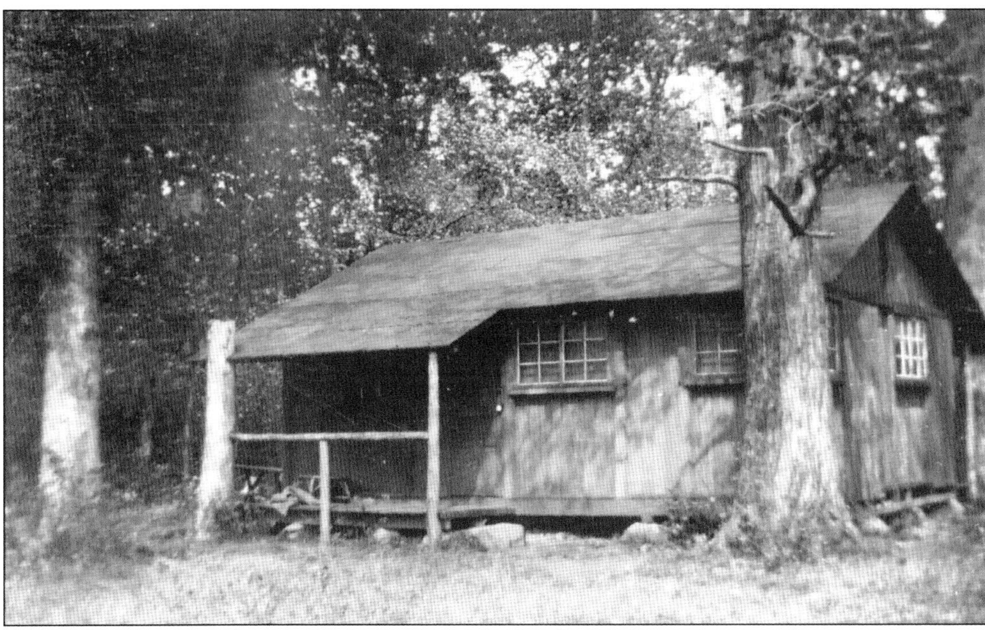

In its earliest incarnation, the Owls Nest was known as Bower's Bower, the home of the painter Alexander Bower, and the third home built in the community. Bower studied with Thomas Anshutz at the Pennsylvania Academy of Fine Arts from 1900 to 1906, which is where he most likely met Frank Stephens. Although Bower and his wife can be traced to Cliff Island, Maine, by 1914, they maintained close ties with the community and returned to Arden in the early 1950s. Their Bower was photographed in 1906.

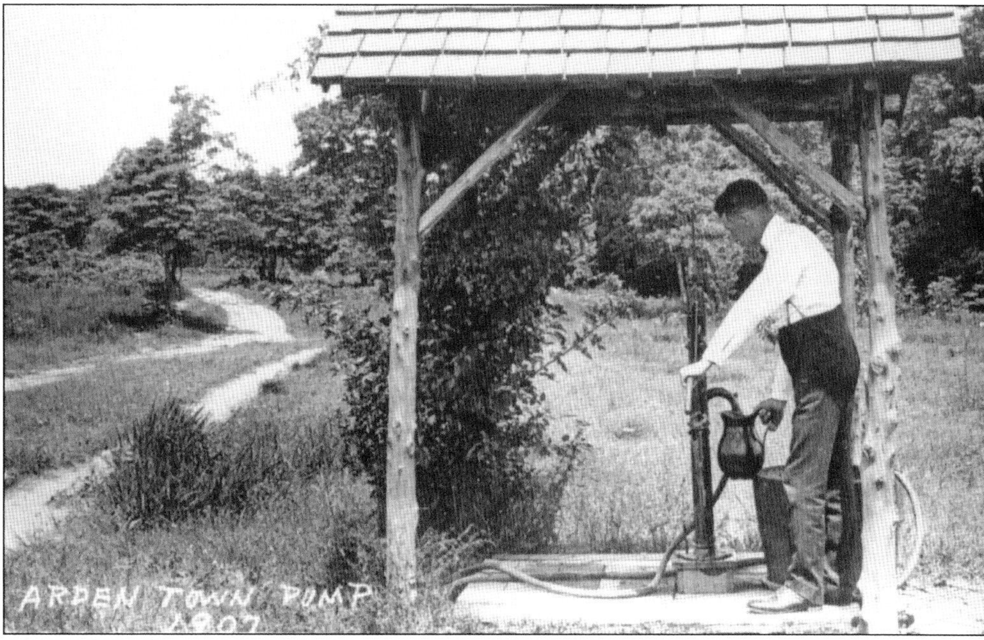

Although its location is unclear, this pump was one of six that were used to provide water for the community. As with Arden houses, town pumps bore names; however, the only one to come down to us is the Practical Farmer, which also happened to be the name of another local watering hole, the Practical Farmer Inn.

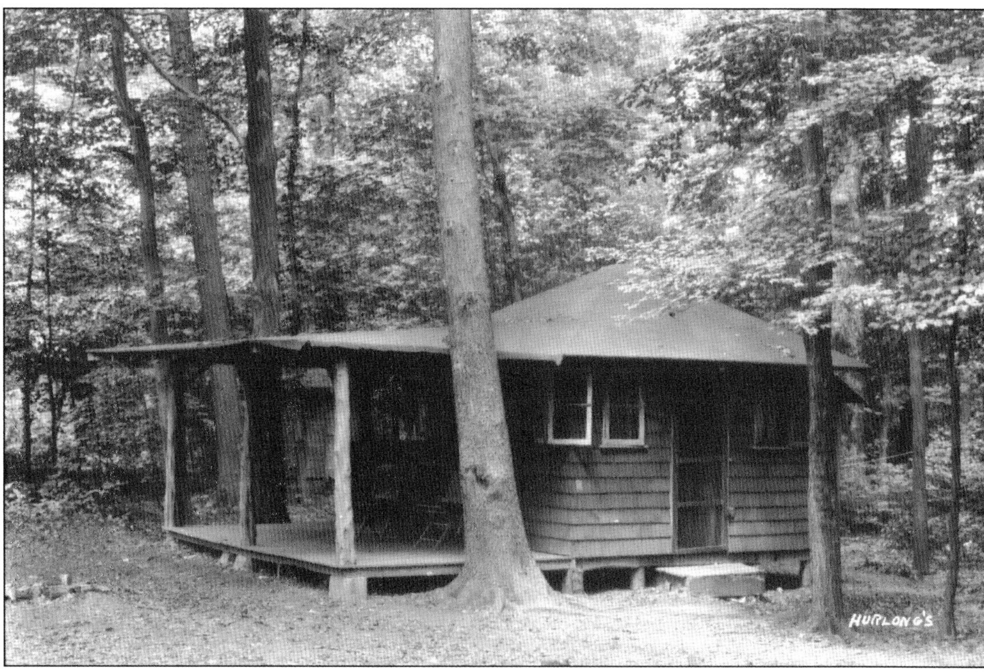

The Camp, located at 2401 Woodland Lane, was the summer residence of the Philadelphia dentist Herman "Doc" Hurlong and his wife Lena, a lawyer and suffragette. Like many of the Arden pioneers, the Hurlongs lived in a collection of tents on their leasehold. This cabin originally served as a storage shed for their clothing, but was later greatly expanded.

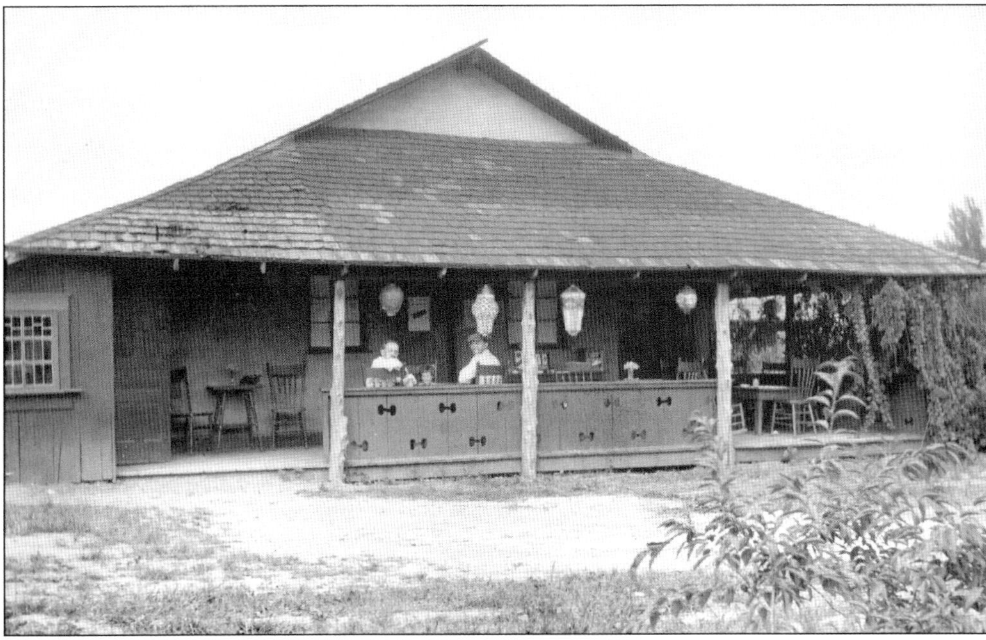

The Cooler, Arden's ice cream parlor, was located just behind the Red House on Miller's Road. The open air porch was a popular gathering spot for residents and visitors alike, as seen here in 1908.

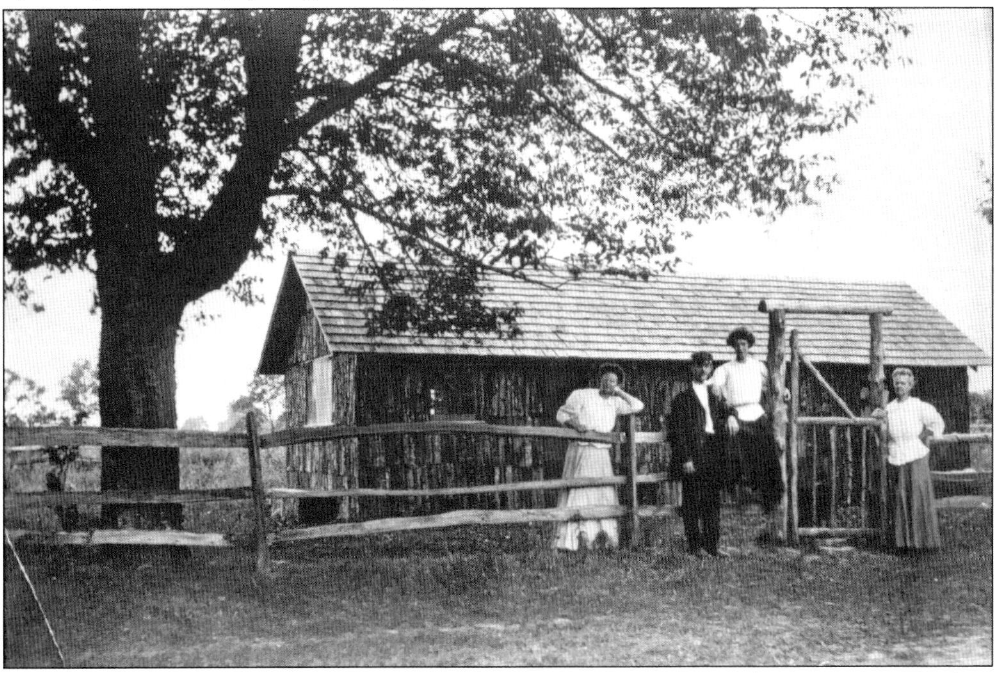

Built with vertical log sheathing, as were many early cottages, Cherry Lodge was home to Arden's first print shop, which was operated by Fred Steinlein and Don Stephens. Their first publication, *Arden Club Talk*, was proposed by Don as a means for Ardenites to remain in contact during the long winter's absence from the community. Issued "try-monthly" beginning in October 1908, it was superseded by the *Arden Leaves* in November 1910. Photographed here around 1907 outside Cherry Lodge is the Kumme family.

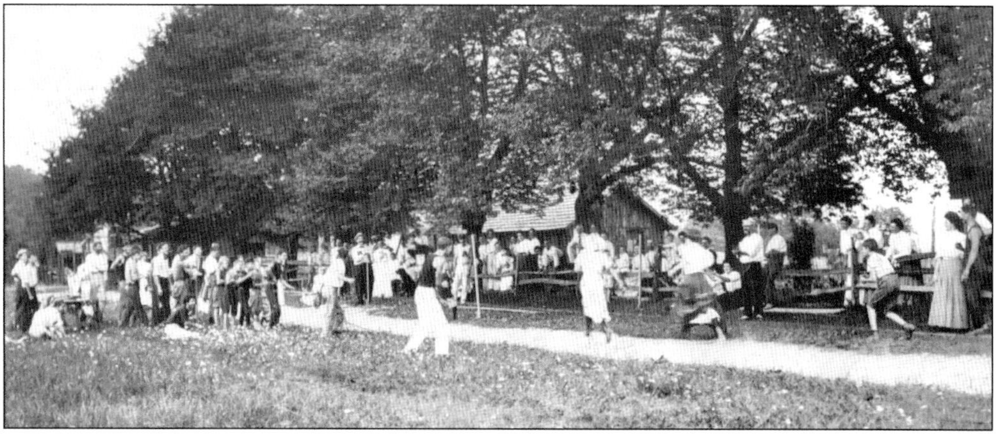

Arden's First Annual Field Day was held August 15, 1908, along Cherry Lane. Pictured here is Jimmie Ware leading her sister Mabel to the finish line in the women's 100-yard dash, an event she won with a time of 15 seconds. Other events that year included the men's sack race (pictured below), men's and women's nail driving, baseball throwing, and a pie eating contest. The latter was won by Hal Ware, who managed to devour 35 pies in 2 minutes and 40 seconds. (Courtesy of Terry Colgan.)

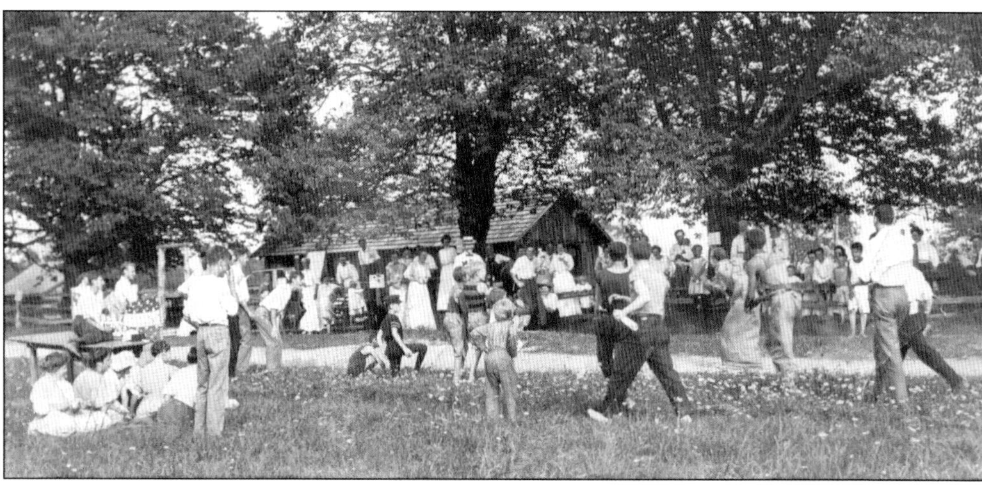

An unidentified pair of boys jump the stile steps on Arden's tennis court in the annual Hare and Hounds race. The photograph is dated 1907 and is titled *First Hounds In*.

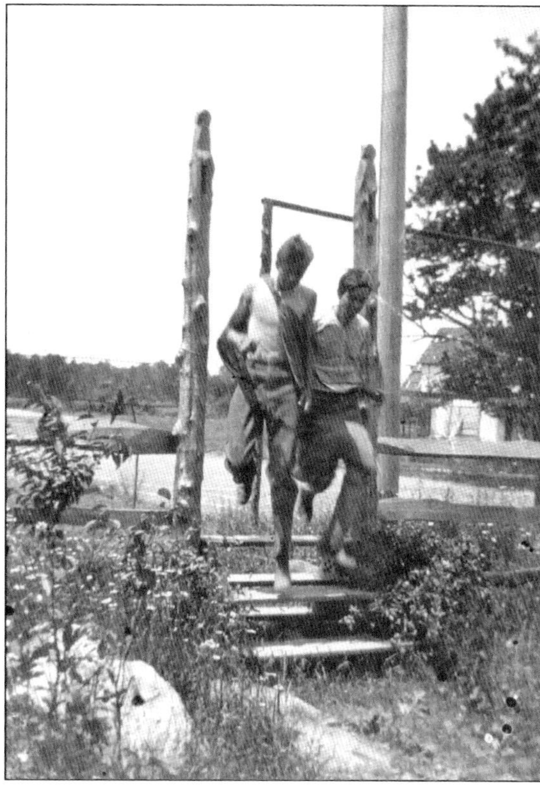

In an effort perhaps to bring attention to the new community, Frank Stephens and Rose Valley resident Henry Hetzel ran a boy's summer camp in Arden from 1905 to 1908. In a 10-week program, boys 16 and under studied theater, gardening, carpentry, crafts, and the international language Esperanto. Meals were served in the open air dining room attached to the Arden Inn.

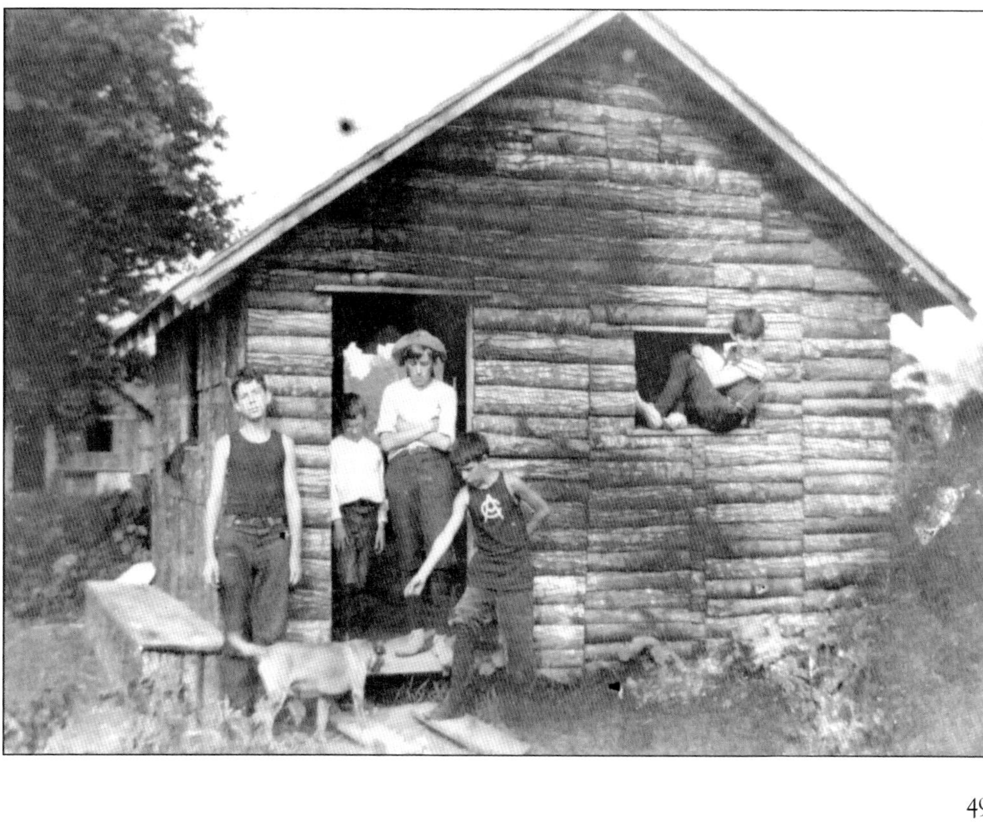

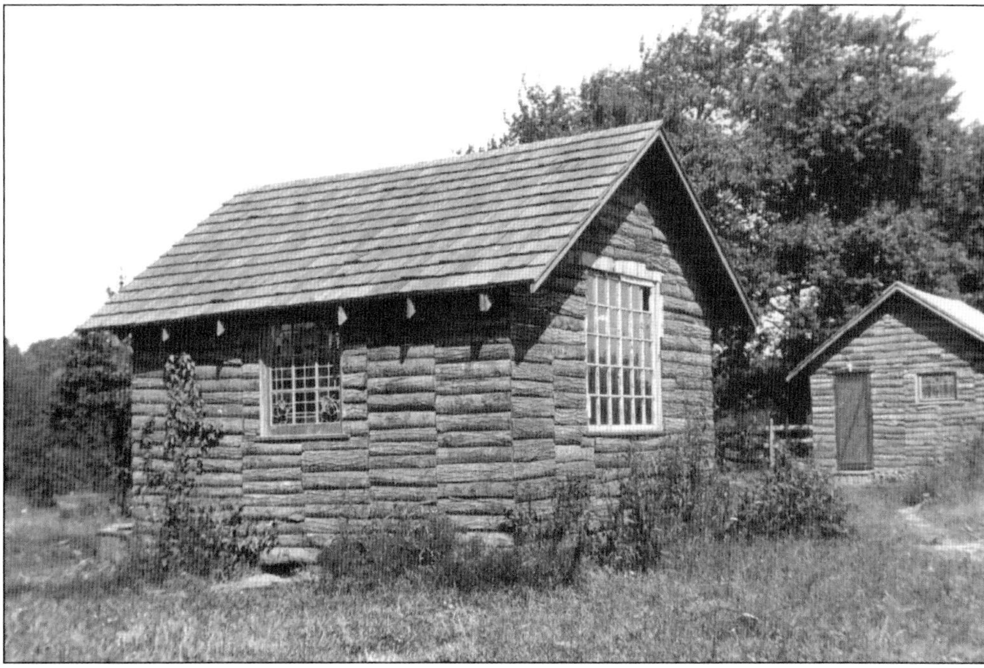

In 1909, Don Stephens began converting one of the former boys' camp cabins for his new residence, which he called the Monastery. The cabin featured leaded windows designed by Buzz Ware with caricatures of two seated monks. The windows were made by Elena Darling and can be seen in the foreground of the photograph above. The bottom photograph shows the Monastery's interior. The library table and footstool were both made by Don.

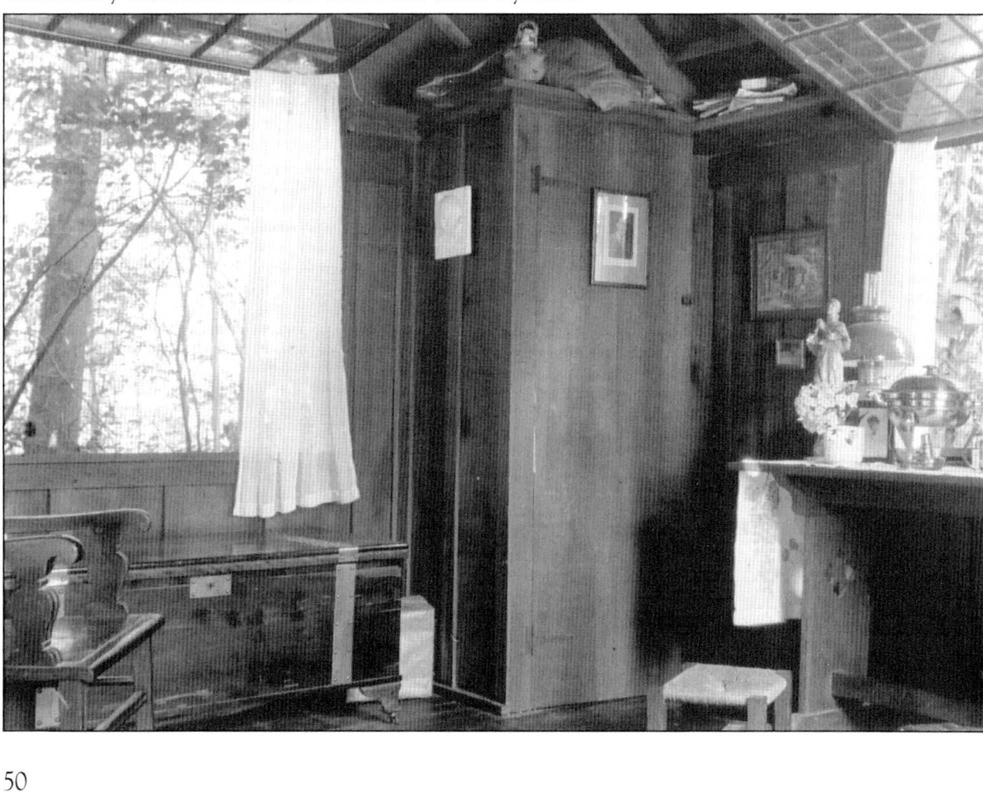

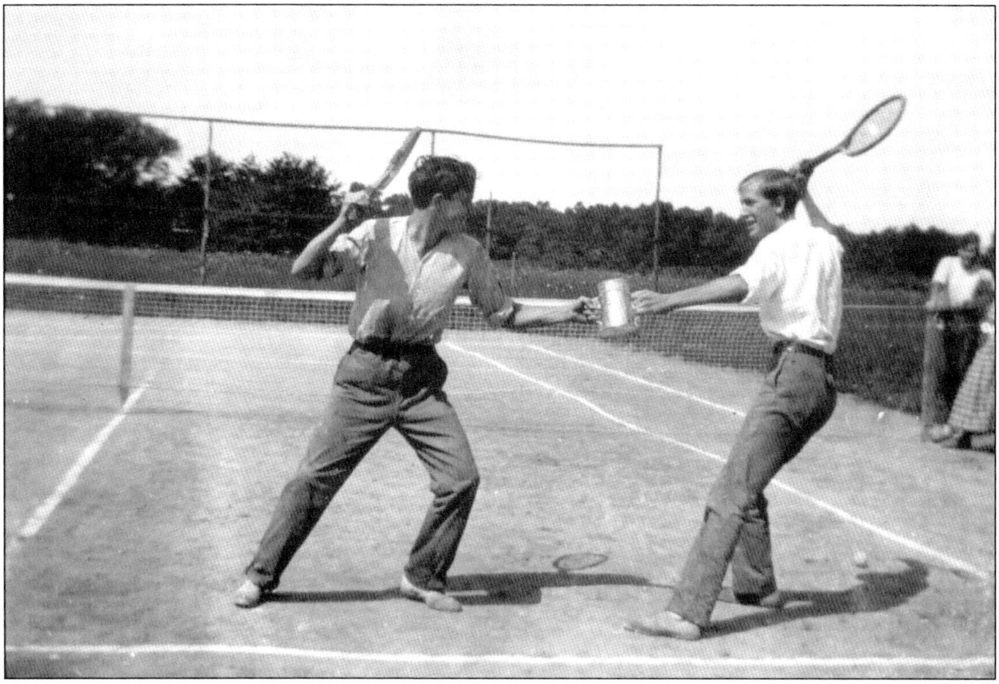

Tennis was a popular sport in the early years. Here Don Stephens (right) and his brother Roger battle over rights to the 1907 Arden tennis trophy. The trophy, now part of the permanent collection of the Arden Museum, has Don Stephens listed as Grand Champion in 1904, 1905, and 1907.

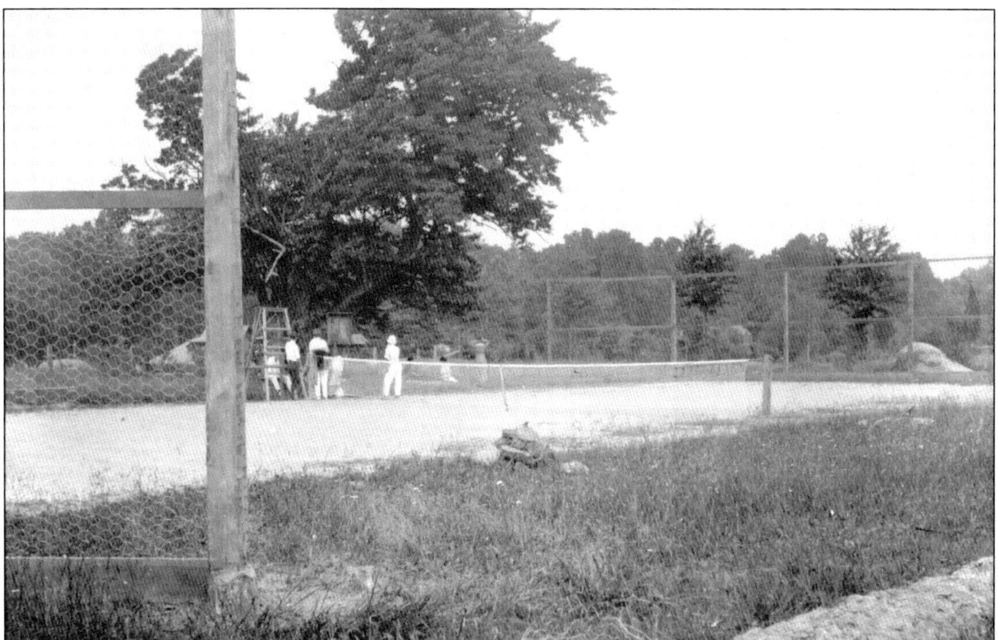

Arden's tennis court, which no longer exists, was located just at the end of the Village Green near the intersection of Miller's Road and the Milky Way. The Milky Way, one of the many walking paths throughout the community, was so named because it was the path the Derricksons had formerly used to take their milk cows to pasture.

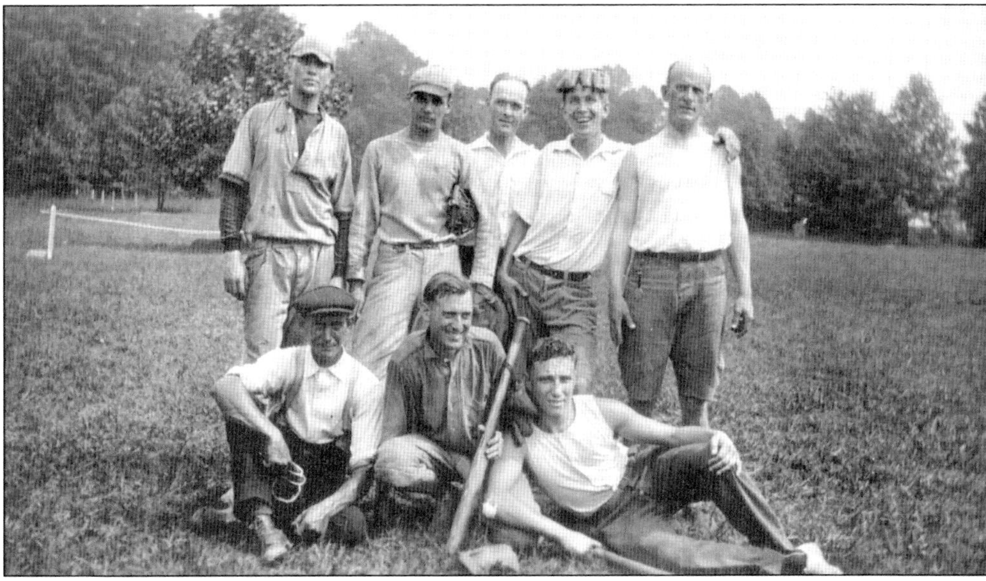

Along with tennis, baseball was a popular sport for both players and spectators. Home and away games were held most Saturdays throughout the summer against Rose Valley, B & O Railroad, Knights of Columbus, Claymont, and other teams. In this Arden team photograph taken around 1911 on the Village Green, Don Stephens stands with his glove on his head. Catcher Buzz Ware can be seen second from left, also in the back row. (Courtesy of Terry Colgan.)

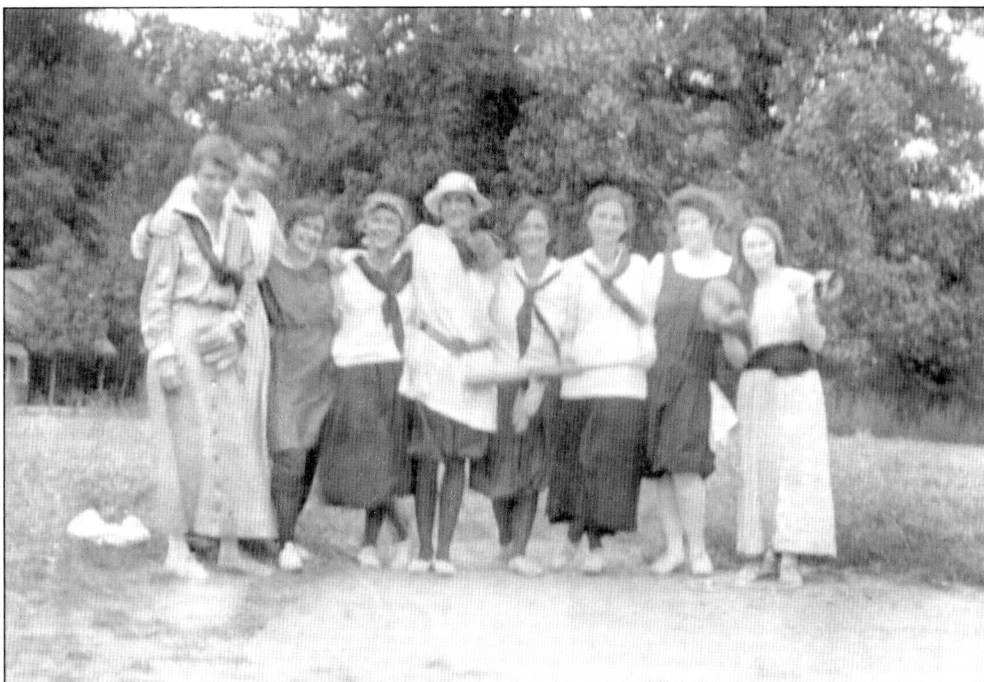

Not to be outdone, Arden women formed their own baseball team in 1909. The team members seen here from left to right are Connie Kiehel, unidentified, Nellie Nearing, Connie Farrell, Jimmie Ware, Peach Worthington, Mary Nearing, Chris Smith, and unidentified. (Courtesy of Terry Colgan.)

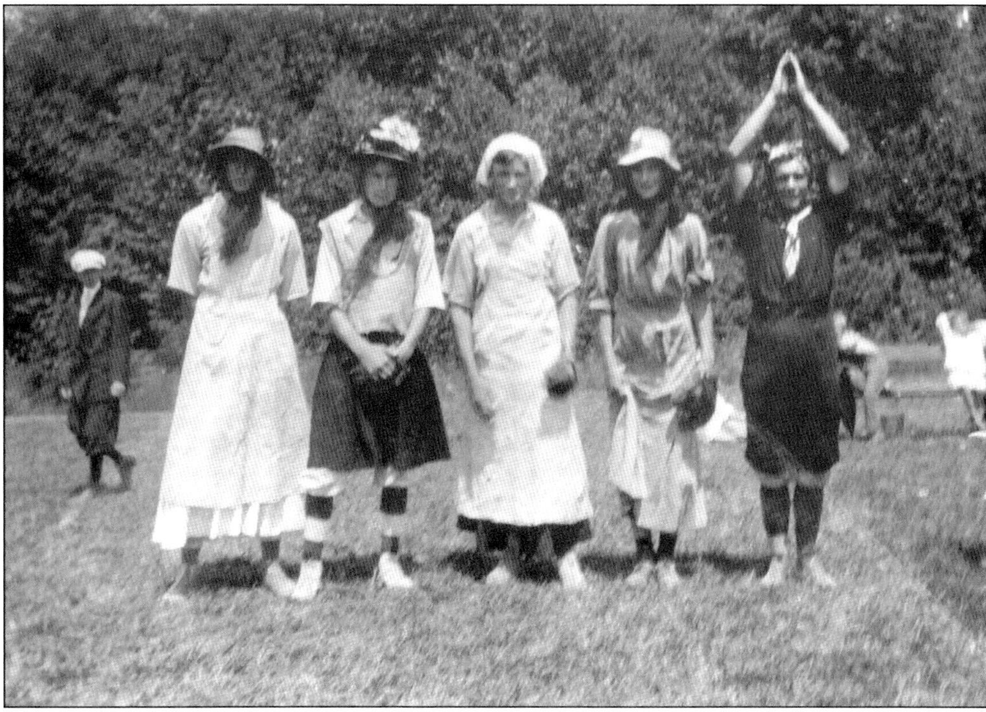

When other games were not scheduled, the men's and women's ball teams often challenged each other, which may explain the team uniform on the men's side for this particular game in 1912.

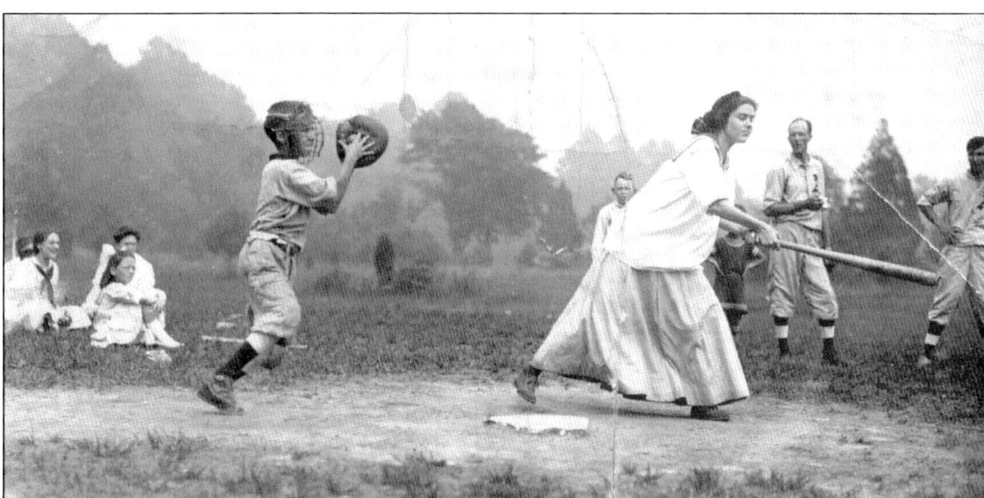

Margaret Stephens takes her turn at bat in this 1909 photograph of a game in progress. The catcher is Buzz Ware. (Courtesy of Terry Colgan.)

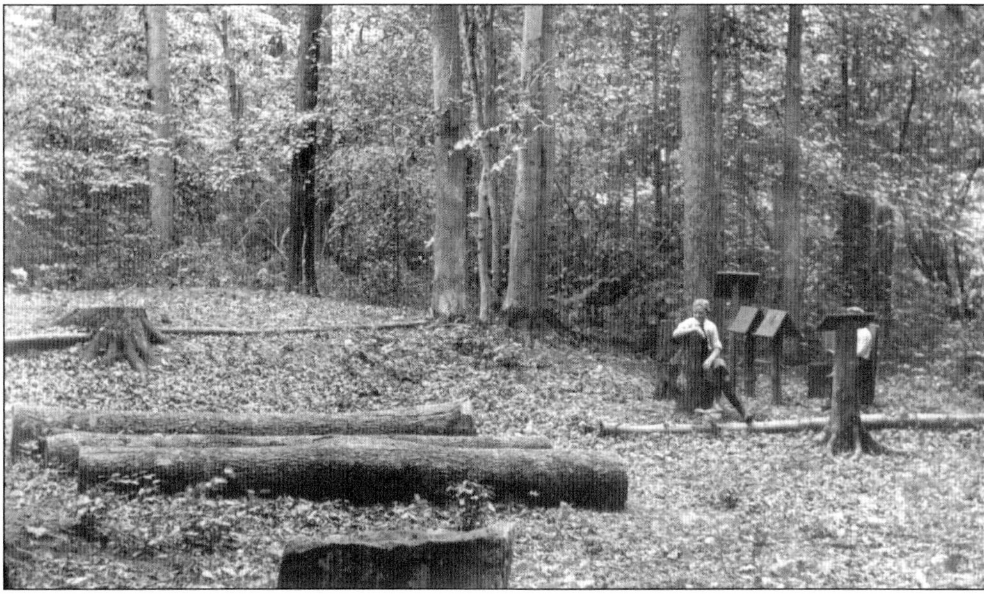

This clearing, located at the foot of Woodland Lane, was the site of Arden's Sunday evening campfires. Here at dusk, in an informal woodland setting, residents and visitors shared songs, recitations, and music. According to Don Stephens, the old Arden campfires embodied more of the Arden spirit than any other institution.

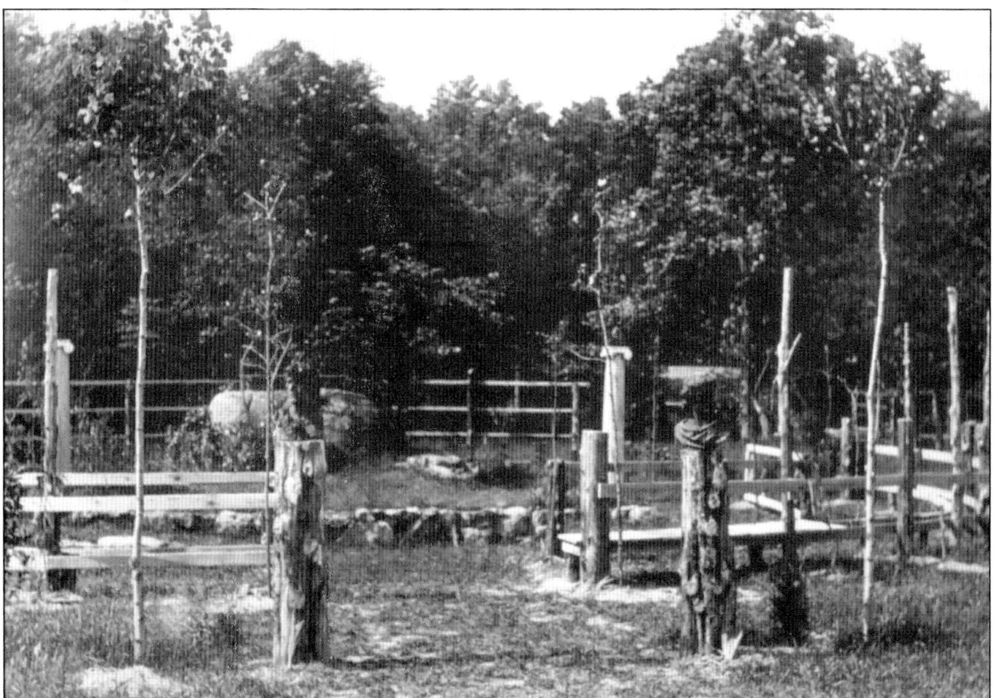

Although there were only a handful of cottages in Arden when the Field Theater was constructed, it immediately became a focal point of village life. On most Saturday evenings throughout the summer, Ardenites gathered there for Shakespearean performances, followed by an ice cream party on the Village Green, and a dance at the Red House. The theater is seen here around 1906.

Lighting for the Field Theater was provided by Japanese candle lanterns, which also illuminated the walkway between the Field Theater and the Red House. In this 1909 photograph, Buzz Ware and an unknown actress perform a scene from *As You Like It* by William Shakespeare. An accomplished artist as well as an actor, Buzz was responsible for much of the illustration work used in Arden's promotional material during the 1910s and 1920s.

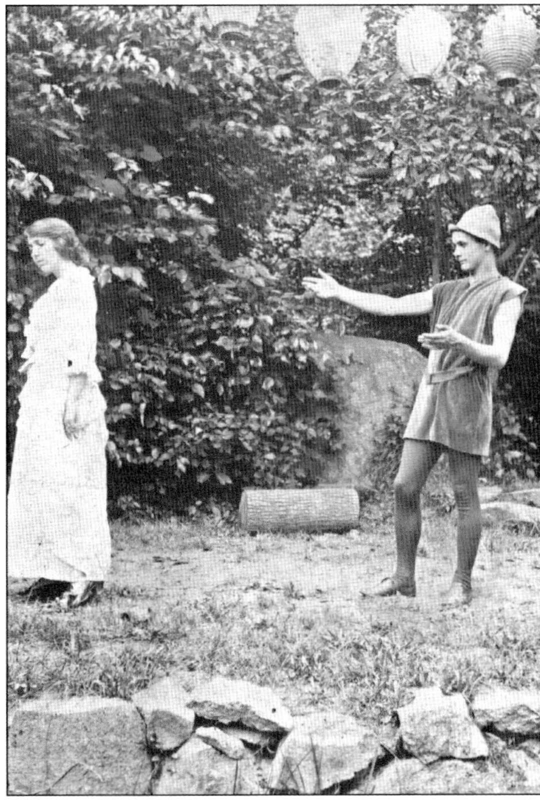

The large boulder on the stage of the Field Theater provides a dramatic setting for the balcony scene from *Romeo and Juliet*. Fred Whiteside takes the role of Romeo, but his Juliet is unknown.

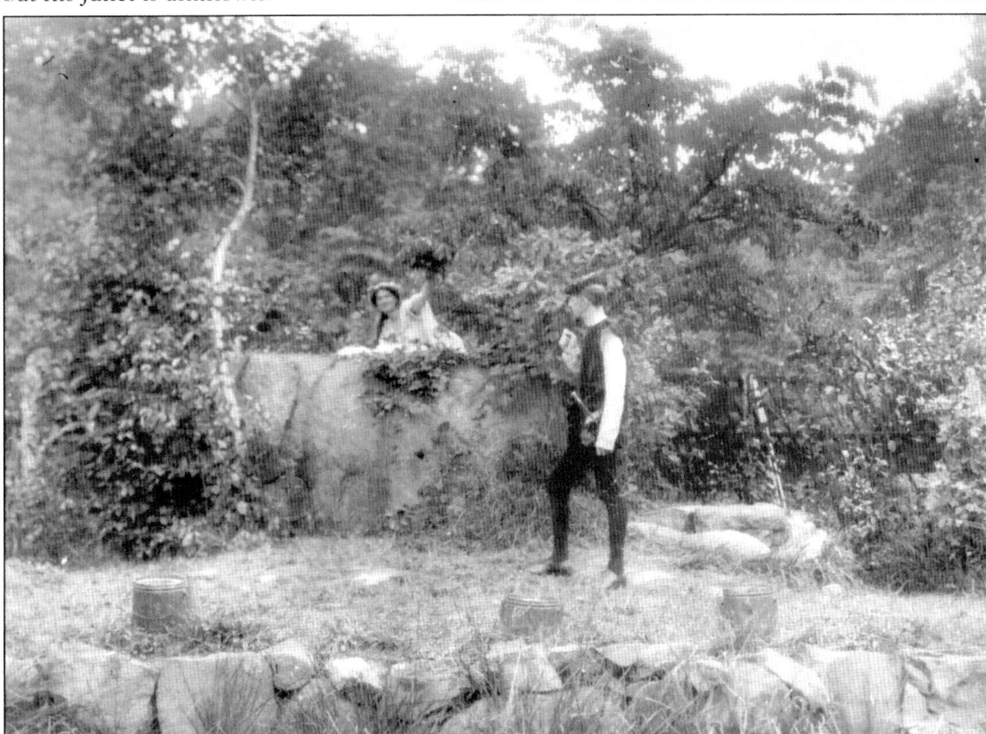

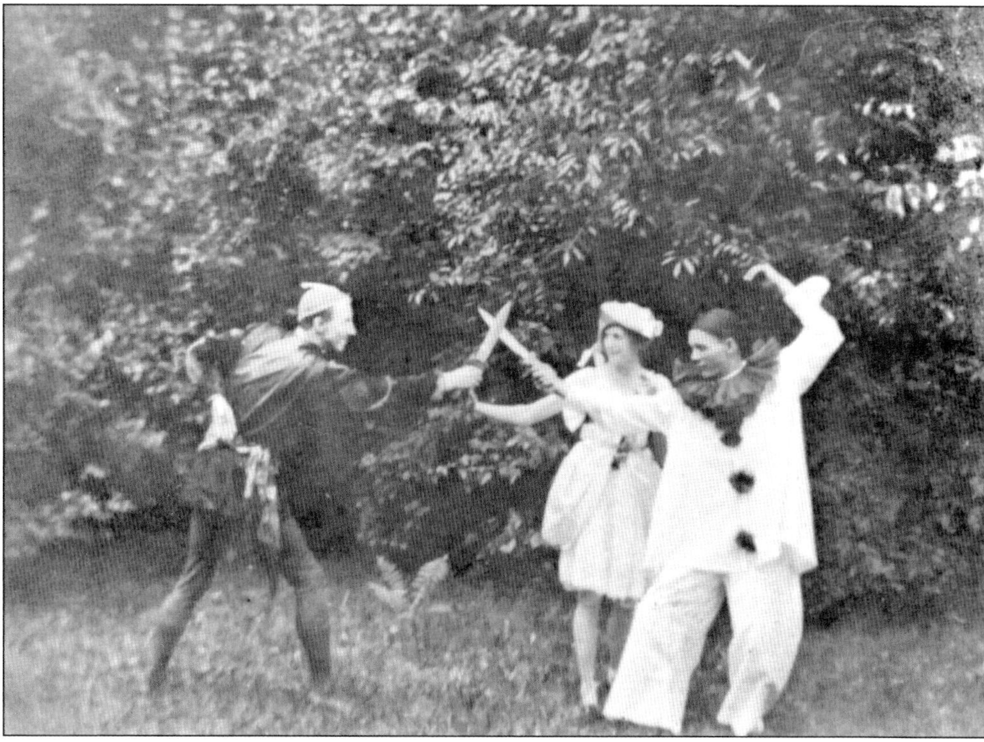

The action is Shakespearean, but the source for this Field Theater production is unknown. From left to right are Earl Broadbent, Jimmie Ware, and an unknown clown.

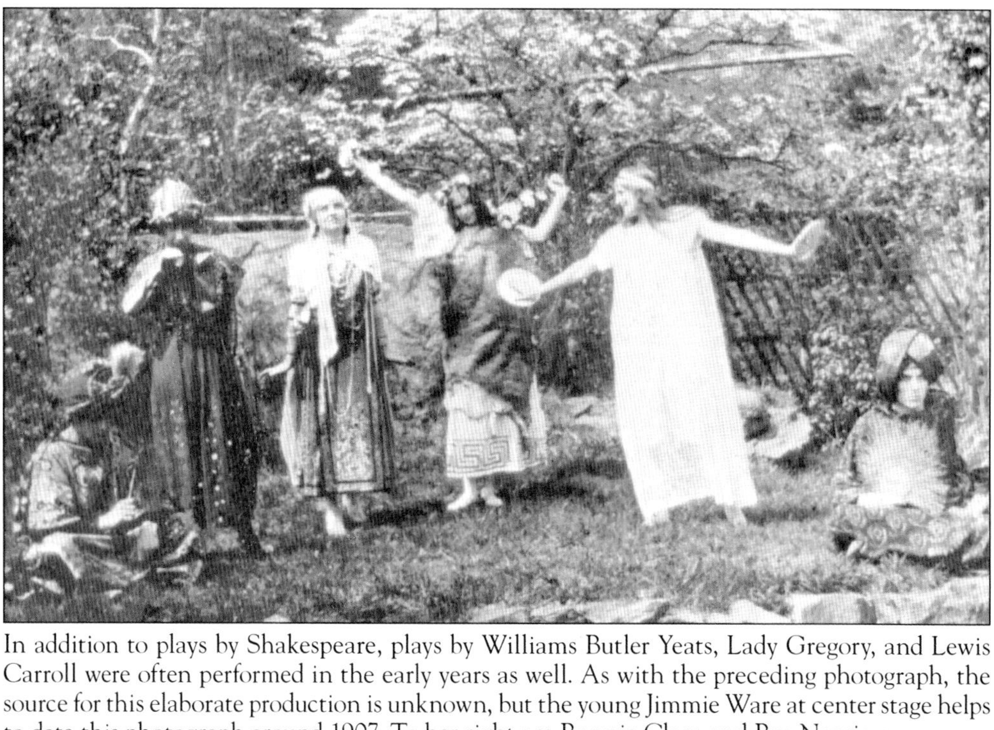

In addition to plays by Shakespeare, plays by Williams Butler Yeats, Lady Gregory, and Lewis Carroll were often performed in the early years as well. As with the preceding photograph, the source for this elaborate production is unknown, but the young Jimmie Ware at center stage helps to date this photograph around 1907. To her right are Bonnie Clare and Bea Nearing.

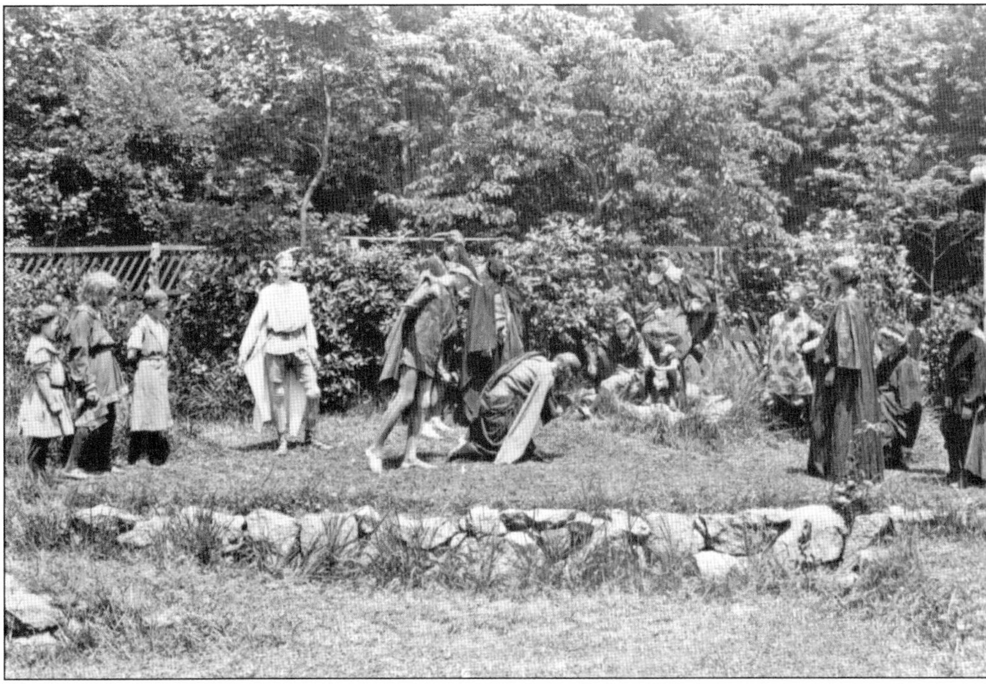

The Merchant of Venice was among the most popular of the Shakespearean plays performed in Arden. In this 1907 production, Frank Stephens as Shylock bows to the Duke, while his daughter Margaret, in the role of Portia, looks on.

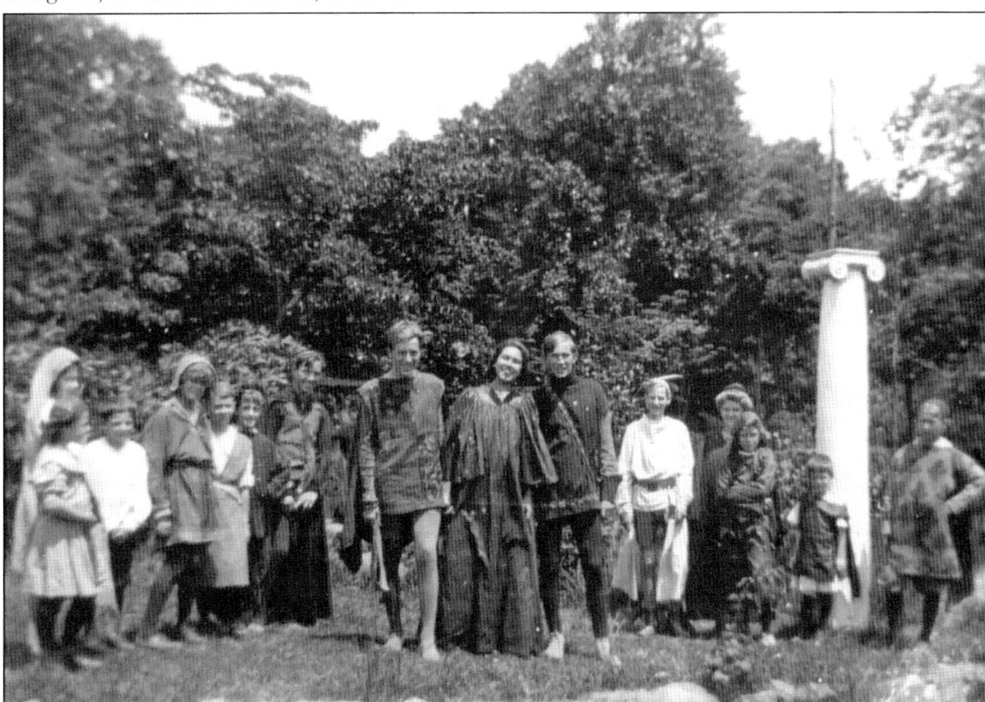

The performance concluded, the cast is all smiles for their curtain call. From left to right in the center are an unidentified actor, Margaret Stephens, and Don Stephens.

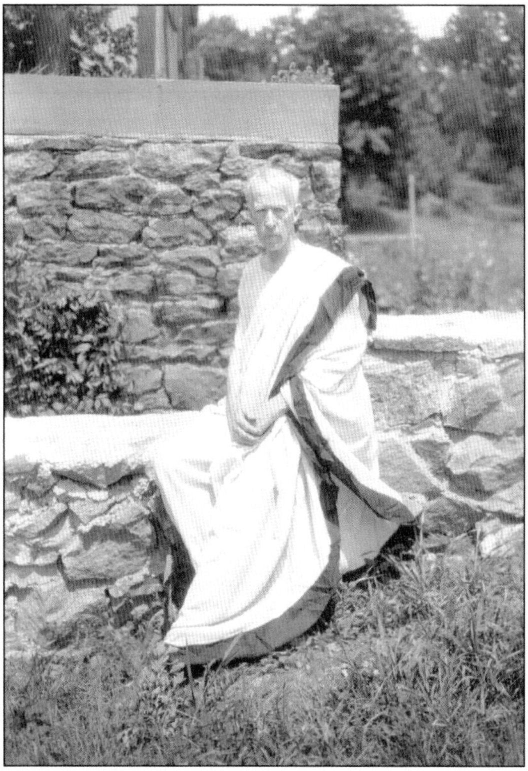

Frank Stephens by all accounts was an extremely accomplished and highly regarded actor and orator. He is pictured here in 1930 at the age of 71 in one of his favorite roles, Cassius, from *Julius Caesar*. Stephens was the founder of the Players Gild, which performed not only in Arden, but in the surrounding community as well. A favorite stage of his in the Philadelphia area was the large baronial hall at Rosslevyn, the home of Charles Winter Bailey.

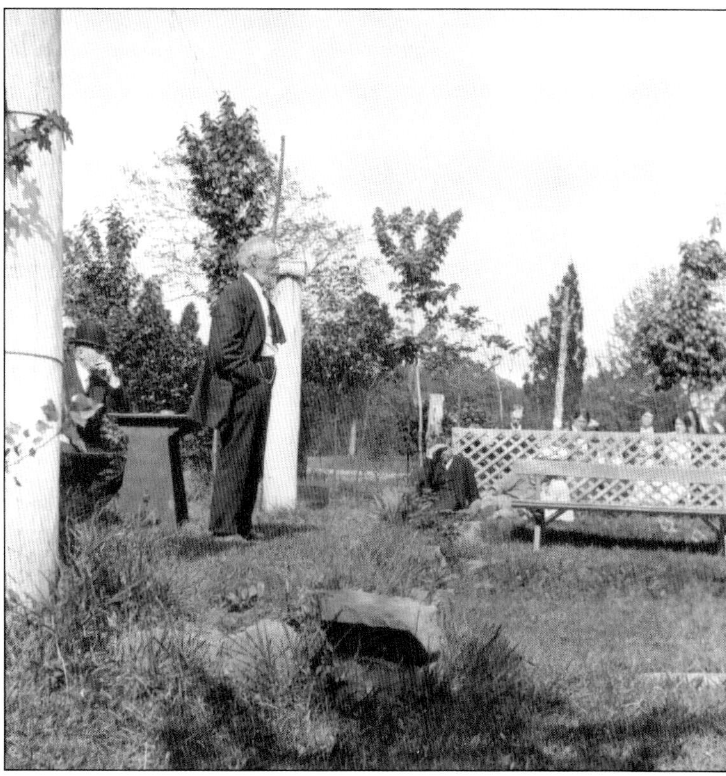

Along with theatrical presentations, the Field Theater was frequently used for lectures. Will Price, pictured here around 1910, was always a featured speaker at the Henry George birthday celebration held the first Sunday in September. The celebration was an important date on the village calendar, and single tax luminaries such as Bolton Hall and Louis Post were often in attendance.

Three

The Great and Glorious City

I cannot play upon any stringed instrument, but I can tell you how of a little village to make a great and glorious city.

—Themistocles

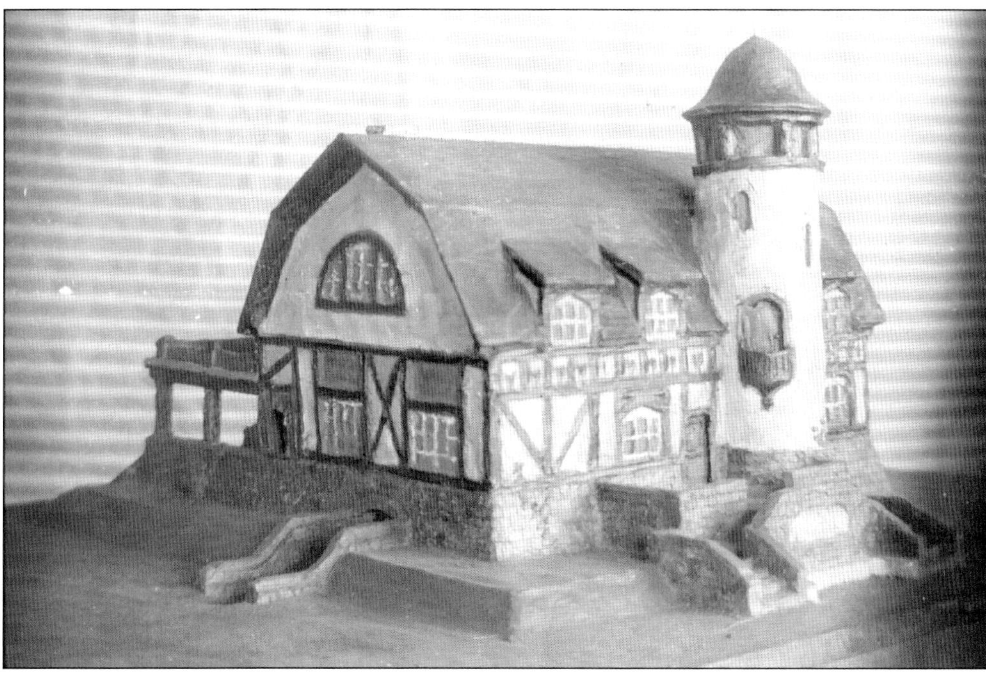

By 1908, the Arden Club had outgrown its temporary quarters in the Red House, and plans were made that year for a new clubhouse, just south of the tennis courts on Miller's Road. This wax model for the proposed structure was sculpted by Frank and Don Stephens from a design by Will Price. Unlike the other buildings that dotted the Arden landscape, the new clubhouse was to have been made of concrete.

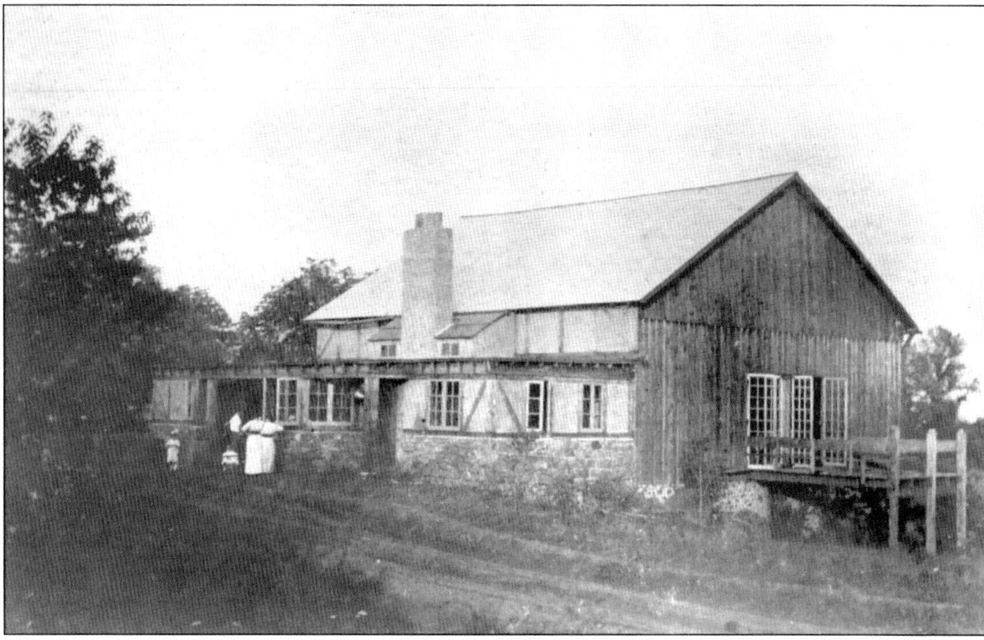

By the spring of 1909, plans for the new clubhouse had dramatically altered. Earlier that year, Joseph Fels had released his mortgage on the land southwest of Grubb's Road, now making the Sherwood side of the community available for settlement. With this in mind, Stephens and Price donated the Derrickson barn to the club in exchange for stock, effectively making the new clubhouse the center of the village. Renovations began almost immediately, and the new clubhouse opened officially with an inaugural dance on July 4, 1910. The building was originally known as the Gild House, with the Arden Club now organized into interest groups or Gilds.

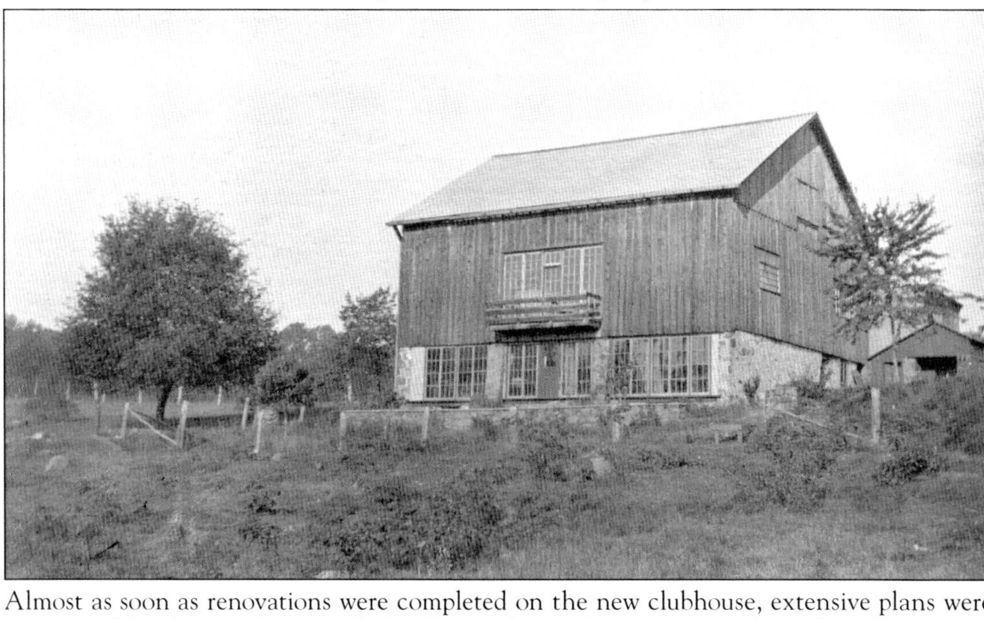

Almost as soon as renovations were completed on the new clubhouse, extensive plans were announced for the exterior grounds. To the north, tennis courts were planned; to the west, an outdoor theater; and to the south, a classical rostrum and stadium. The sloping hillside seen here in 1910 was to be sodded over to provide seating for a thousand spectators.

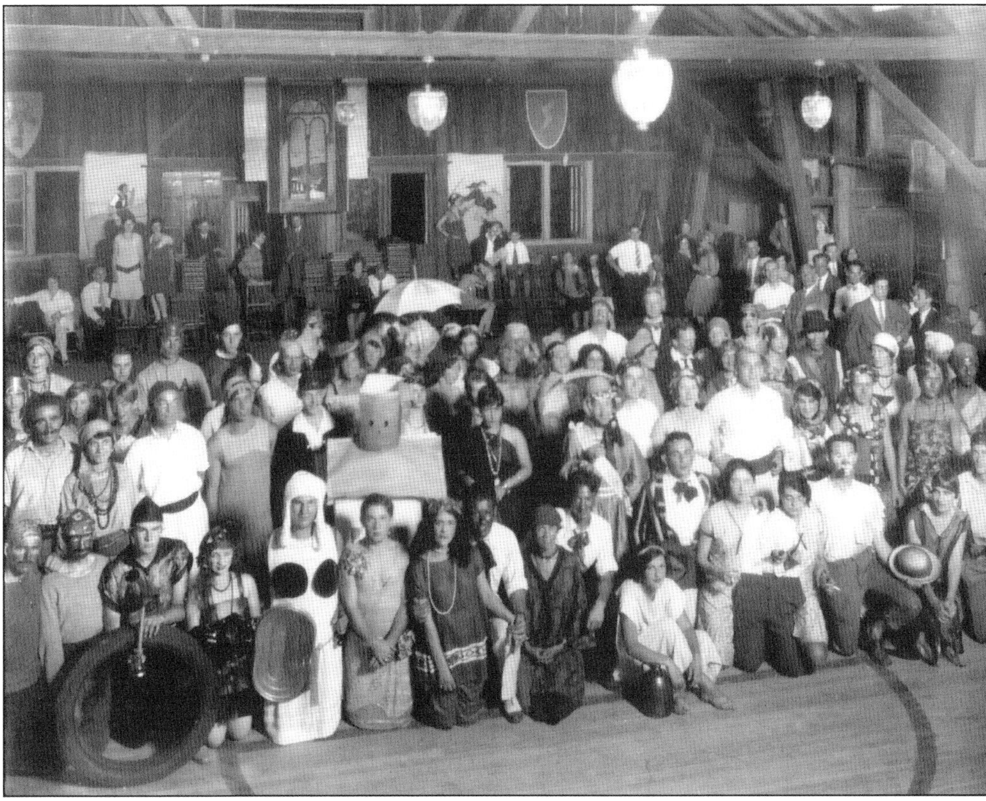

This 1929 masquerade party provides an early view of the Gild House interior, literally the Gild Hall. Visible on the rear wall are two Gild shields; however, their symbols are unclear. In later years, the entire building became known simply as the Gild Hall.

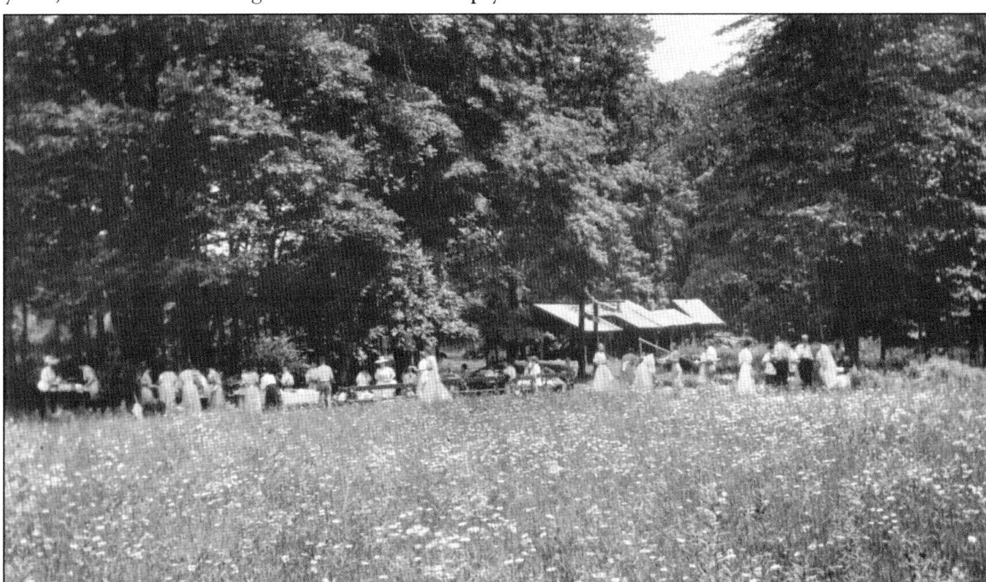

Much of the renovation on the new clubhouse was done by volunteer labor. In this 1910 photograph, a work party enjoys a picnic in the Meadow Green. The sawmill is visible in the distance.

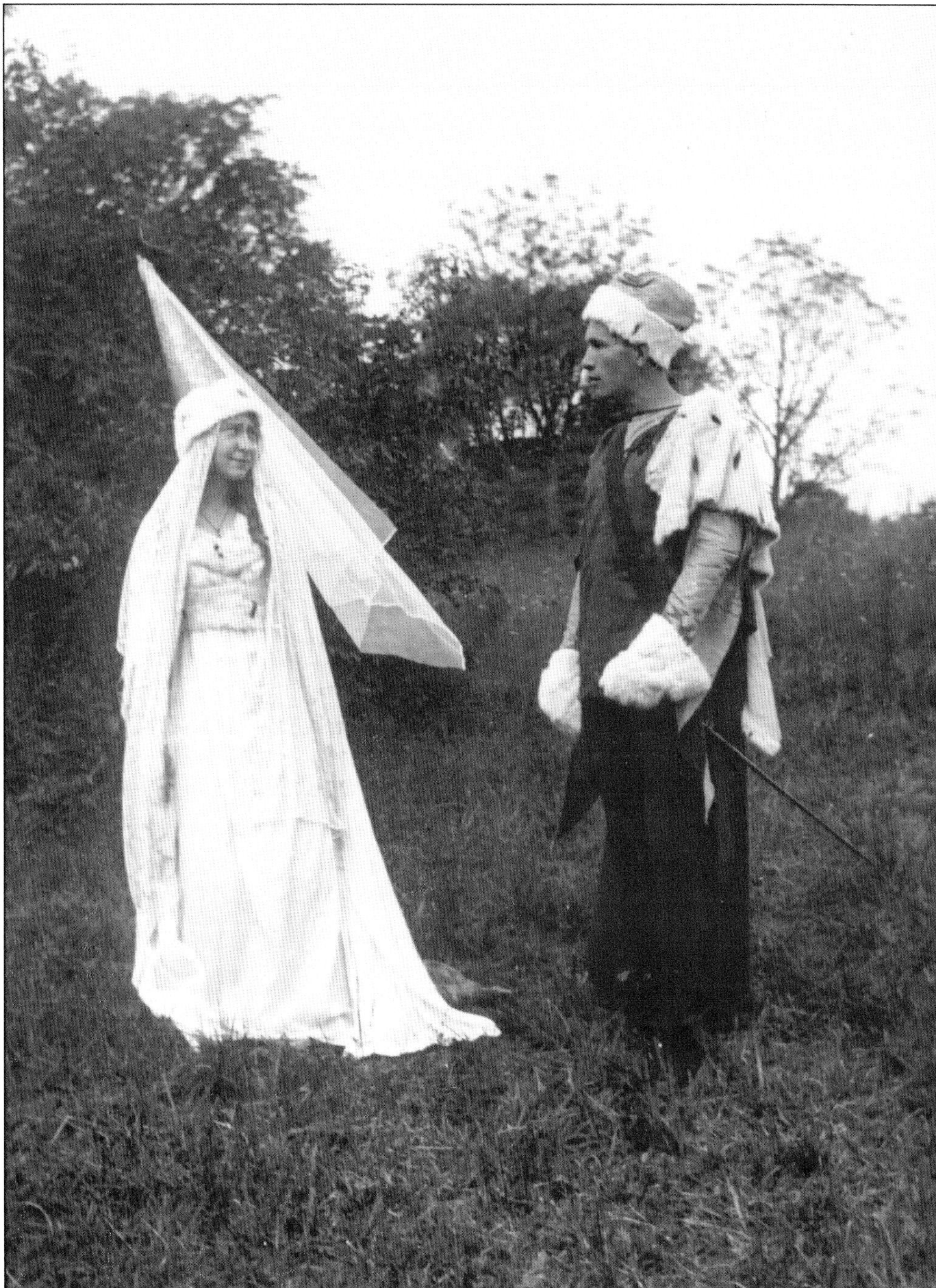

One of the first activities of the reorganized Arden Club was a medieval pageant, which was held September 5, 1910. The pageant portrayed the journey of the lord and lady of the manor and their attendant retinue, including jesters, huntsmen, knights, and pages to a nearby manorial village. Upon arriving, they were ceremoniously received by town officials, gild officers, craftsmen, and villagers. Don Stephens and Hildegarde Clark, seen here, were the Lord and Lady of the Manor.

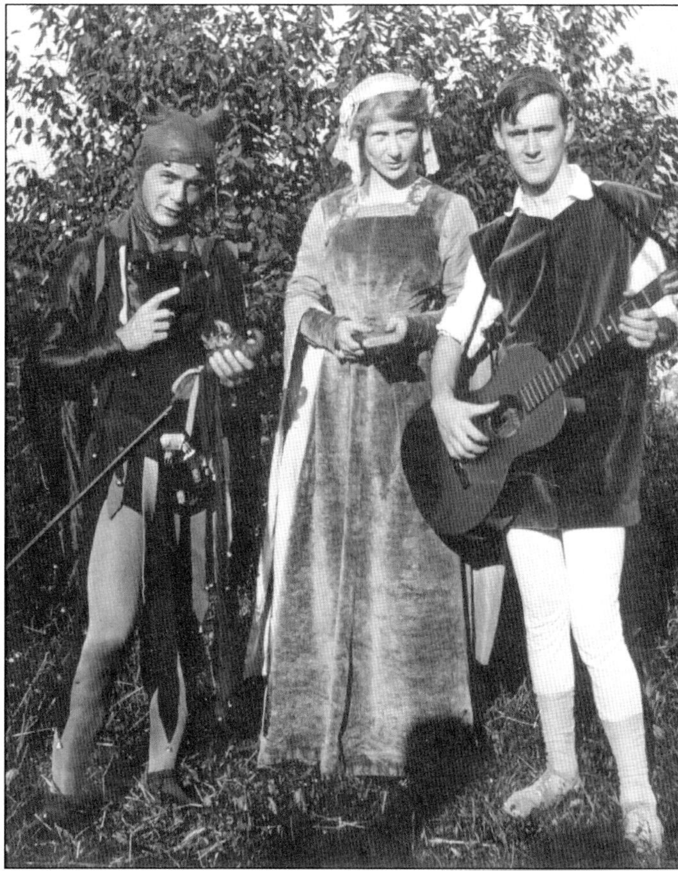

Pictured here from left to right, Buzz Ware, Elena Darling, and an unknown musician pose for a photograph before the pageant commences.

As a symbolic gesture of its move to a new home, the pageanteers assembled at the Red House, circled the Village Green, and made their way to the Gild Hall, where the lord and lady held court. In this photograph, two horsemen pass the Arden Inn. The rider on the left is William Lightbown.

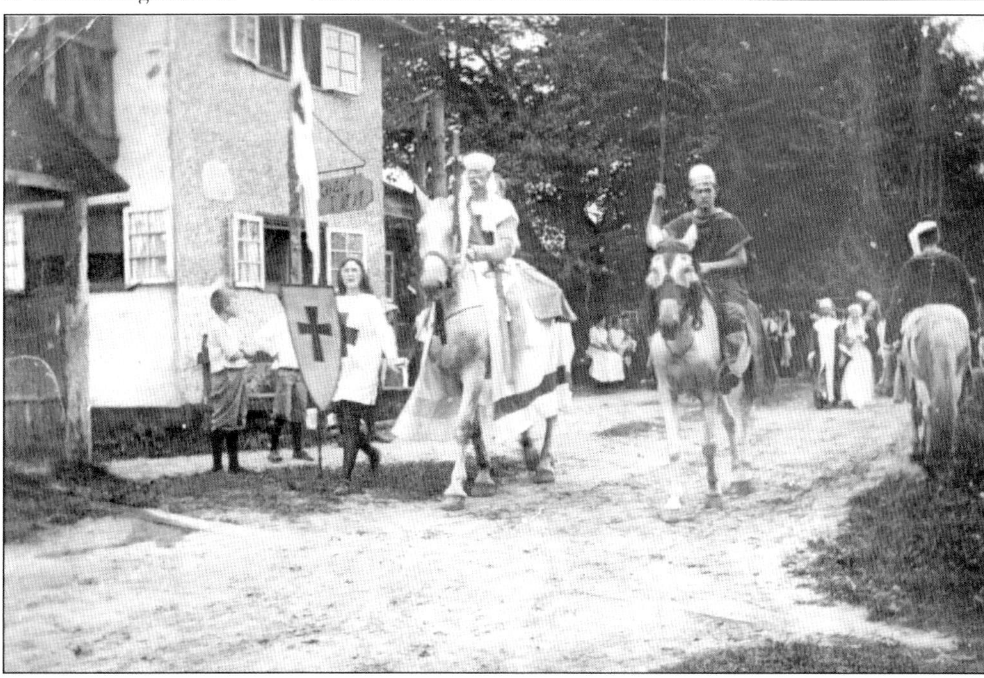

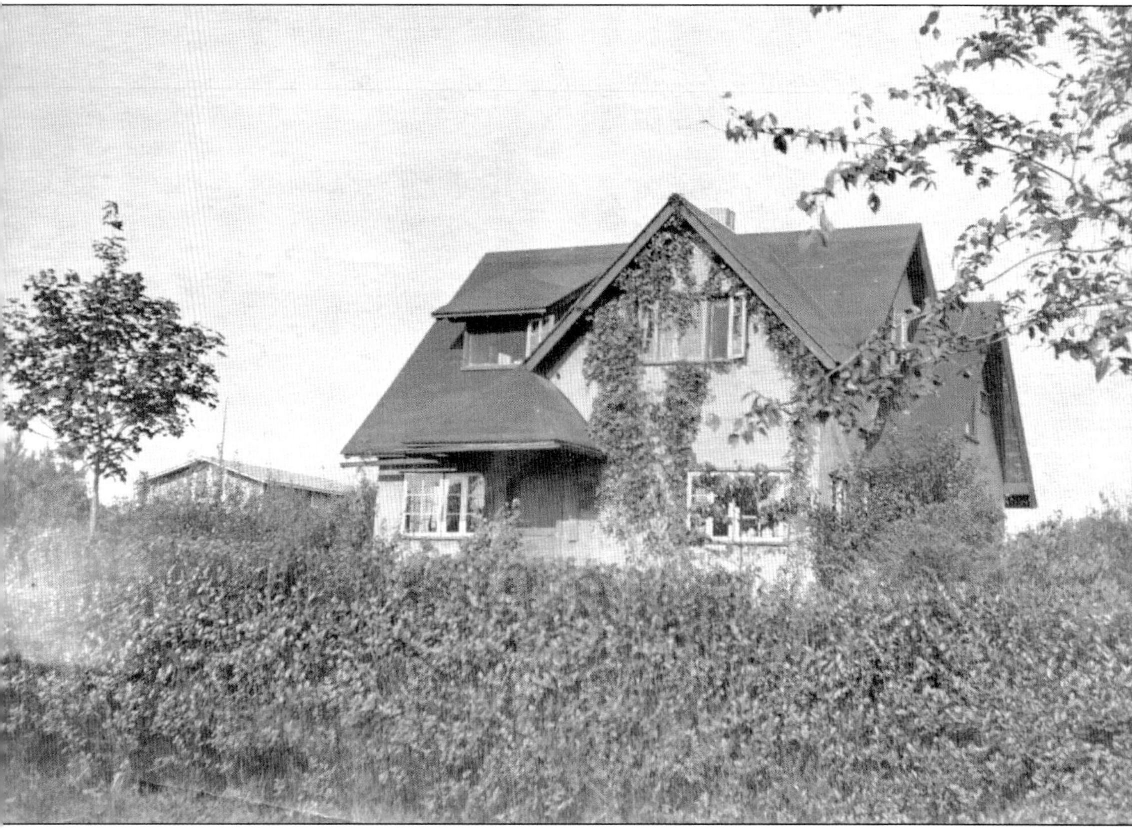

In 1909, in addition to releasing the mortgage on the Sherwood side of Arden, Joseph Fels also donated "several thousand dollars" towards home building. Fels stipulated that the cottages should be designed by Will Price and must be "permanent and artistic in character with stone foundations and cellars, hollow brick and concrete walls, and above all, literally, the red tiled roofs so beautiful in the scenery of England and the Netherlands." The first of these so called "Fels Cottages" to be completed was Friendly Gables, seen here in 1910, the home of Alice and Fred Steinlein. It is located on Little Lane.

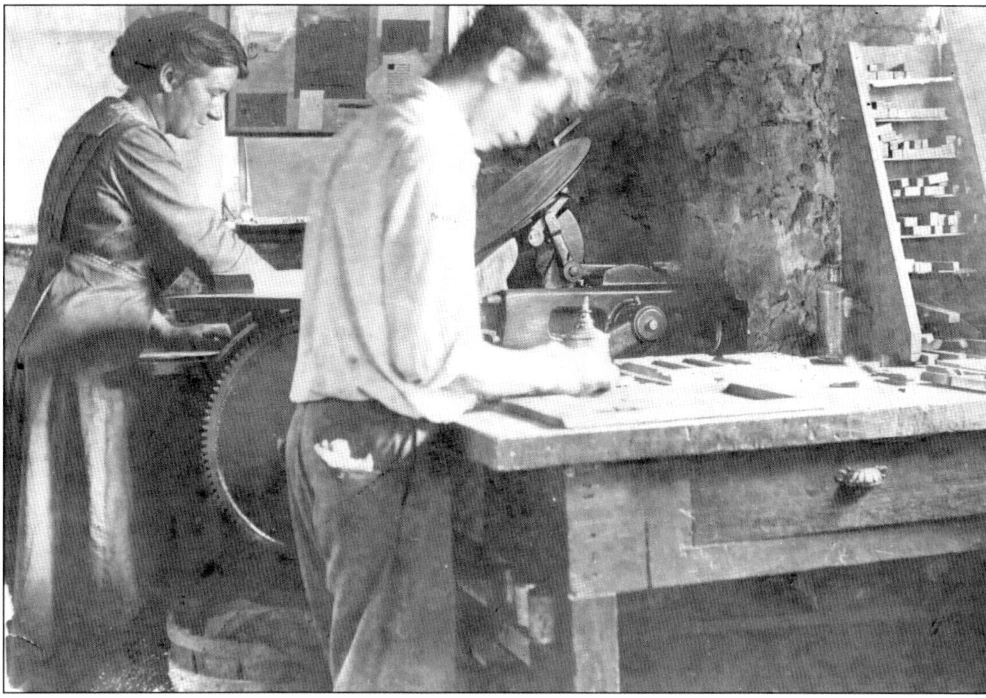

Fred and Alice Steinlein are seen here in 1910 working at the Arden Printery, which had been moved from Cherry Lodge to the basement of Friendly Gables. Friendly Gables also served as home to Arden's cooperative kitchen club, the precursor to the community's current Dinner Gild.

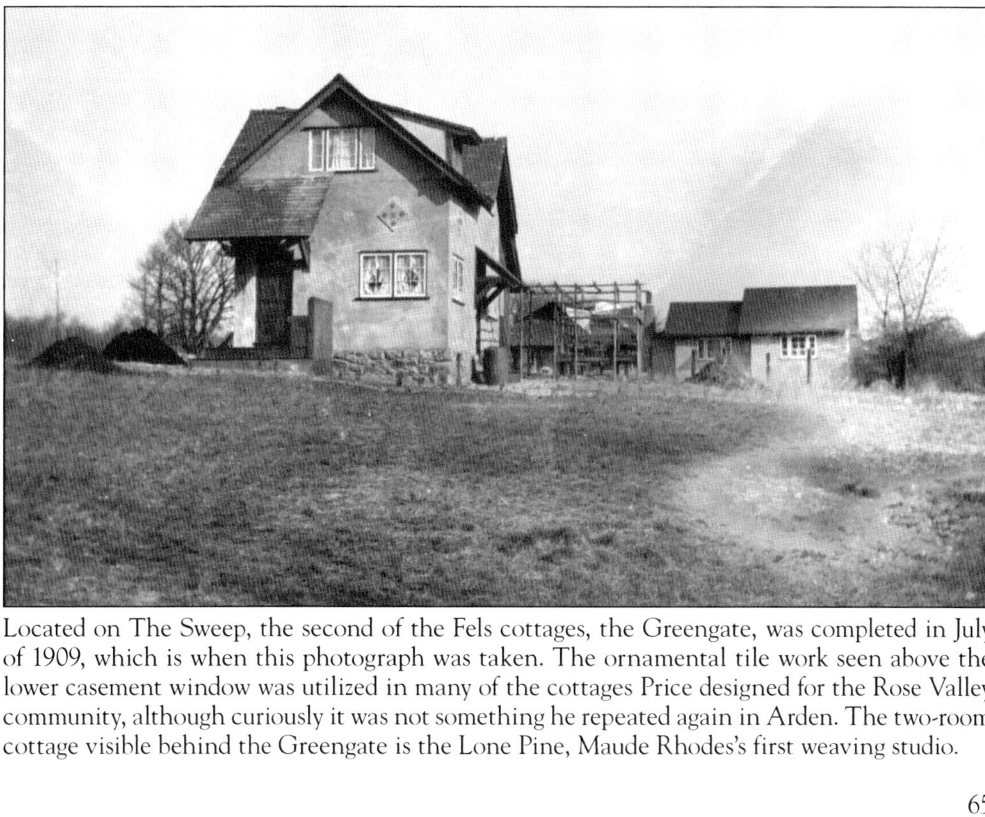

Located on The Sweep, the second of the Fels cottages, the Greengate, was completed in July of 1909, which is when this photograph was taken. The ornamental tile work seen above the lower casement window was utilized in many of the cottages Price designed for the Rose Valley community, although curiously it was not something he repeated again in Arden. The two-room cottage visible behind the Greengate is the Lone Pine, Maude Rhodes's first weaving studio.

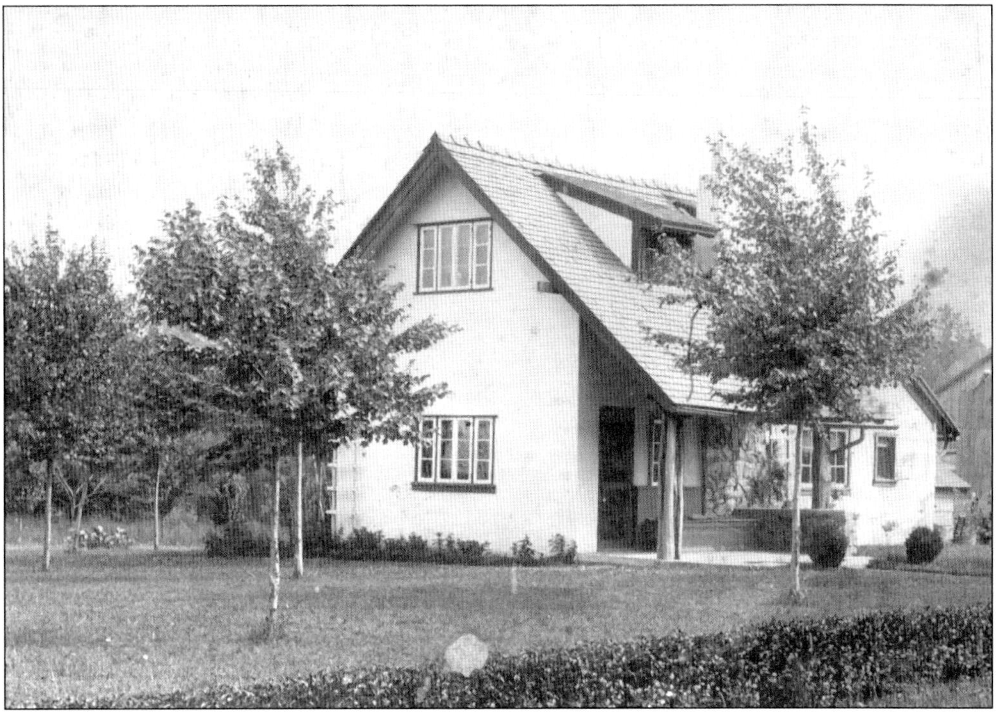

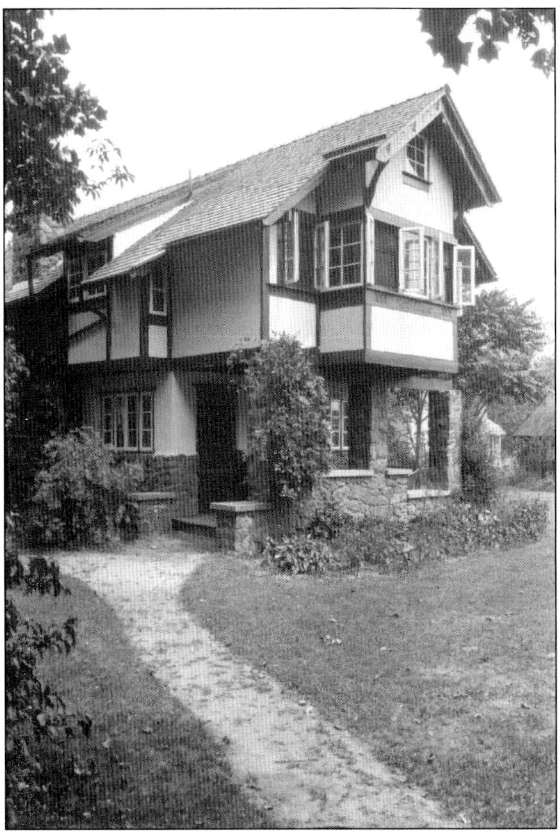

The third Fels cottage, the only one built on the Sherwood side of the village, was completed August 1, 1909. It sits at the corner of The Highway and Grubb's Road.

Believed to be the last of the Fels cottages, Rest Cottage faces the Village Green at its southeast corner. With its stone walls, wide shed roofs, and picturesque half timbering, it stands as one of Will Price's most charming Arden designs. The cottage became the home of Margaret Stephens and Hal Ware after their marriage in 1912.

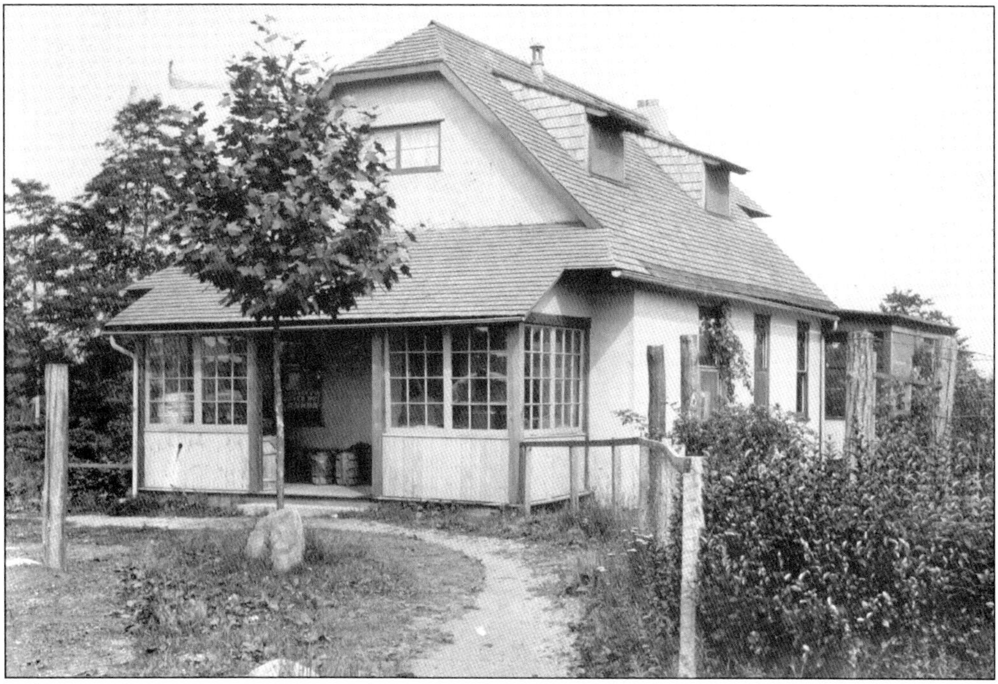

Robert Woolery's grocery store, seen here around 1918, was located on Little Lane along the Grocery Path, which ran from Hillside Road to the Milky Way. It is likely that the business opened in 1910, as an advertisement placed in the May issue of that year's *Arden Club Talk* refers to the grocery as "a new Arden industry." Mr. Woolery is remembered by many for his overwhelming generosity, which is known to have carried several Arden residents through the Depression of the 1930s.

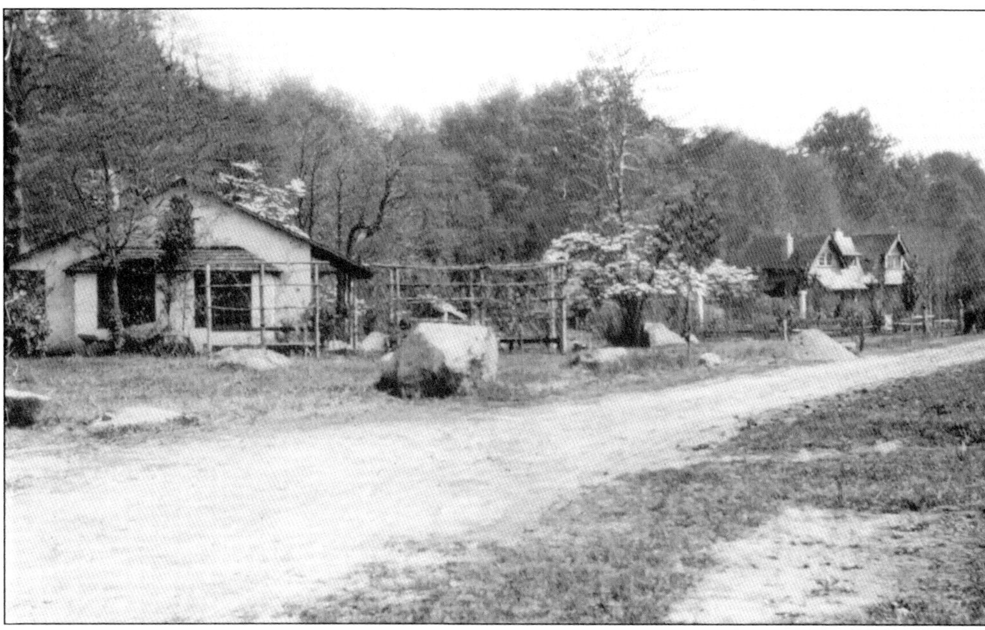

The Admiral Benbow, Field Theater, and Founder's House can clearly be seen in this spring photograph of Woodland Lane taken in 1910. The dogwood blossoms stand in stark contrast to the late winter tree line.

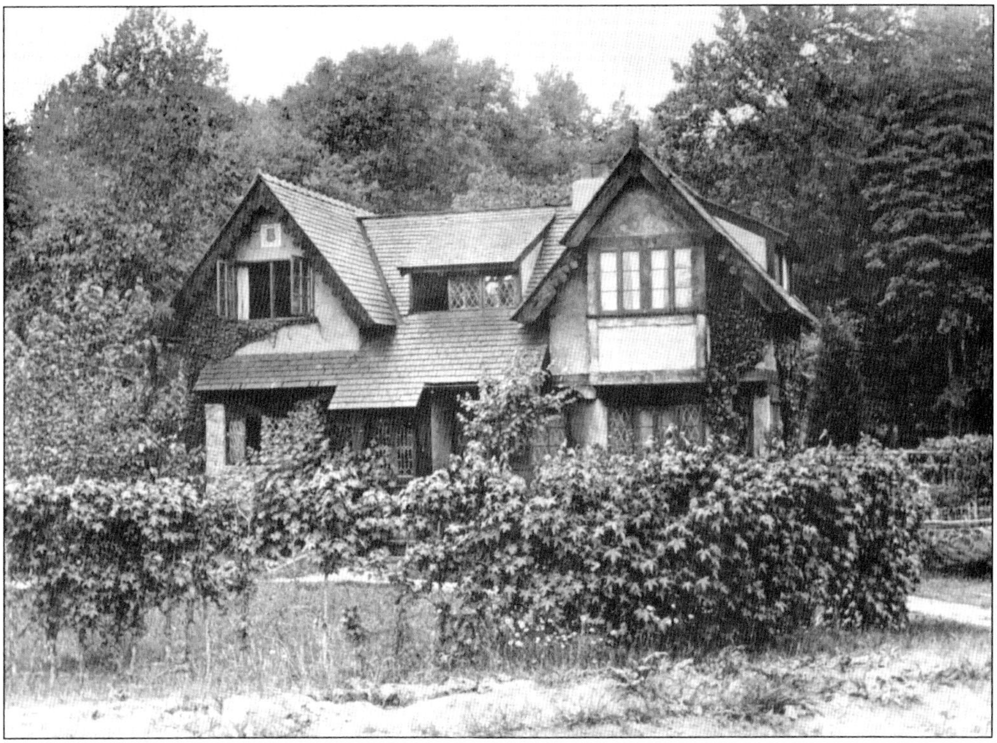

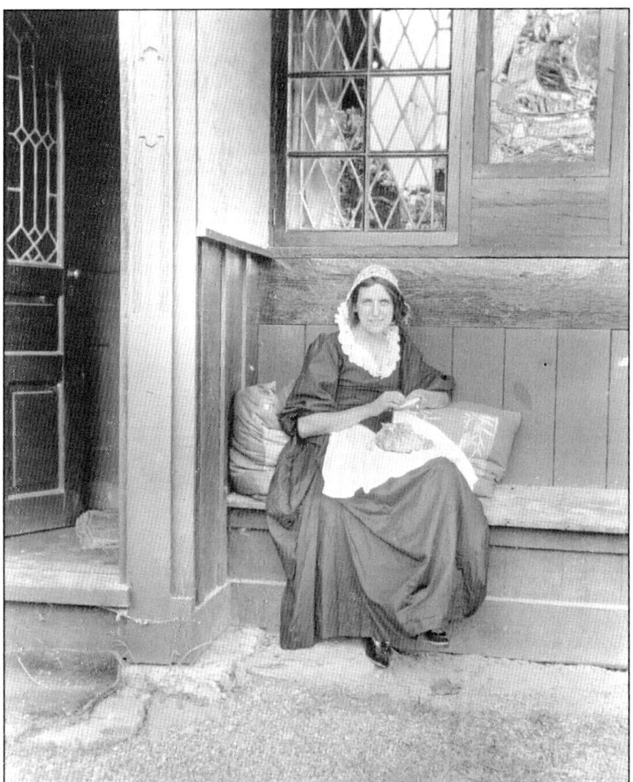

The Founder's House or Second Homestead was home to Frank and Eleanor Stephens. Built in 1909, it was designed by Will Price from a sketch that Frank had drawn on a trip to England the prior year. The motto board visible above the downstairs window on the right reads "Tomorrow is a New Day" and was carved by Don Stephens, as were the figures on the roof peaks.

Jimmie Ware poses in costume in front of the Founder's House around 1914. The stained glass window is by Alexander Bower, and was a gift to Frank Stephens from the artist. The sailing ship was a popular motif during the Arts and Crafts era, equating the explorer's quest for new lands with the reformer's quest for a better life.

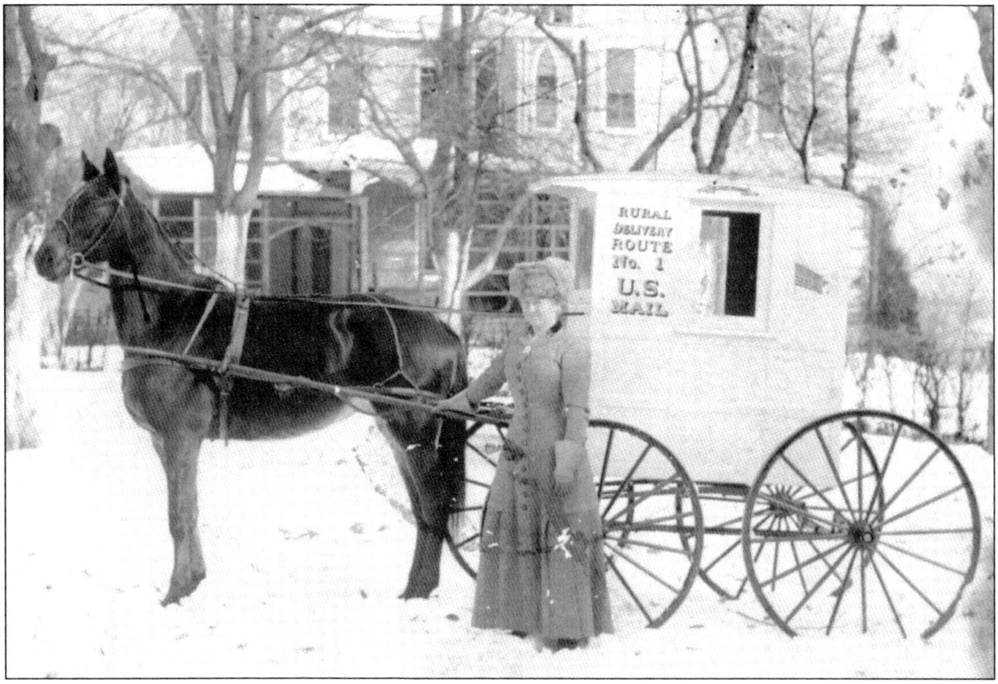

Lily Donohue, Delaware's first female postal carrier, delivered mail to Arden with her horse and buggy. Prior to 1909, residents waited for her on Grubb's Road. It wasn't until February of that year that she was authorized by the United States Postal Service to deliver mail within the community, but only along Miller's Road between the Red House and the town pump.

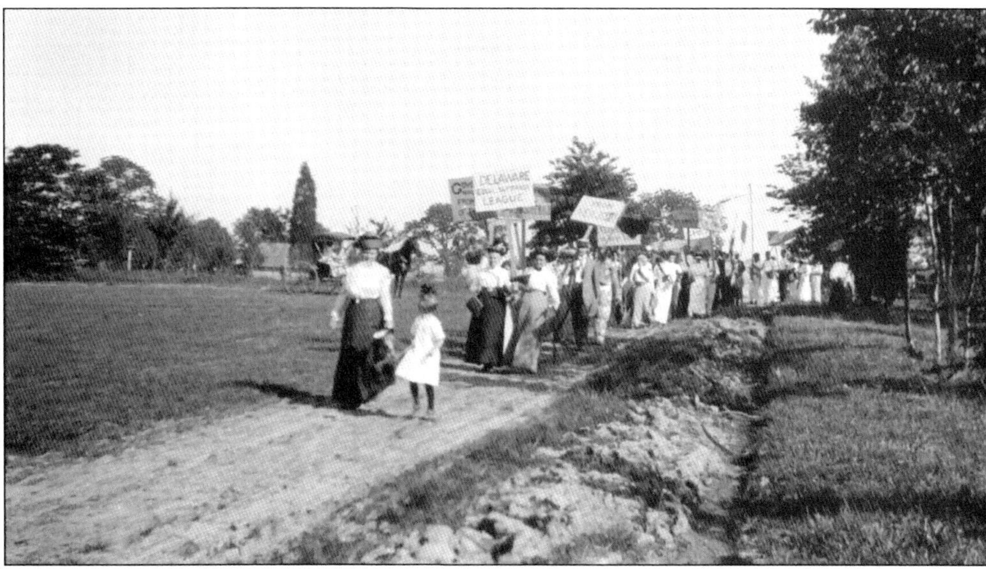

On June 1, 1911, Arden held its first Equal Suffrage Day, and according to an account published in the village newspaper, the *Arden Leaves*, over 100 residents and visitors attended. The day's festivities began with a march around the Village Green, pictured here, followed by speeches, a performance of William Shakespeare's *The Merchant of Venice*, and an Equal Rights Dance at the Gild Hall, where the author notes "the women seemed indeed to enjoy and take advantage of their extended privileges, the proportion of feminine wall flowers being noticeably smaller.'

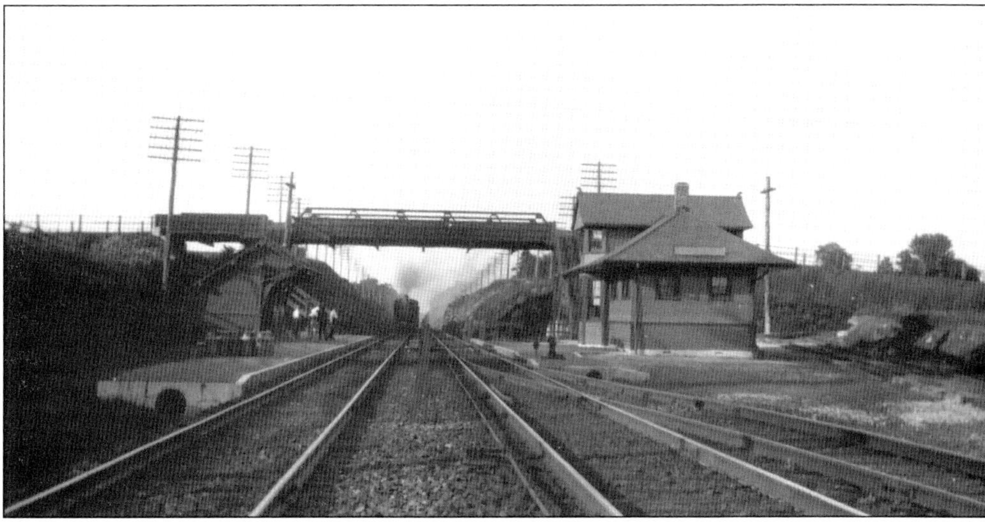

The new Harvey Station opened in May 1911 and included an attached cottage for the station master and her family. Gone, however, was the picturesque country road that meandered by the tracks during Arden's first decade. It had been replaced by a much wider road that was now diverted over what many Ardenites considered a "most hideous modern iron bridge."

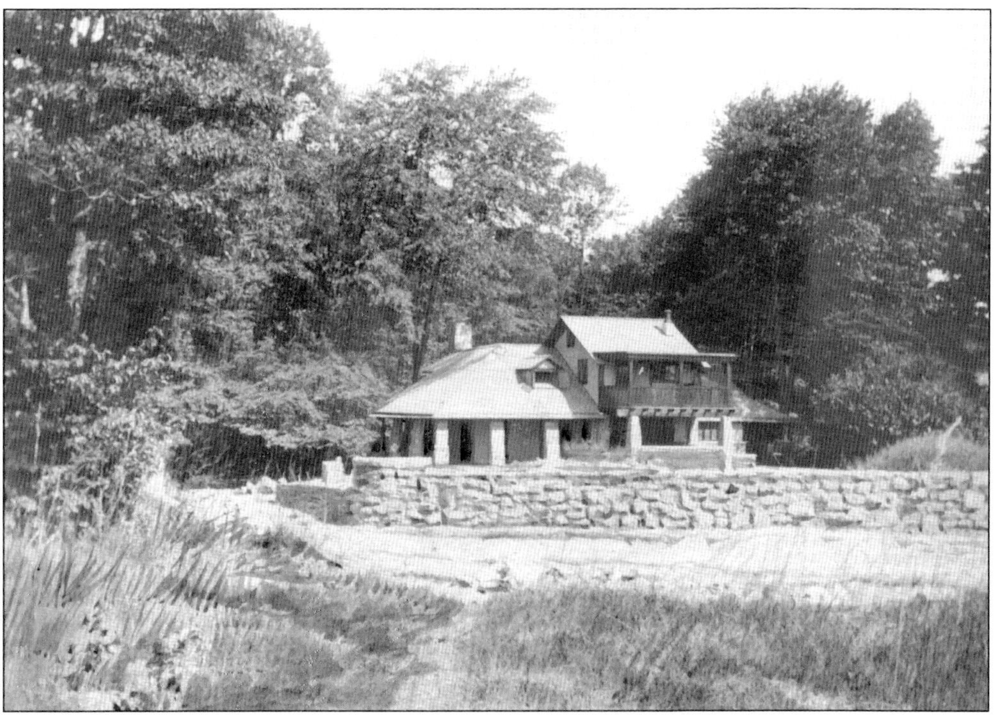

In 1910, a major renovation was undertaken of the Brambles by its new owner Frank Downs. Mr. Downs is known to have been an amateur musician of some note and held orchestral rehearsal most Sunday mornings in his home. (Courtesy of Mike Curtis.)

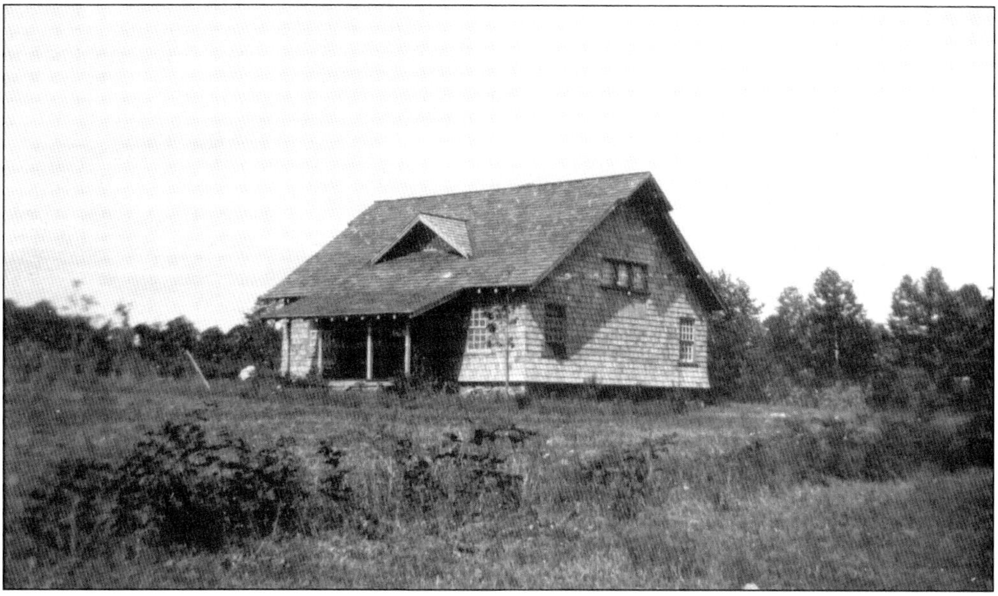

Artist Annora Kiehel's wonderful shingle-style bungalow on Hillside Road was built sometime around 1912. This photograph was taken shortly after the home was completed.

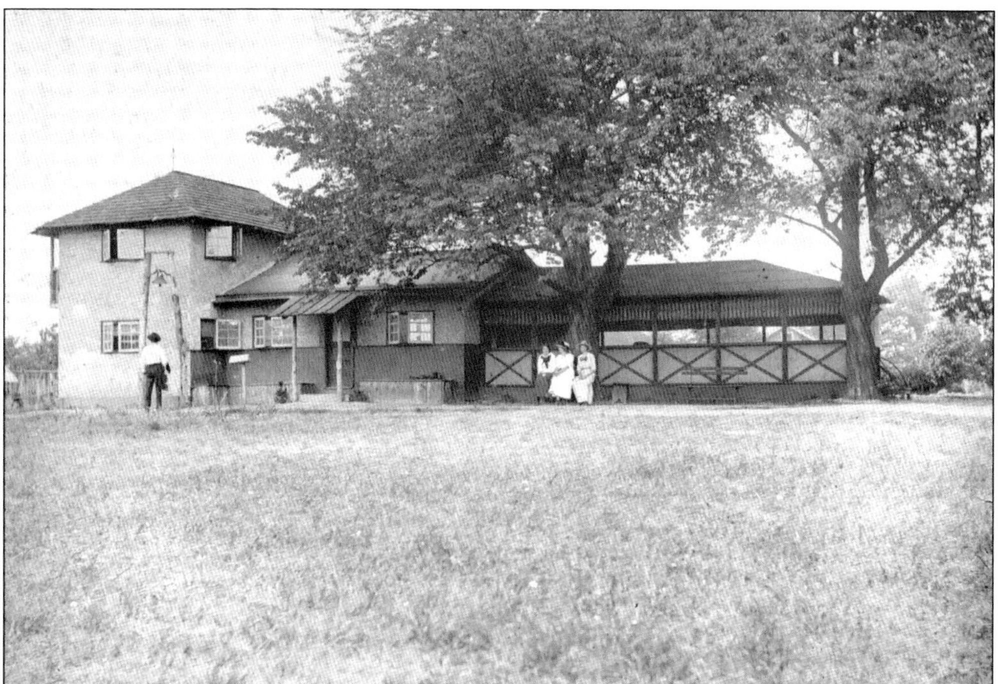

In 1907, this open-air dining pavilion was a welcome addition to the Arden Inn. This photograph dates from around 1914

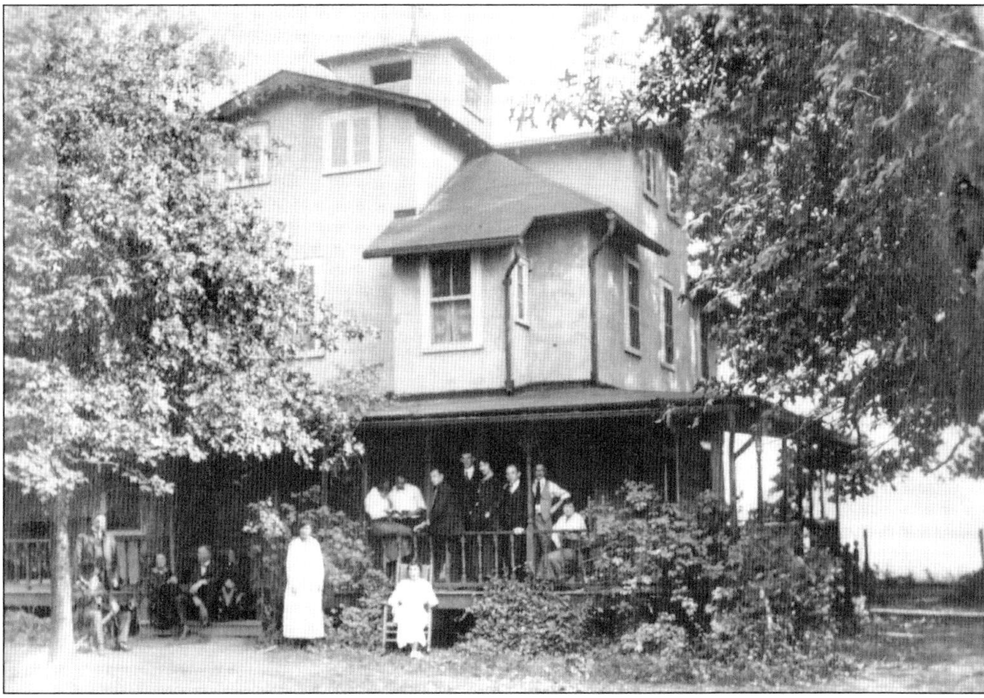

Built in 1910, the Spreading Oak guesthouse was located at the intersection of Lower Lane and Miller's Road just down the road from the Cooler. Its proprietress was Louise Kumme, who offered her guests "16 bedrooms and a large reception hall in the shade of the spreading oak." Most of her guests took their meals at the Arden Inn.

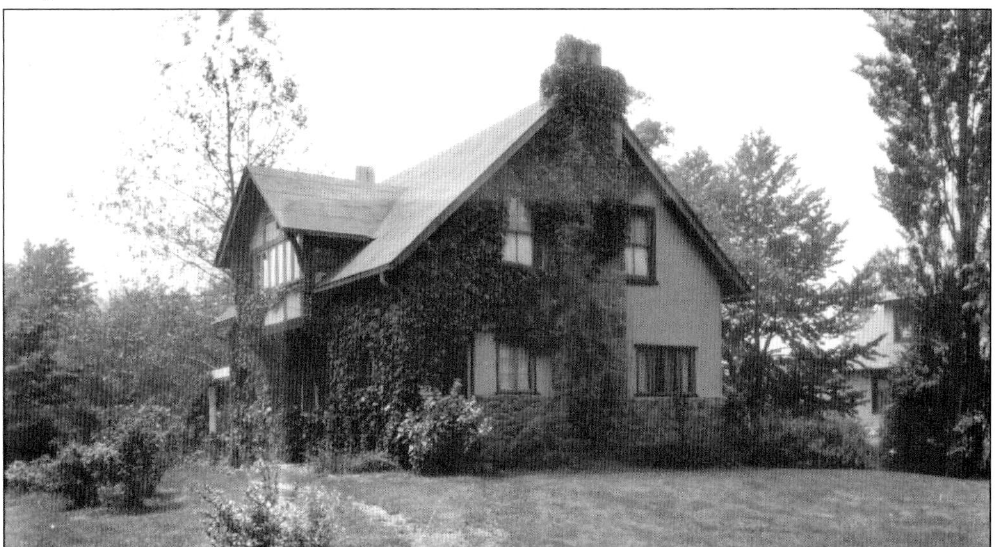

The Lodge, located on The Sweep at the corner of the Village Green, is another house designed by Will Price and is noteworthy for its large central dormer. The dormer's row of vertical windows provides an appealing decorative touch and is reminiscent of those used by Price on the Founder's House. The Lodge was built for Elena Darling, who took occupancy in 1914. This photograph is believed to date from the 1930s.

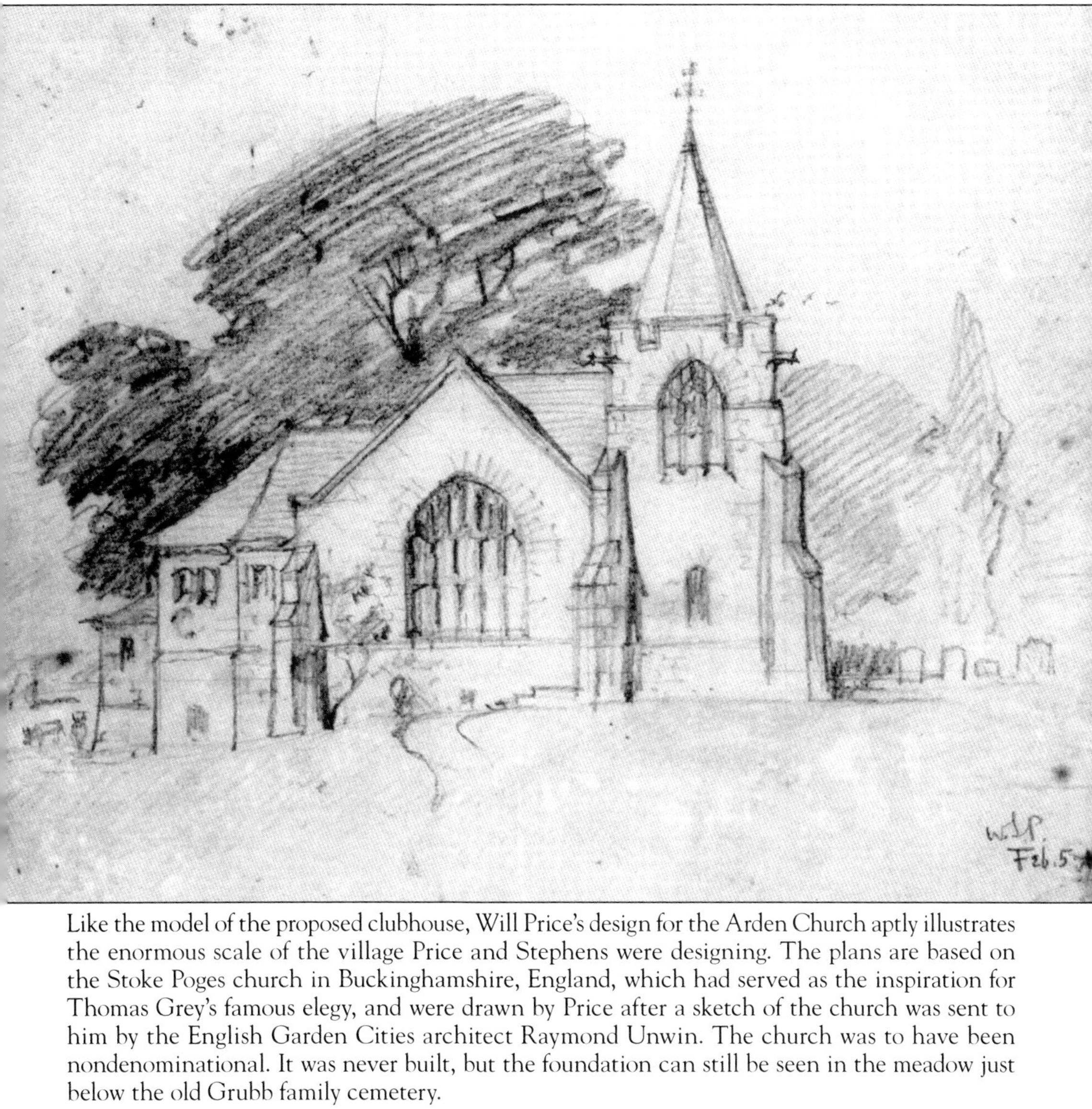

Like the model of the proposed clubhouse, Will Price's design for the Arden Church aptly illustrates the enormous scale of the village Price and Stephens were designing. The plans are based on the Stoke Poges church in Buckinghamshire, England, which had served as the inspiration for Thomas Grey's famous elegy, and were drawn by Price after a sketch of the church was sent to him by the English Garden Cities architect Raymond Unwin. The church was to have been nondenominational. It was never built, but the foundation can still be seen in the meadow just below the old Grubb family cemetery.

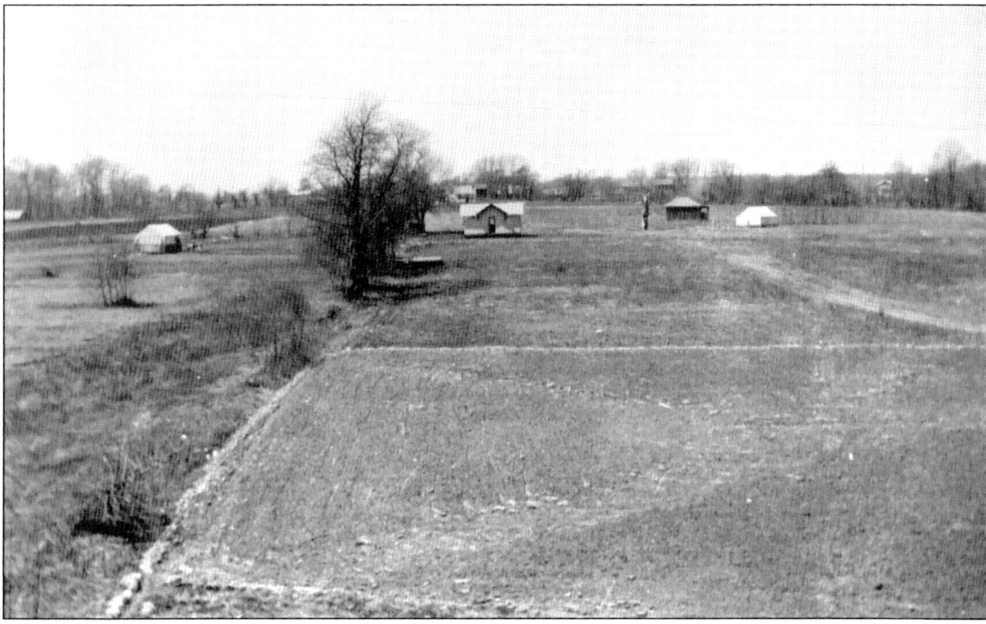

The following four photographs were taken from the roof of the Gild Hall in 1912, and clearly illustrate the evolving Arden landscape. Moving from left to right, the first photograph in the series looks toward Lovers Lane. Development on this side of the community has barely begun.

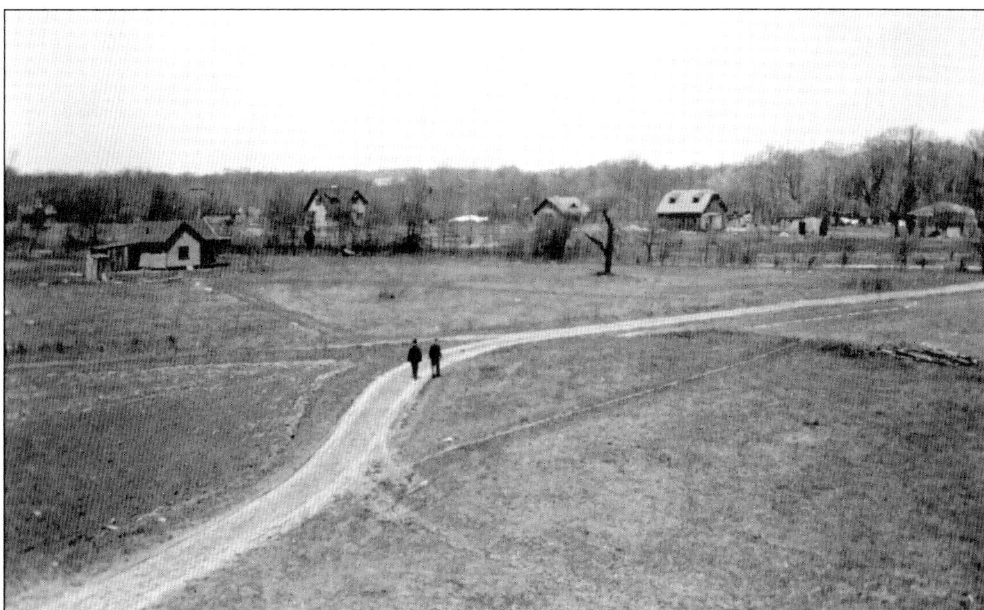

In the second photograph, two figures approach the intersection of The Highway and Orleans Road. The Steinlein's home, Friendly Gables (page 64), can be seen in the distance, second from the left in the rear.

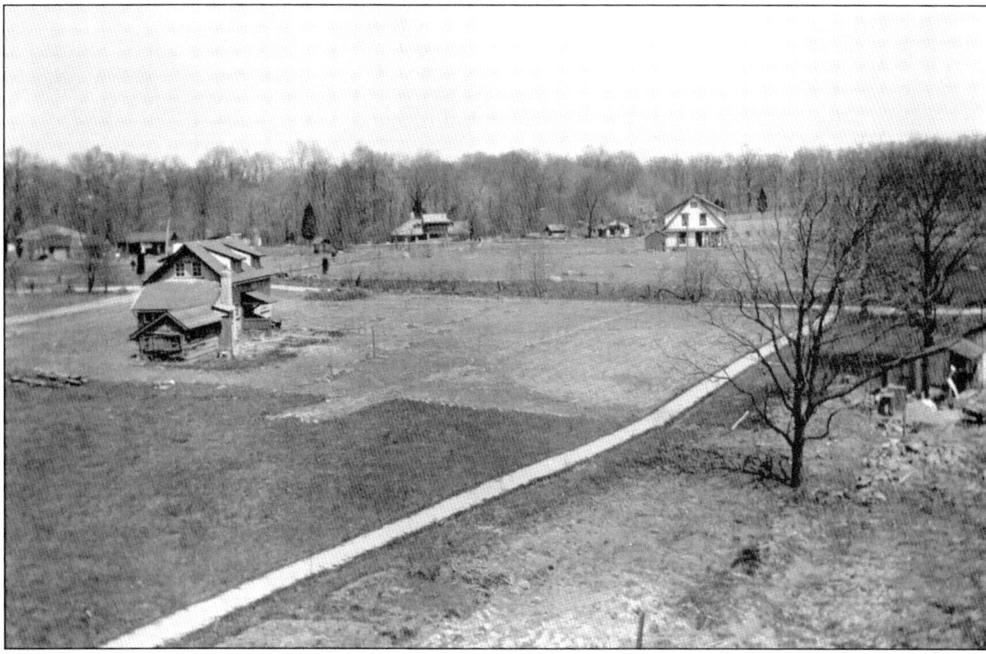

Grubb's Road, the Club House Path, Miller's Road, and Orleans Road can all be seen in the third photograph in the series. The house in the foreground is the Fels cottage (page 66), which was owned by Alex Ervin. The Brambles (page 70), Homestead (page 68), and Admiral Benbow (page 37) can all be seen in the distance. Of particular note is a hitherto undocumented town water pump, which can be seen between the Fels cottage and the Brambles.

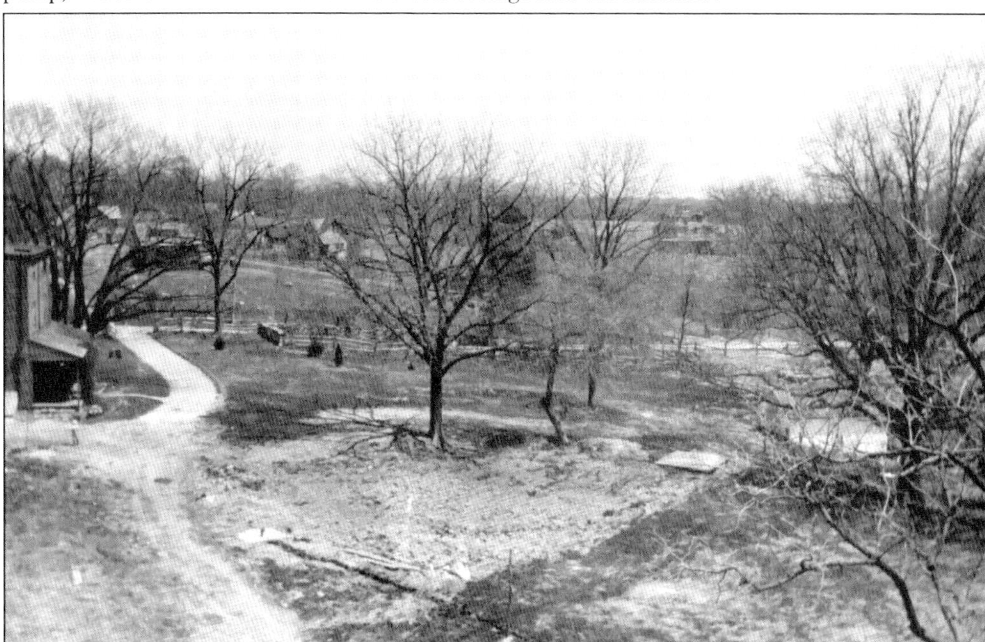

The last photograph in our series looks behind the Gild Hall toward Grubb's Road. The Greengate (page 65) can be seen in the center of the photograph with the Spreading Oak (page 72) to the far right.

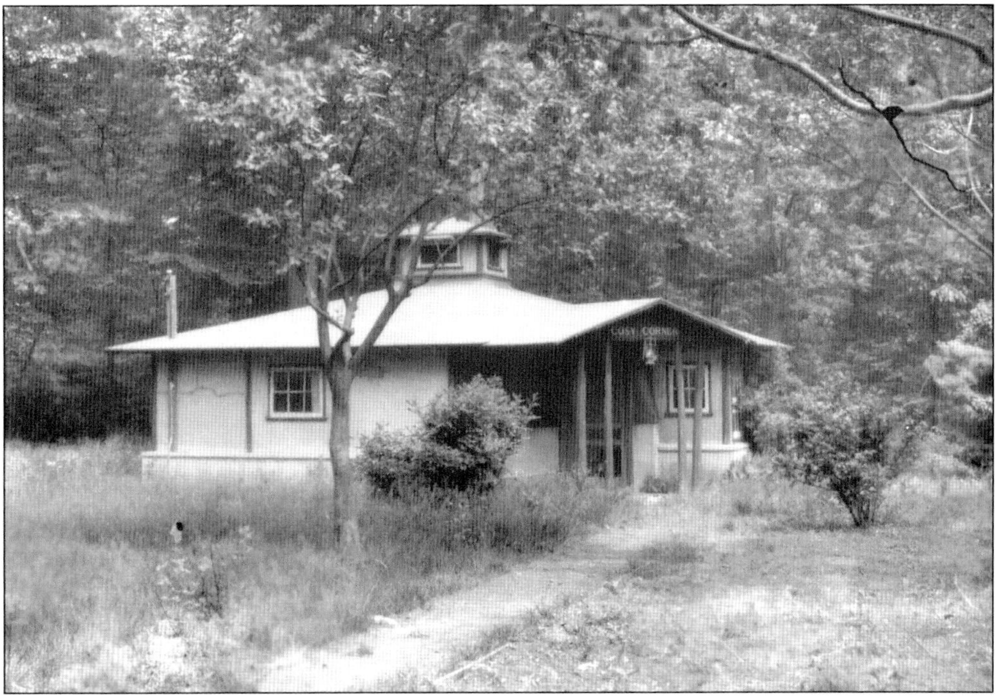

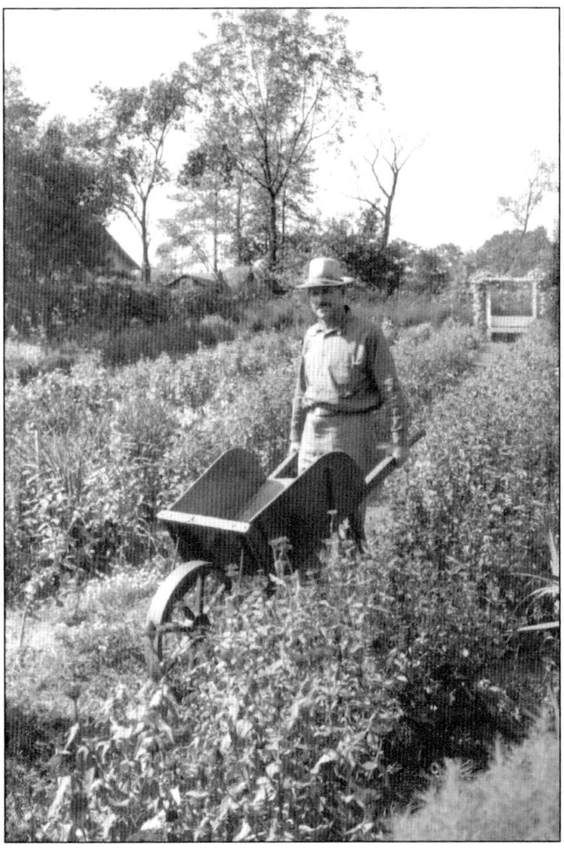

Self-sufficiency and simple living were values that many early Ardenites aspired to. When W. L. Lightbown's cottage Cosy Corner was put on the market in 1912, it was described as "an attractive, substantial bungalow with lease to one and a half acres of good garden land in high state of cultivation and well stocked with good varieties of fruits, berries, nuts, etc."

Thoreau scholar Ira Hoover is seen here around 1930 in his extensive garden on Walnut Lane. Many early residents grew market gardens. Produce was sold both in the community and at Wilmington's Farmers Market on King Street.

Born in Germany, Robert Rautenberg studied wood and stone carving in Berlin, Paris, Vienna, and Rome. Rautenberg came to this country in 1887, working with Augustus St. Gaudens and other prominent sculptors. It was through St. Gaudens that he reputedly met Frank Stephens, moving to Arden in 1911. Rautenberg's best known work is the statuary and figural work for the main staircase of the Congressional Library in Washington, D.C. Local commissions included altars for St. Agatha's Church in Philadelphia and Trinity Church in Wilmington. He is pictured here in his garden on Orchard Road around 1920.

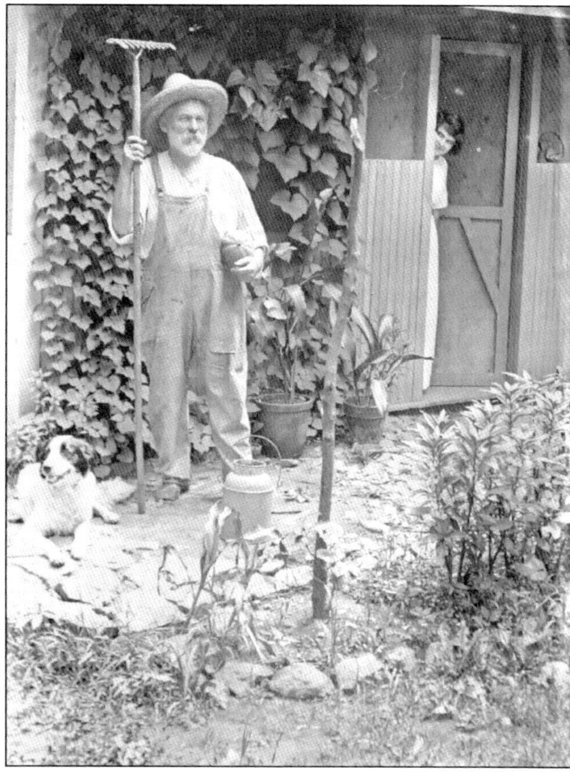

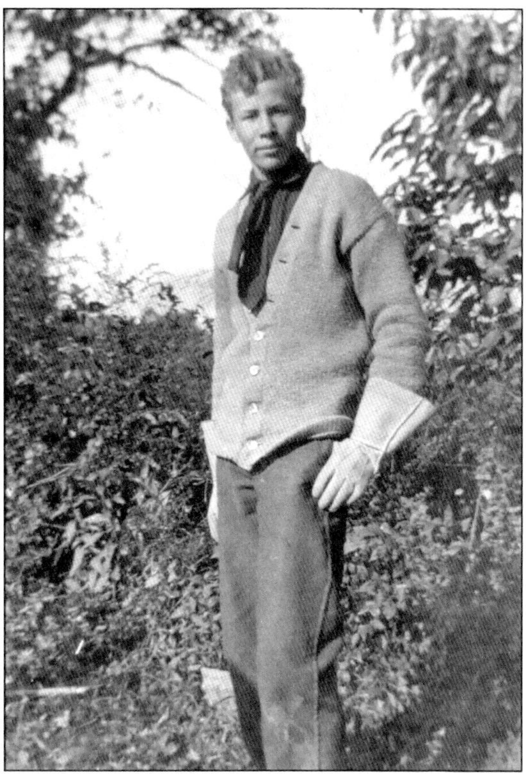

Hal Ware, Mother Bloor's eldest son, developed a love for both politics and farming during his Arden years. A communist like his more famous mother, Hal founded Russian Reconstruction Farms in 1922, an organization designed to teach Russian farmers modern American farming techniques as an aid to famine relief. He spent much of the 1920s in Russia, and was later thanked by Russian leader Vladimir Lenin for "successes which must be recognized as quite exceptional." He is seen here in 1909.

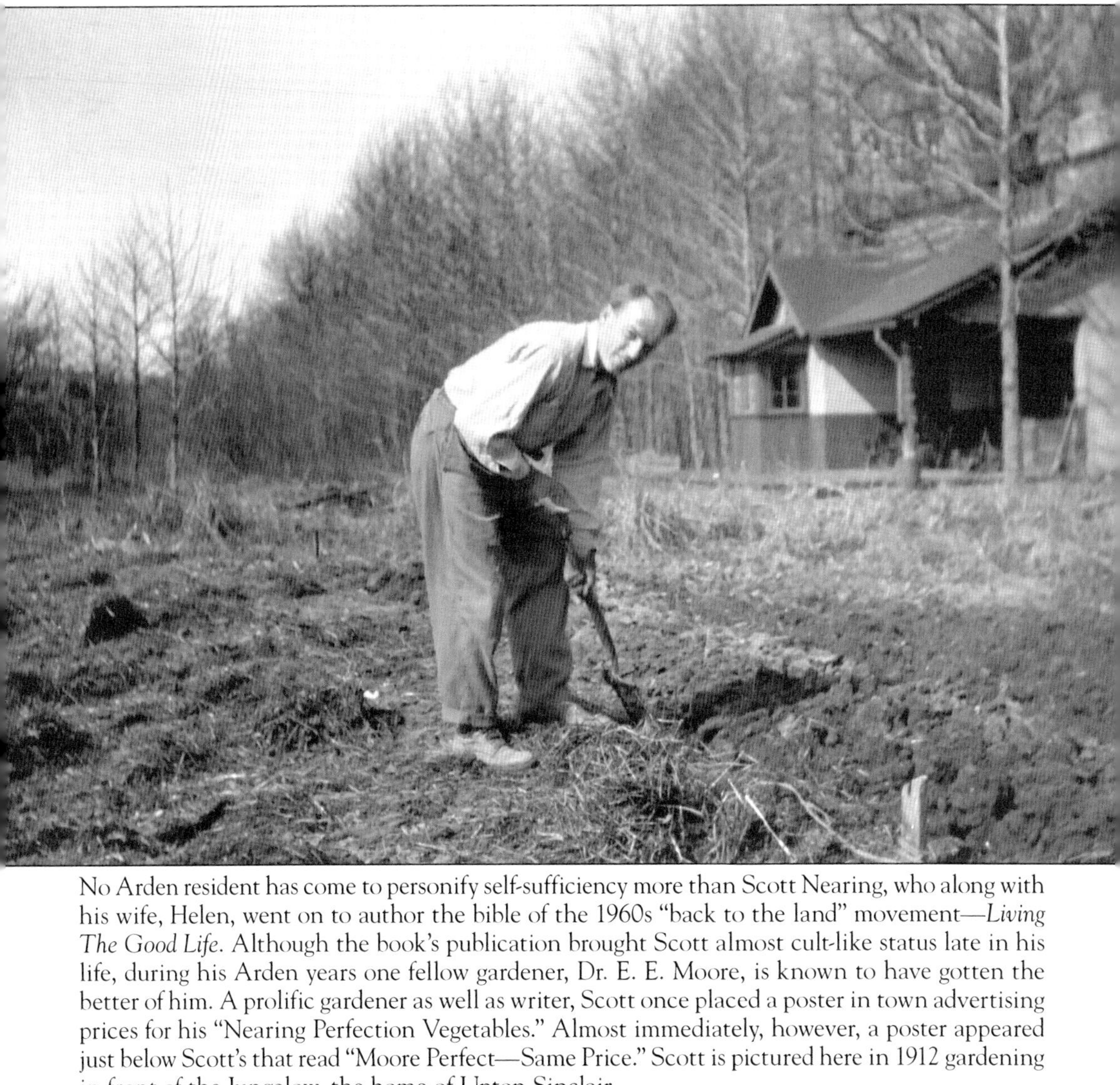

No Arden resident has come to personify self-sufficiency more than Scott Nearing, who along with his wife, Helen, went on to author the bible of the 1960s "back to the land" movement—*Living The Good Life*. Although the book's publication brought Scott almost cult-like status late in his life, during his Arden years one fellow gardener, Dr. E. E. Moore, is known to have gotten the better of him. A prolific gardener as well as writer, Scott once placed a poster in town advertising prices for his "Nearing Perfection Vegetables." Almost immediately, however, a poster appeared just below Scott's that read "Moore Perfect—Same Price." Scott is pictured here in 1912 gardening in front of the Jungalow, the home of Upton Sinclair.

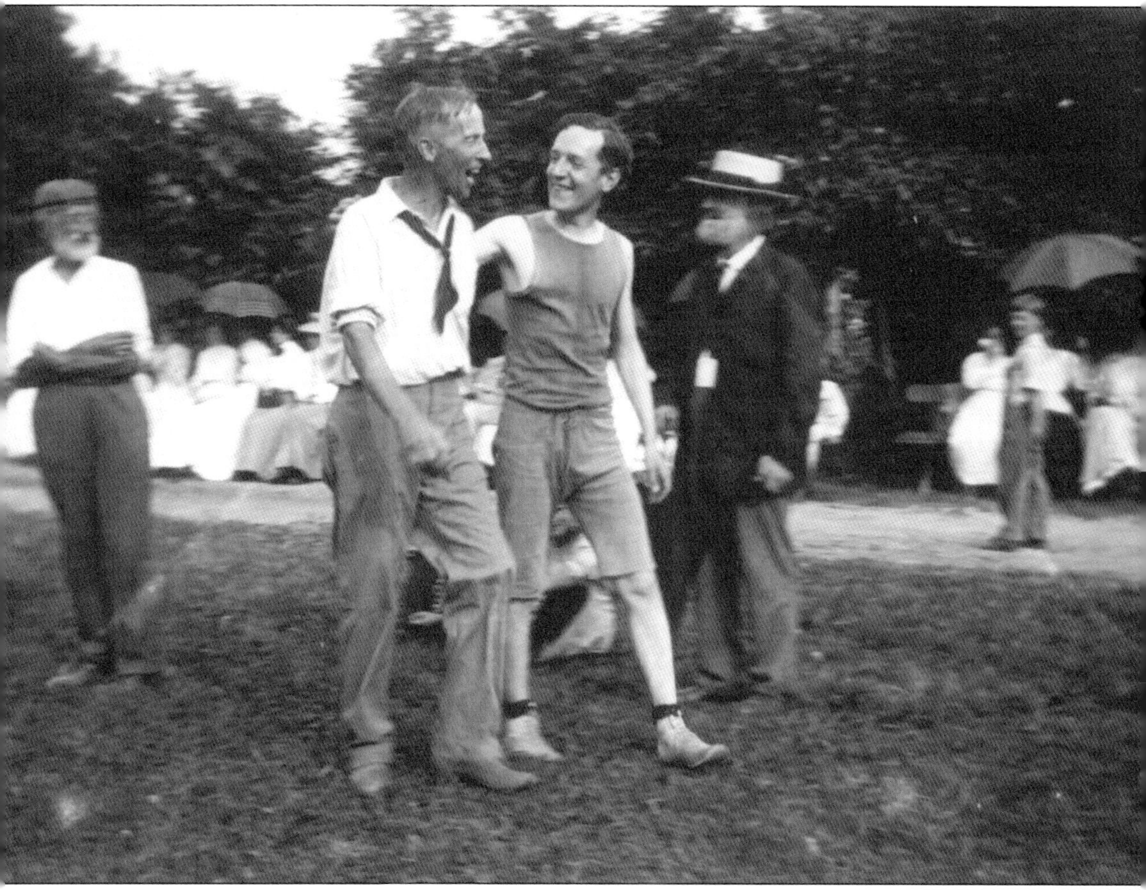

Upton Sinclair arrived in Arden in the spring of 1910 shortly after his own utopian experiment, Helicon Hall in Englewood, New Jersey, burned to the ground. According to his autobiography, Sinclair came to Arden to work on a sequel to his book *Loves Pilgrimage*, the purpose of which was "to illustrate the new attitude toward love and marriage in which the equal rights of both parties to experiment and self-discovery are recognized." The book was never finished and exists today only in manuscript form. In this photograph, Frank Stephens and Upton Sinclair share a rare moment of lighthearted camaraderie at Arden's 1910 Field Day.

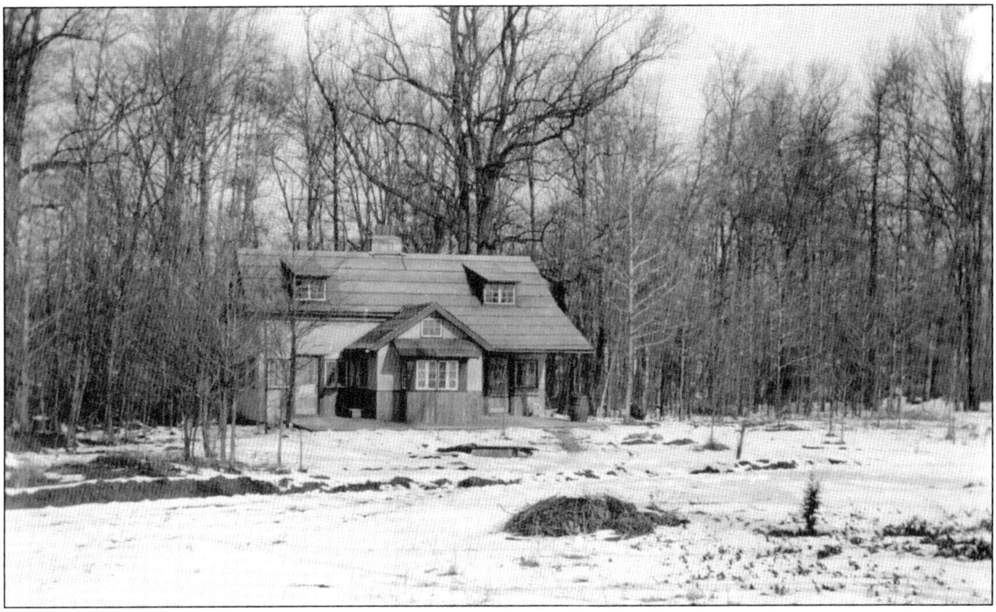

Upton Sinclair's house was completed in December 1910 and was immediately nicknamed the Jungalow by Arden residents. The author apparently appreciated the joke, going so far as to have stationery printed with the name. Frank Stephens built the house at a cost of $2,600, a price the builder grossly underestimated, according to Sinclair.

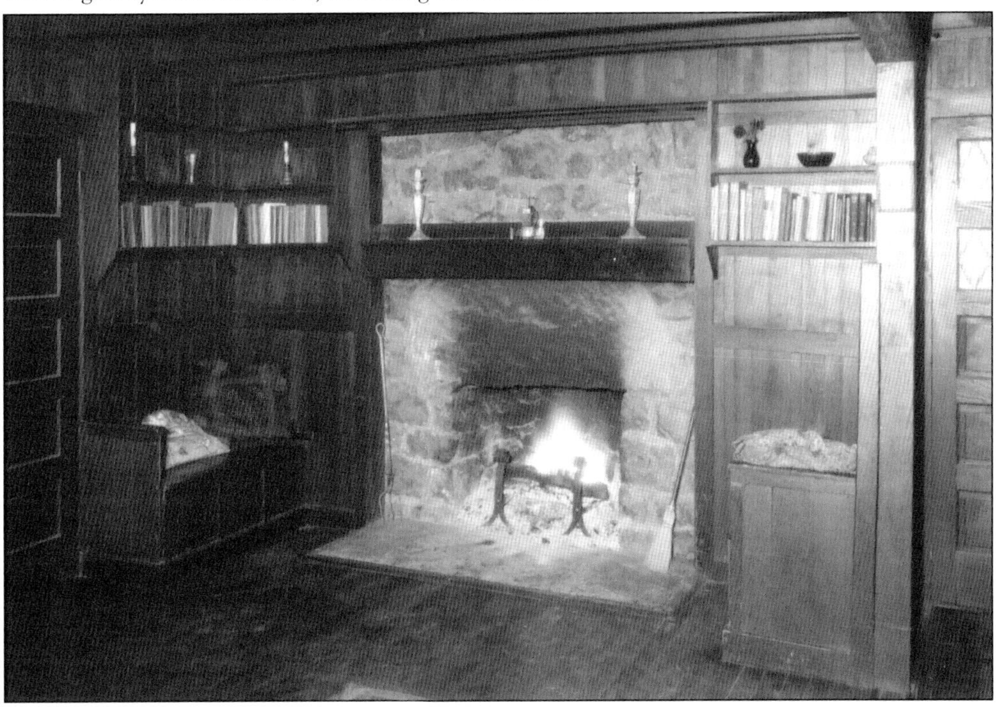

Although this photograph of the Jungalow's interior was most likely taken after Sinclair left the community, it appears to have been staged to document the author's description: "There was a living room in front with an open fireplace and a chimney that smoked. High on the wall, a shelf ran all the way around, and held most of my books."

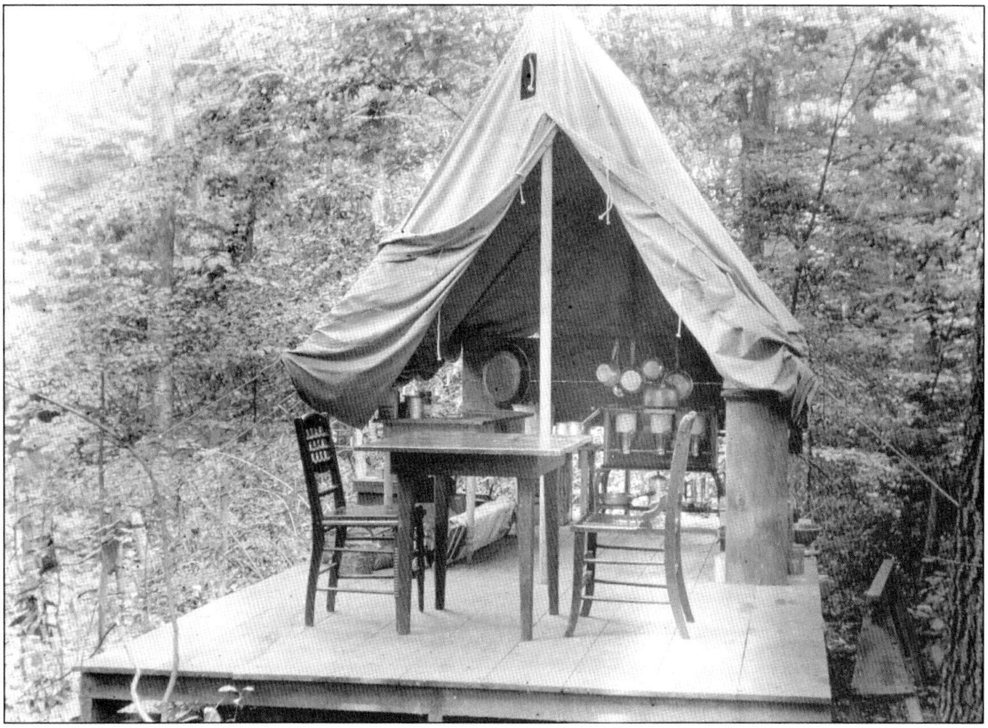

In addition to the Jungalow, Sinclair frequently used Scott Nearing's cottage as an office. His leasehold also included a number of tents, of which this is believed to be one.

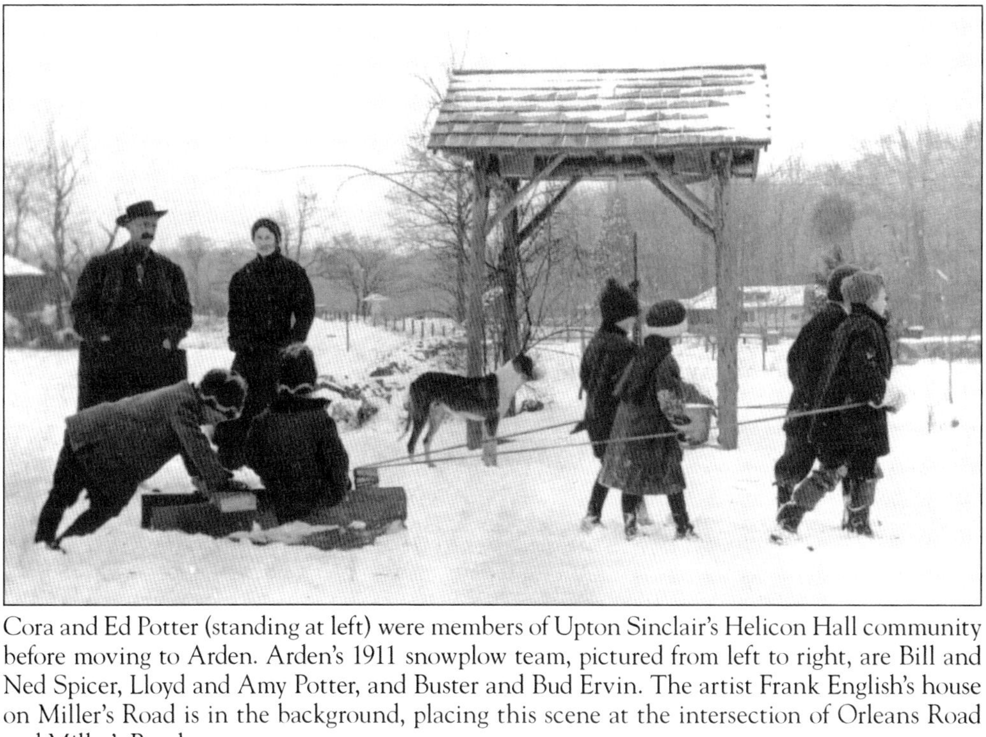

Cora and Ed Potter (standing at left) were members of Upton Sinclair's Helicon Hall community before moving to Arden. Arden's 1911 snowplow team, pictured from left to right, are Bill and Ned Spicer, Lloyd and Amy Potter, and Buster and Bud Ervin. The artist Frank English's house on Miller's Road is in the background, placing this scene at the intersection of Orleans Road and Miller's Road.

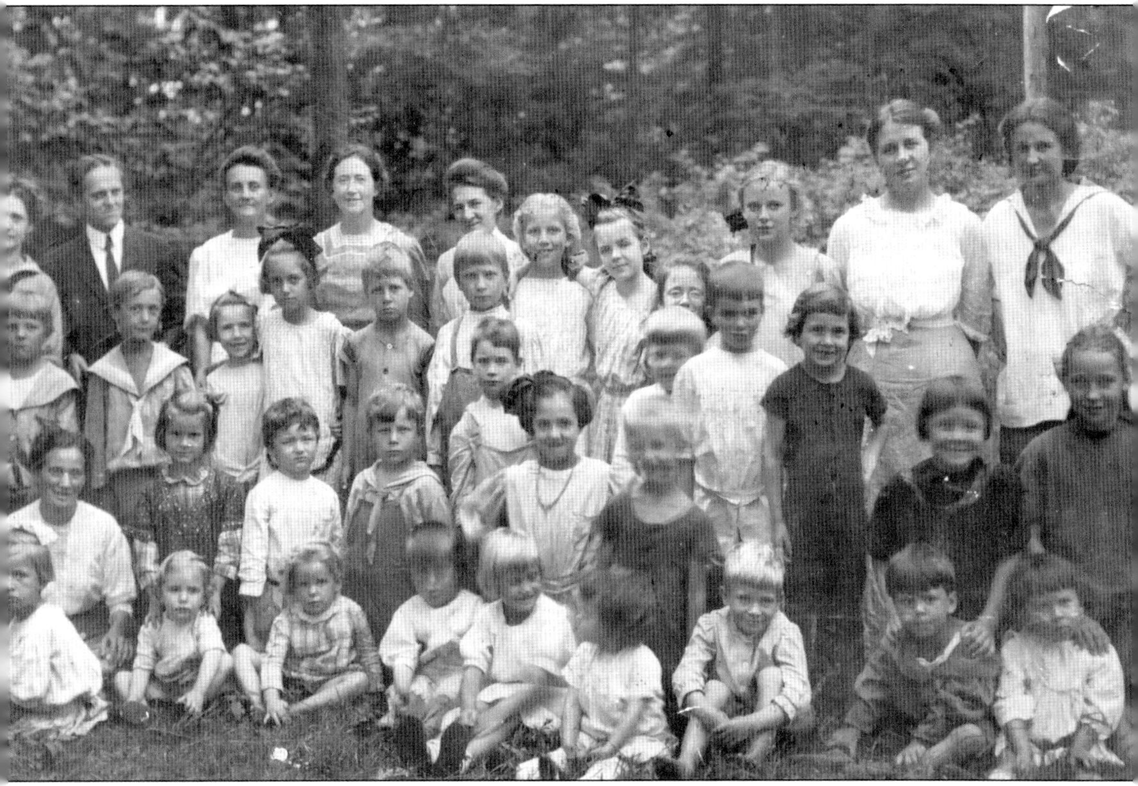

Prior to their move to Arden, Cora and Ed Potter had run the Living House at Elizabeth and Alexis Ferm's Playhouse School, an anarchist educational experiment in Brooklyn, New York. In Arden, with the Ferms as inspiration, Cora started Arden's first kindergarten, the Playground School, which met at the Red House beginning in 1910. The school met for five hours a day with classes in nature study and the arts, as well as reading and writing. Students were supervised but self-directed, and were free to leave the schoolroom at any time. Weather permitting, part of the day was always spent outdoors with sports and games. Although Cora served as principal, many Arden women (and men) volunteered their time including Mary Hansen, Louise Kumme, Alice Steinlein, and Ed Potter. The children and their instructors in this 1911 photograph remain unidentified; however, many of them can also be seen in the Arden family portrait of 1908.

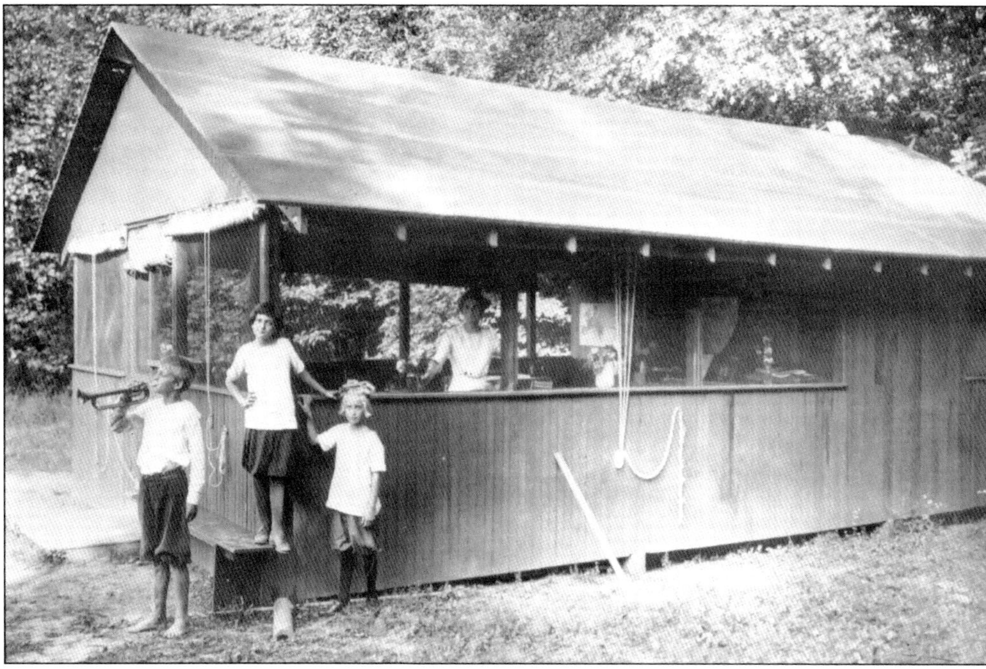

In 1912, Cora Potter started another educational experiment, The Arden Summer Camp School of Organic Education, located at the intersection of Sherwood Road and The Highway. Similar to the Playground School, the Organic School espoused a philosophy of "education for the entire organism." Marietta Johnson, who founded the Organic School movement in 1908 at the single tax community of Fairhope, spent the summer of 1912 in Arden teaching. In this photograph, Cora Potter is seen inside the school dining pavilion. The children, from left to right, are Lloyd Potter, Amy Potter, and an unknown friend.

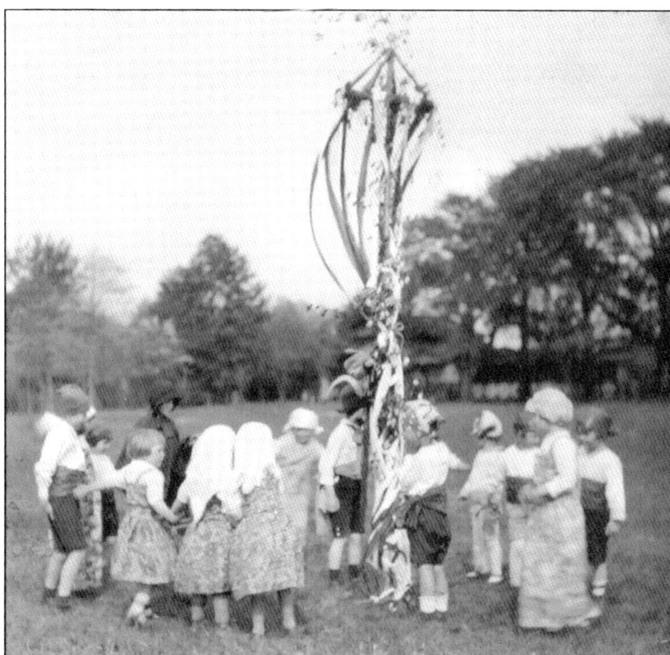

The maypole dance is a popular tradition in Arden and was often performed on Arden Day, which was celebrated in May to commemorate the founding of the village and the beginning of the summer season. Here a kindergarten group learns the steps around 1923. In the foreground, the two girls with kerchiefs are Don Stephens's daughters Hope and Peggy. To their left is Buzz and Jimmie Ware's daughter, Joan. (Courtesy of Terry Colgan.)

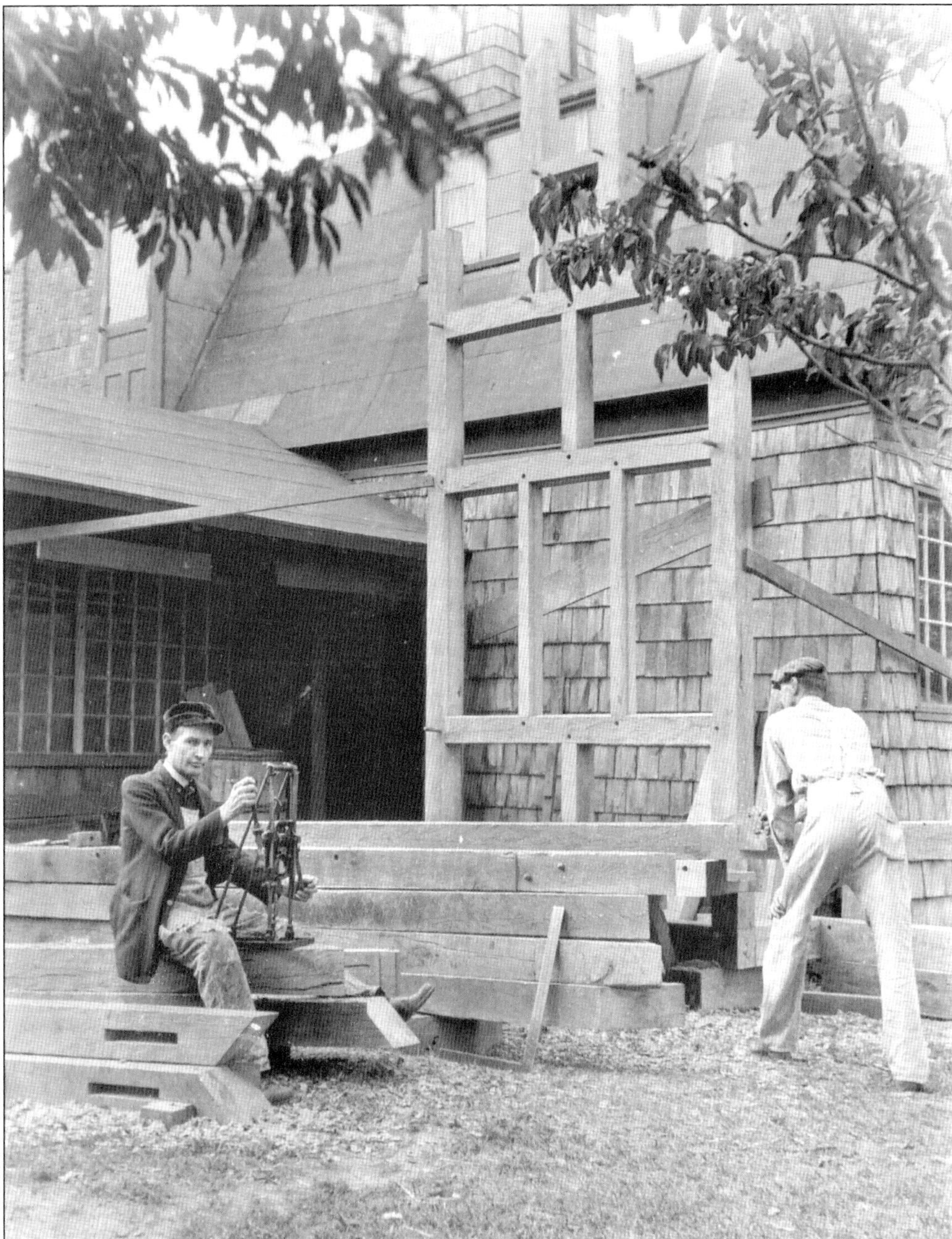

With the village social affairs now firmly ensconced at the new clubhouse, Stephens and Price were able to turn their attention to the development of the arts and crafts in Arden. The Red House on the Village Green now became the industrial center of town, and in 1913, plans were announced for a two-story addition to the building behind the old dance floor. Oak and poplar were sustainably harvested from the Arden Woods with "a view towards the best advantage of the woods themselves." In this 1913 photograph, two workers cut the mortise and tenon joints for a window frame.

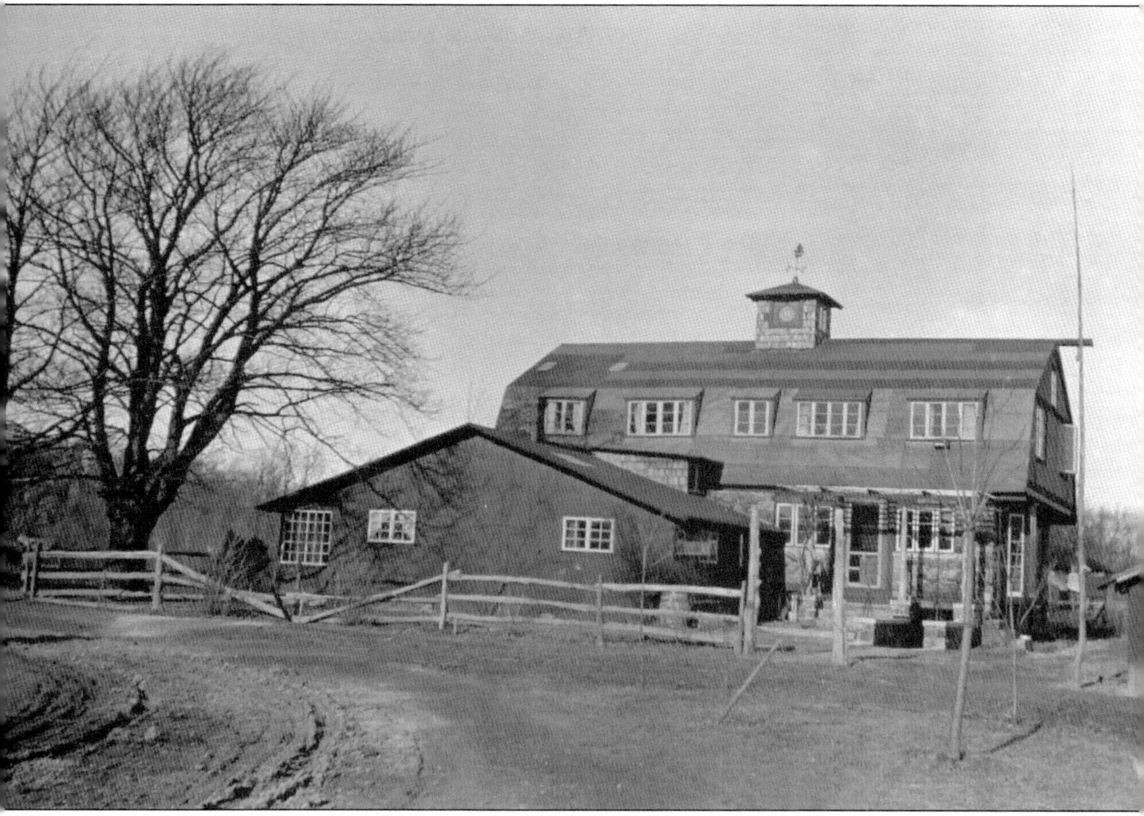

Will Price's architectural drawings for the Craft Shop are dated April 28, 1913. The building's upper floor contained two studios, a weaving room, an art metal studio, and a wood staining room. The main floor contained a workshop for woodcarving, drafting, and modeling, a sales room, smithy, woodworking shop, and sewing room. Surprisingly, it was not the woodworking shop that the architect was most interested in, but rather the sewing room, where he hoped "some designing person will have the courage to make clothing for daily use which will distinguish between draping the human figure and upholstering it, and will do something to put out of fashion the black derby hats and colorless remnants of starched shirts with superimposed suspenders by which the male Ardenites insult the natural beauty of the landscape."

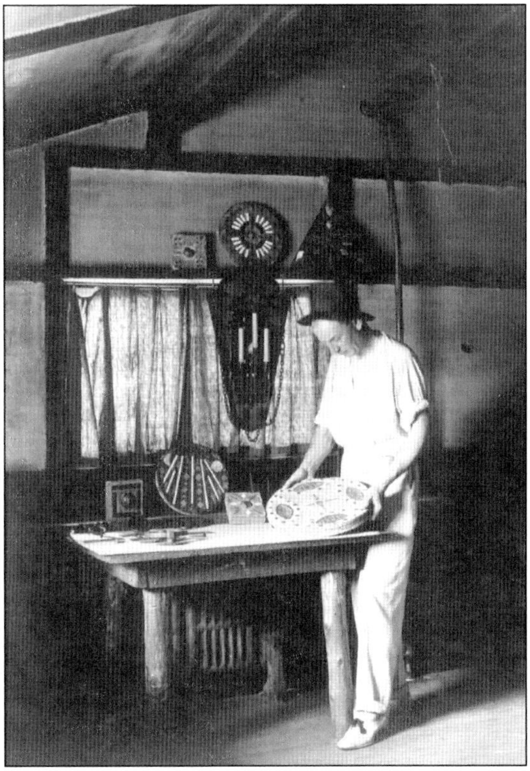

Gildmaster Harry Page proudly displays a cast concrete sundial decorated with American Indian arrowheads. According to a 1914 article on Arden crafts published in the *New York Herald Tribune* from which this photograph is taken, Page also created candleholders, bowls, vases, and sconces in hammered brass and copper. (Photograph by L. A. MacDonnald of Harvey, Delaware.)

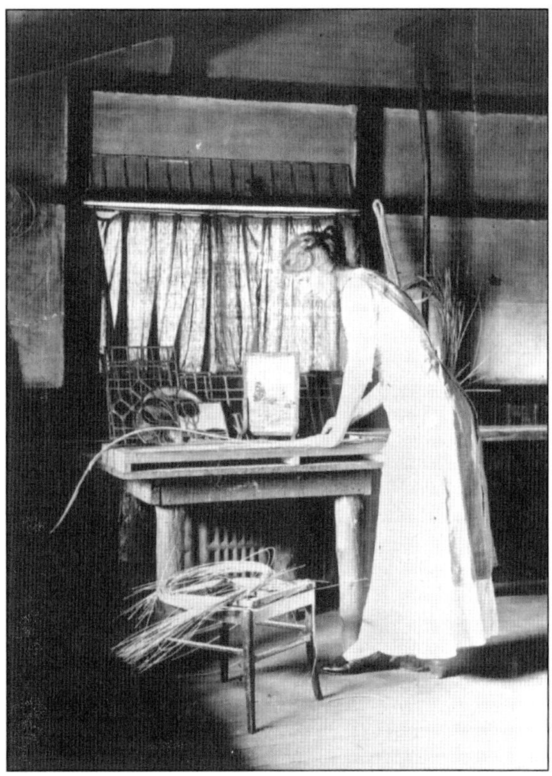

Although in this photograph Elena Darling appears to be caning a chair, she is primarily known for her leaded glasswork, and a few examples can be seen here on her bench. Her firescreens and candlescreens, many done in partnership with Buzz Ware, were particularly sought-after items. (Photograph by L. A. MacDonnald of Harvey, Delaware.)

Margaret Wood's silverwork greatly impressed the writer for the *New York Herald Tribune*. According to the article, Wood made silver trays, bowls, tableware, and jewelry. Although she worked in other metals as well, silver was her preferred medium. (Photograph by L. A. MacDonnald of Harvey, Delaware.)

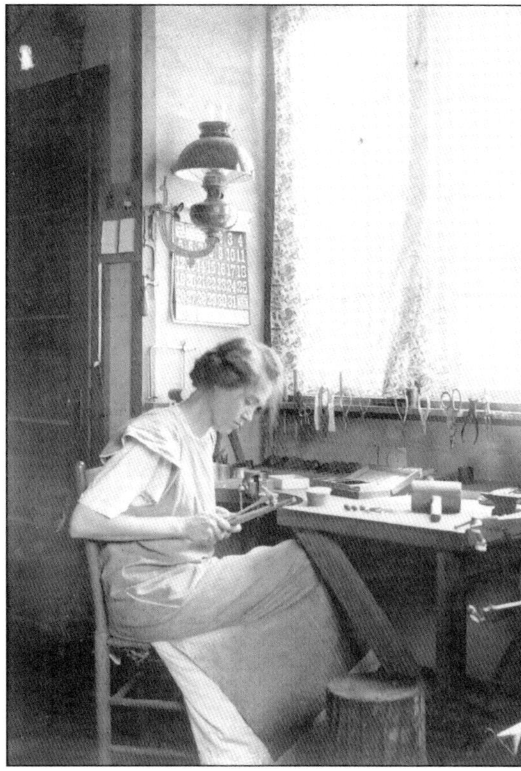

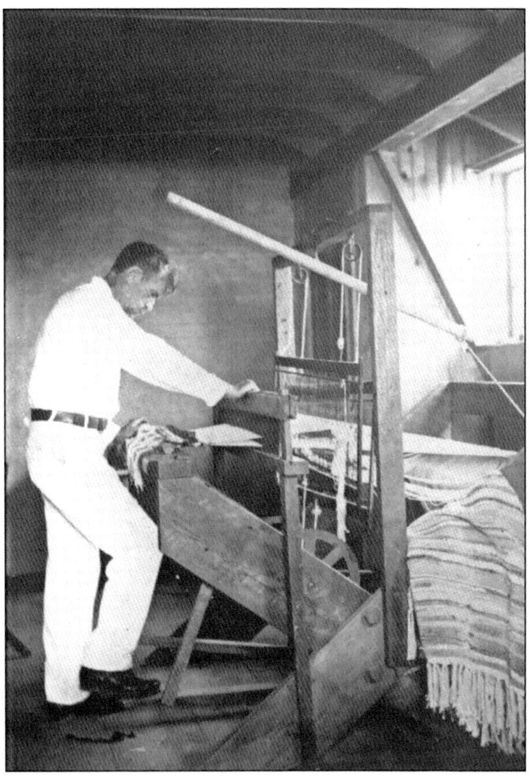

Arden was home to several weavers over the years, beginning sometime prior to 1908 with Dr. E. E. Moore, who wove rag rugs for the community. According to one account, Dr. Moore was a former physician who renounced his profession "when he made the discovery that it was a fraud." (Photograph by L. A. MacDonnald of Harvey, Delaware.)

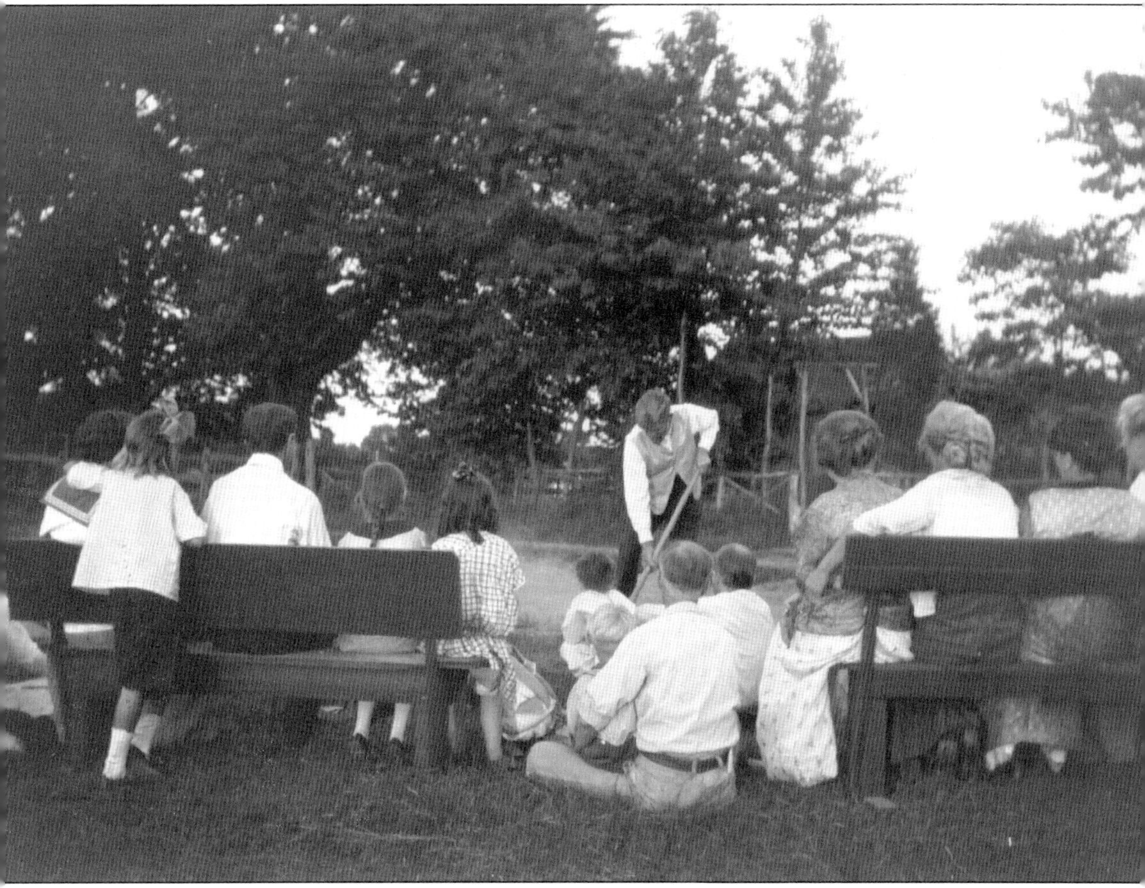

Like many artists and intellectuals of the age, Dr. Moore was a passionate disciple of the poet Walt Whitman, the author of *Leaves of Grass*, and hosted a Sunday discussion group of the poet's works at his home on Walnut Lane. In 1914, Dr. Moore, pictured here digging, and writer David Karsner, who was also an Arden resident, established a memorial to "the Good Grey Poet" by planting a lilac bush on the Village Green. The event marked the beginning of the Arden branch of the Walt Whitman Fellowship International, an organization that had been founded by Whitman's biographer Horace Traubel in 1894.

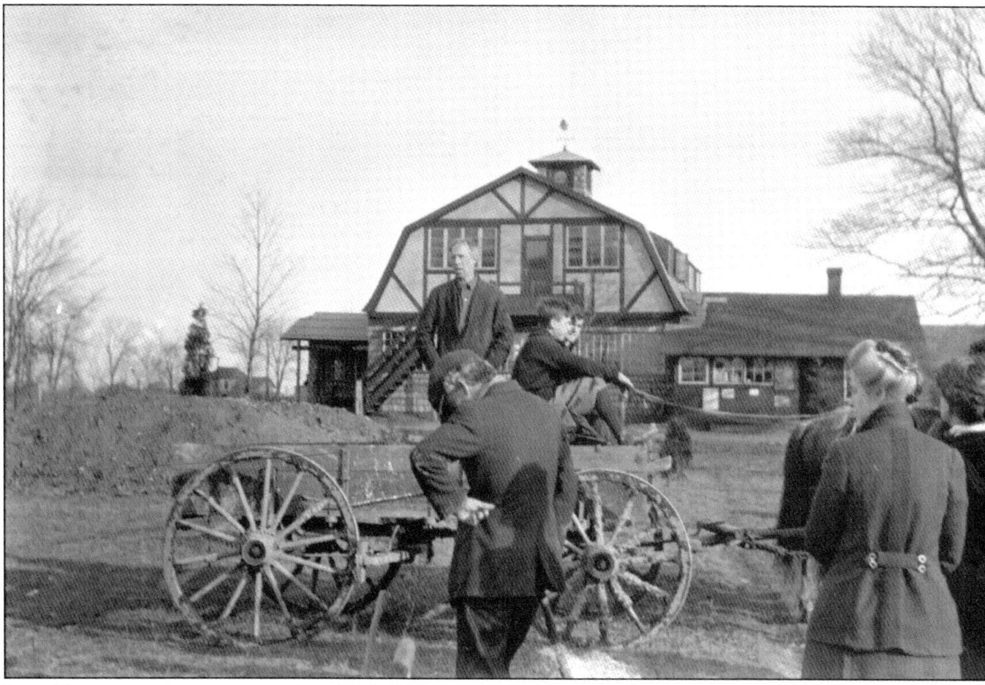

In addition to the memorial to Walt Whitman, memorials to Joseph Fels, William Morris, and Henry George were also planned for the Village Green. Of these three, only the memorial to Fels was completed during Stephens and Price's lifetime. In this 1914 photograph, Frank Stephens addresses the crowd from the now empty wagon used to bring the Fels oak to its new location on the Village Green.

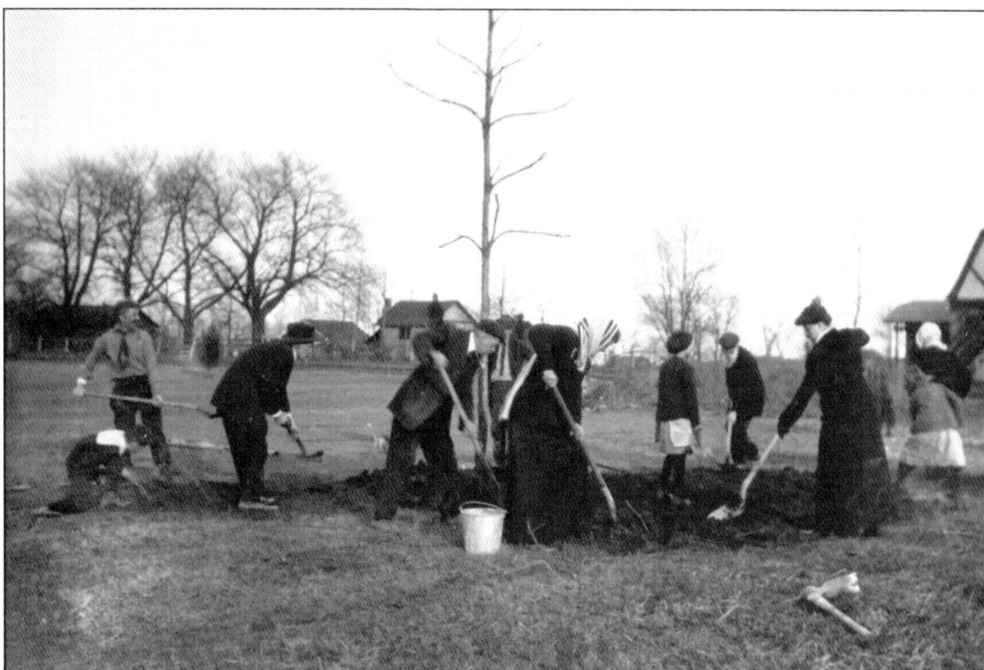

With the tree now planted and night beginning to fall, the workers fill in the last of the soil.

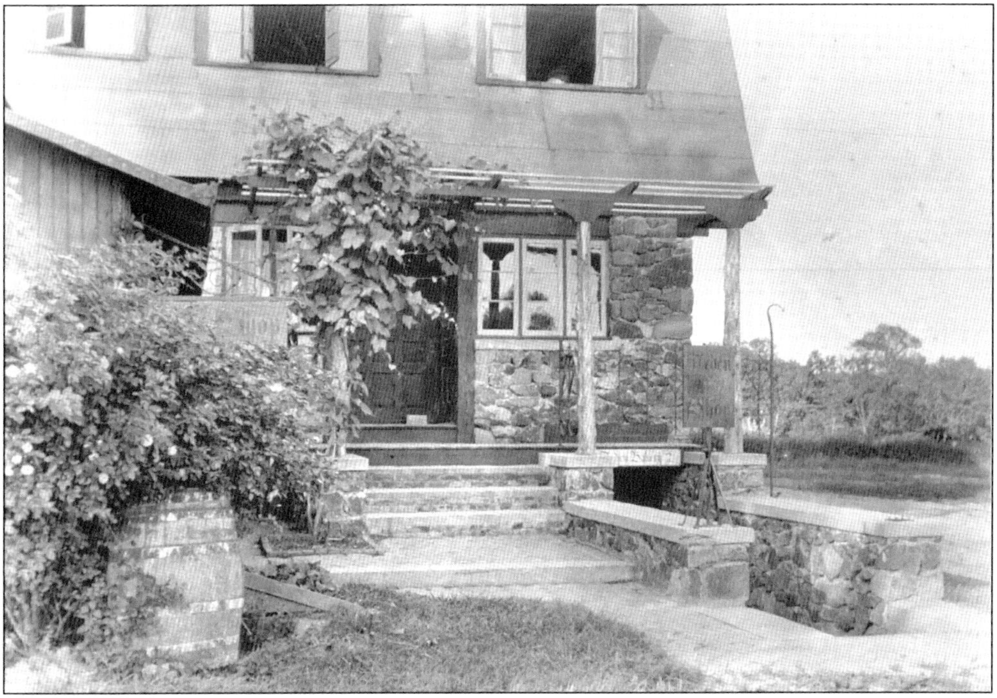

Jane Marcellus opened a bakery in the Craft Shop on August 1, 1913. The door to the left is the entrance to the woodworking shop.

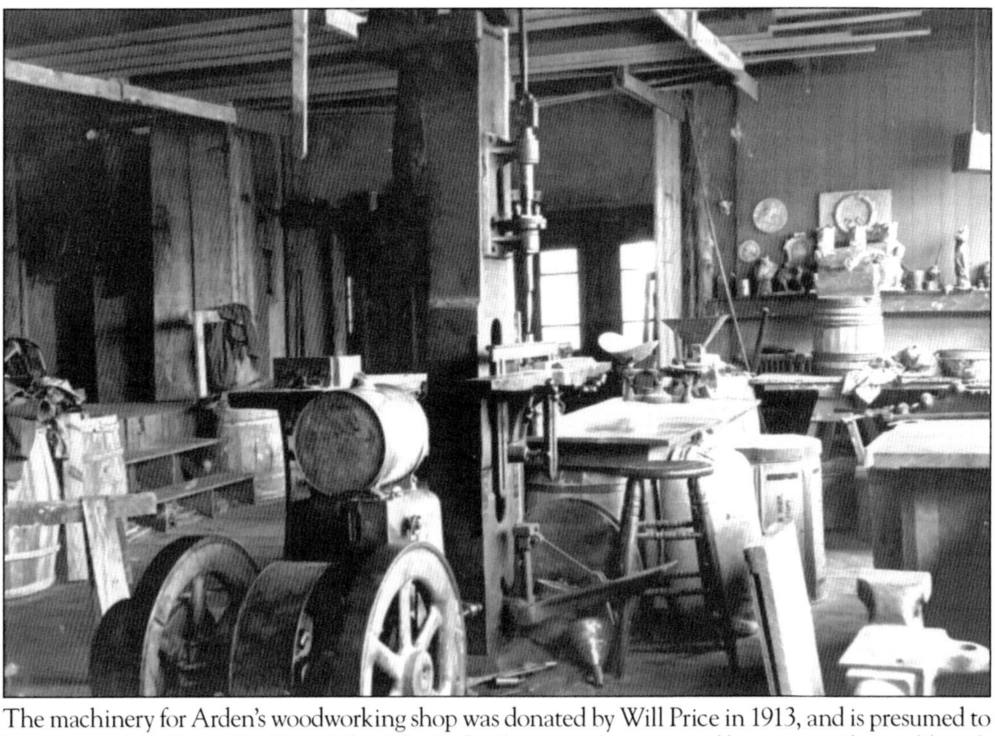

The machinery for Arden's woodworking shop was donated by Will Price in 1913, and is presumed to have been originally used in Rose Valley. The Arden furniture shop was used by many residents, although documentation shows that most of the furniture produced can be attributed to Don Stephens.

Don Stephens dated the photographs of his furniture 1916; however, this music stand can be documented considerably earlier. In the aforementioned article on Arden published in Gustav Stickley's *Craftsman Magazine*, the stand can be seen on the porch of the Roserie.

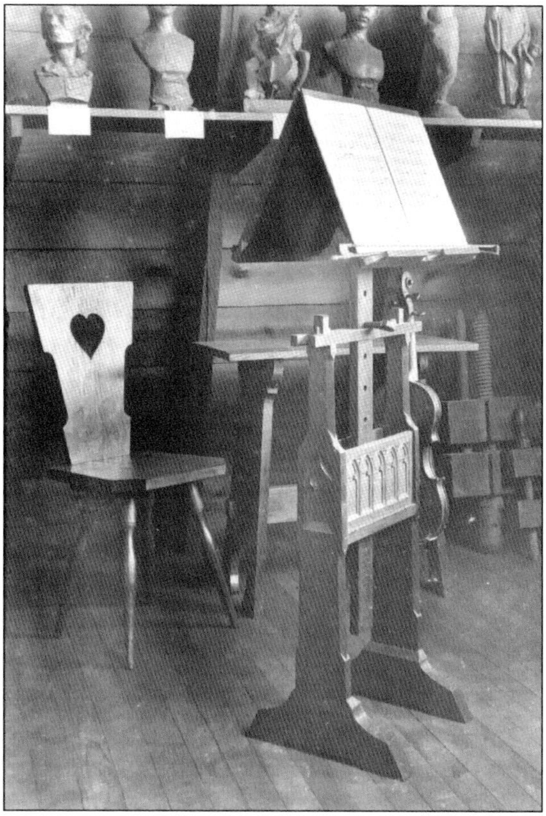

The elaborate wrought iron hinges from the Arden Forge accentuate the ornate carving on this wonderful oak blanket chest. Like much of the Arden furniture, it is considered a one-of-a-kind piece.

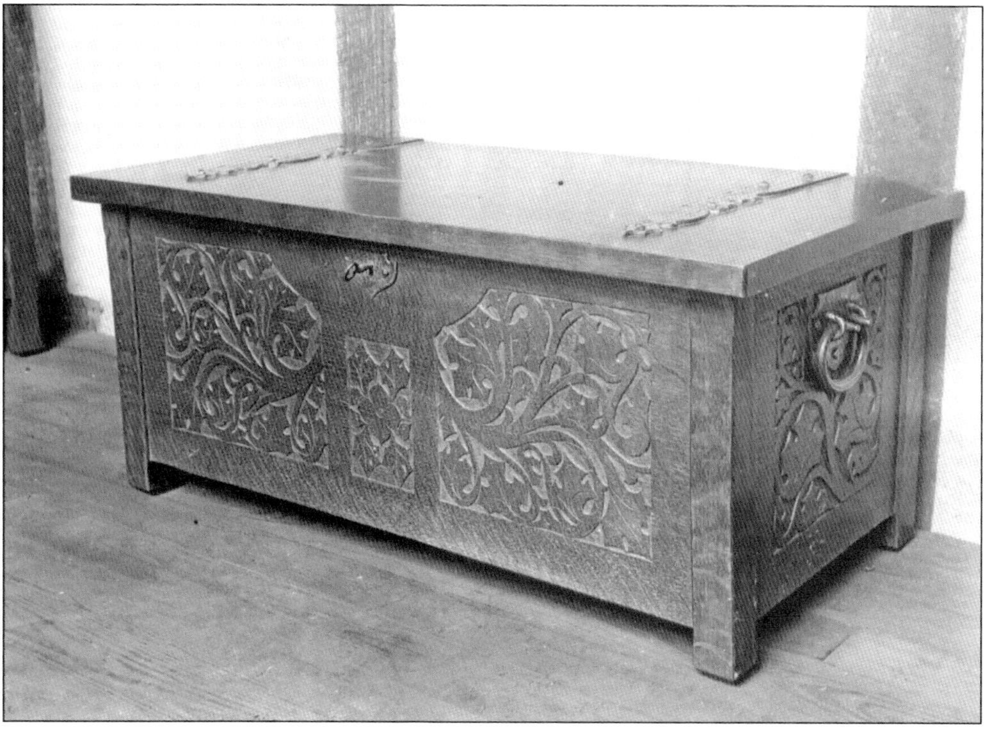

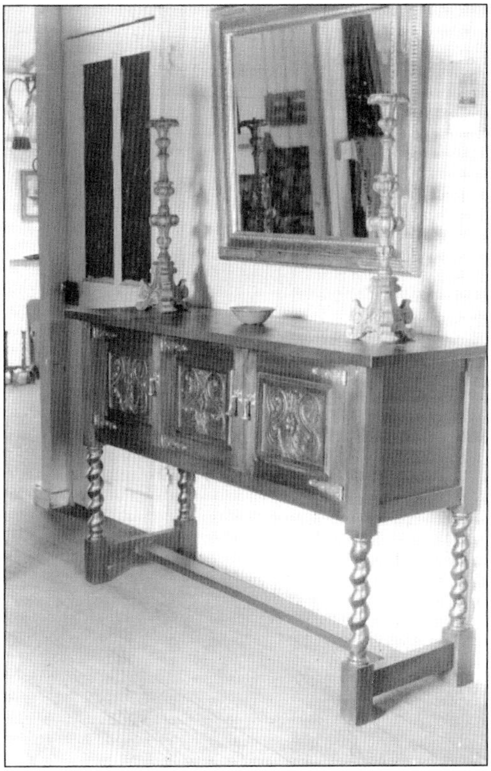

Barley twist turnings were frequently employed on Don's larger case pieces, such as this sideboard. As with the blanket chest, the hinges were made by the Arden Forge. The carved mirror is Don's work as well.

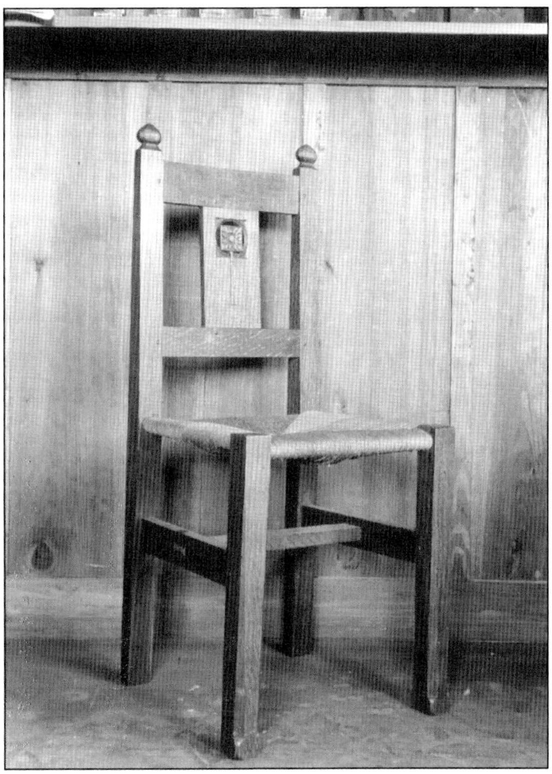

Although at first glance there is little to distinguish this chair from other mission furniture of the period, the stylized flower, carved finials, and chamfered front legs provide a great deal of visual interest.

Inspired by Will Price's Rose Valley Shops, which utilized the wild rose as their symbol, Arden's Craft Gild adopted the dogwood blossom. Don Stephens frequently used the flower for ornamentation, as can be seen in this imposing mirror with its Socratic command.

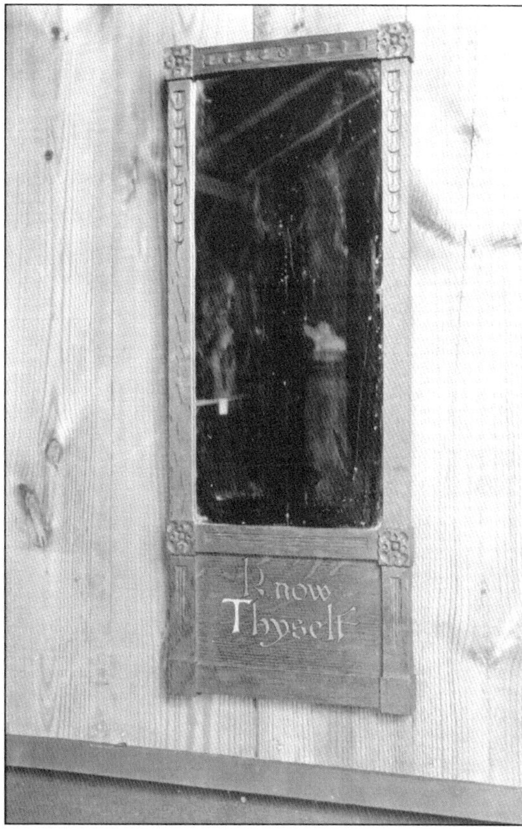

Although this oak library table was made by Don Stephens, its design is attributed to Will Price. It is constructed without glue, using only pegged mortise and tenon joinery. The carving can be traced to several pieces of Rose Valley furniture, thus establishing an important link between Price's work in Rose Valley and Arden.

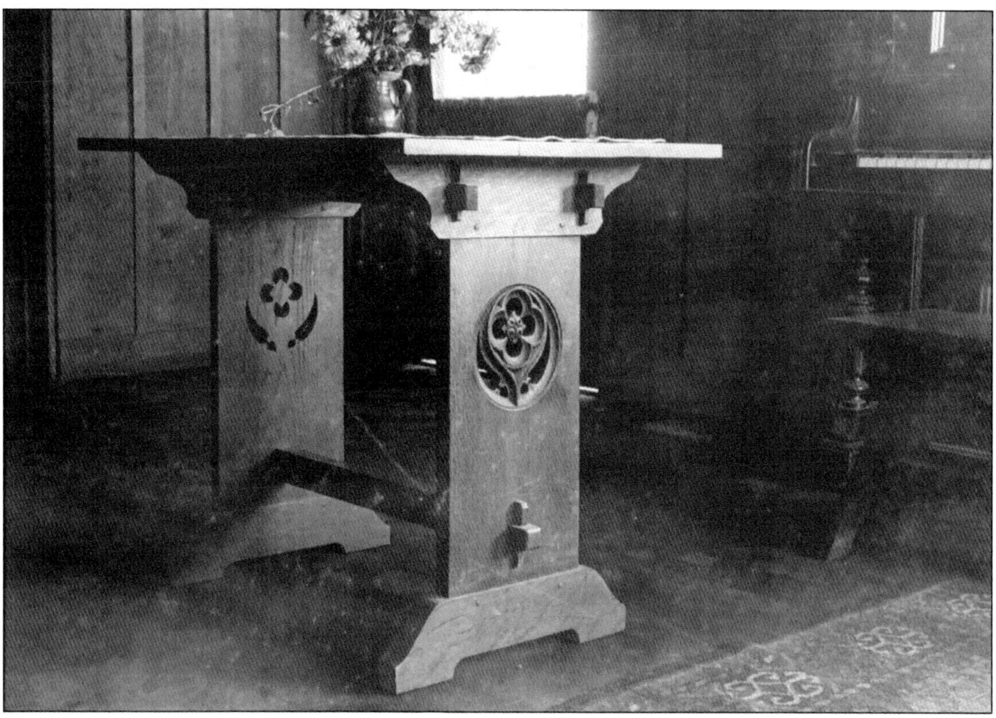

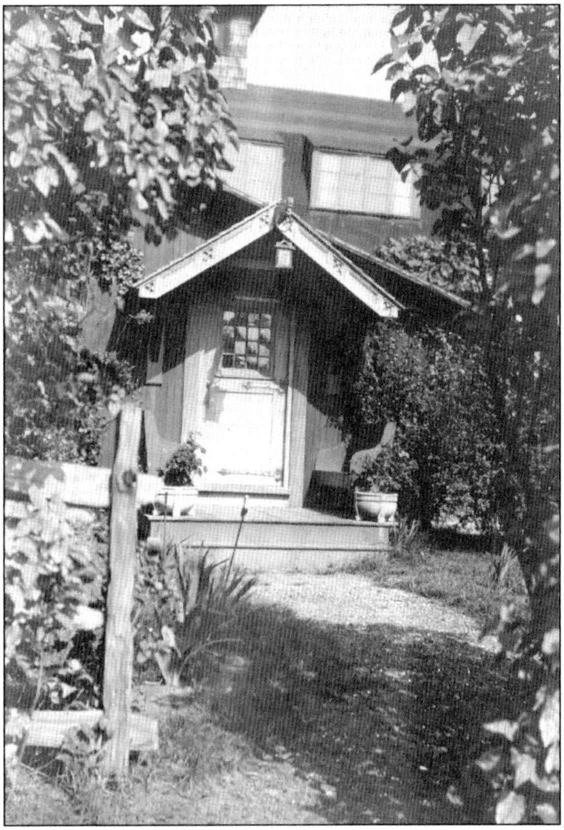

The formal entrance to the Craft Shop, as seen here in the 1920s, opened to Frank Stephens's office and the Arden Salesroom.

In the 1920s, the Arden Salesroom carried work not only from Arden, but from other arts and crafts communities as well, including the Byrdcliffe community in Woodstock, New York. Arden crafts were exhibited and sold throughout the east coast at outlets in Philadelphia, New York, and Boston.

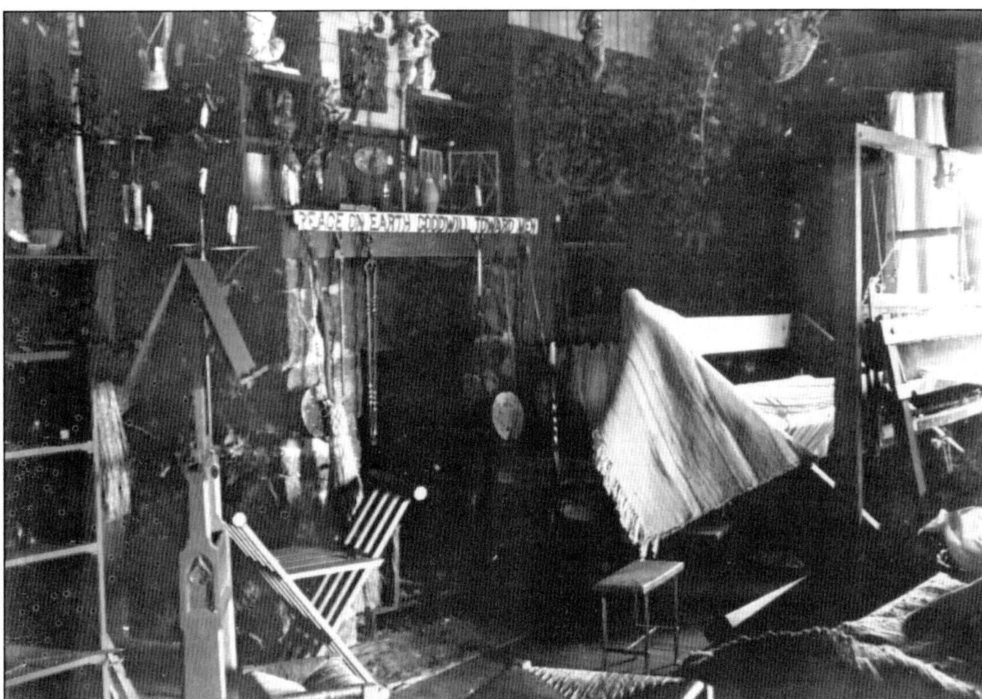

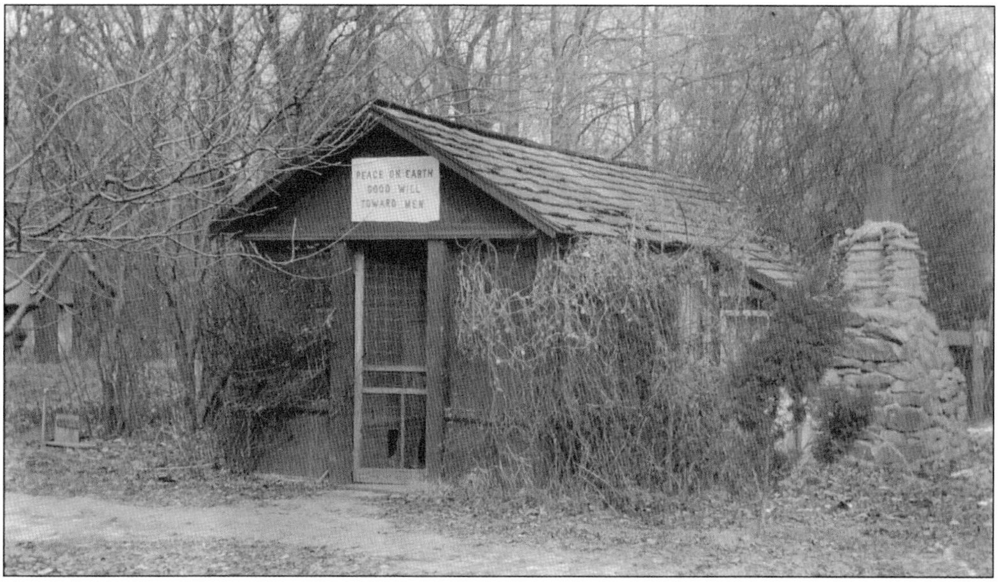

In 1914, Emma Goldman received a request from the Newspaper Enterprise Association for an article on how America could best restore "peace on earth and good will toward men." Her response was published in the January 1915 issue of her magazine, *Mother Earth*, and is most likely the inspiration for the sign seen here over the door to the Roserie, as well as on the mantel in the preceding photograph. Several members of the Arden community published in the pages of *Mother Earth* throughout the years, including Frank Stephens, George Brown, Mary Hansen, and Upton Sinclair.

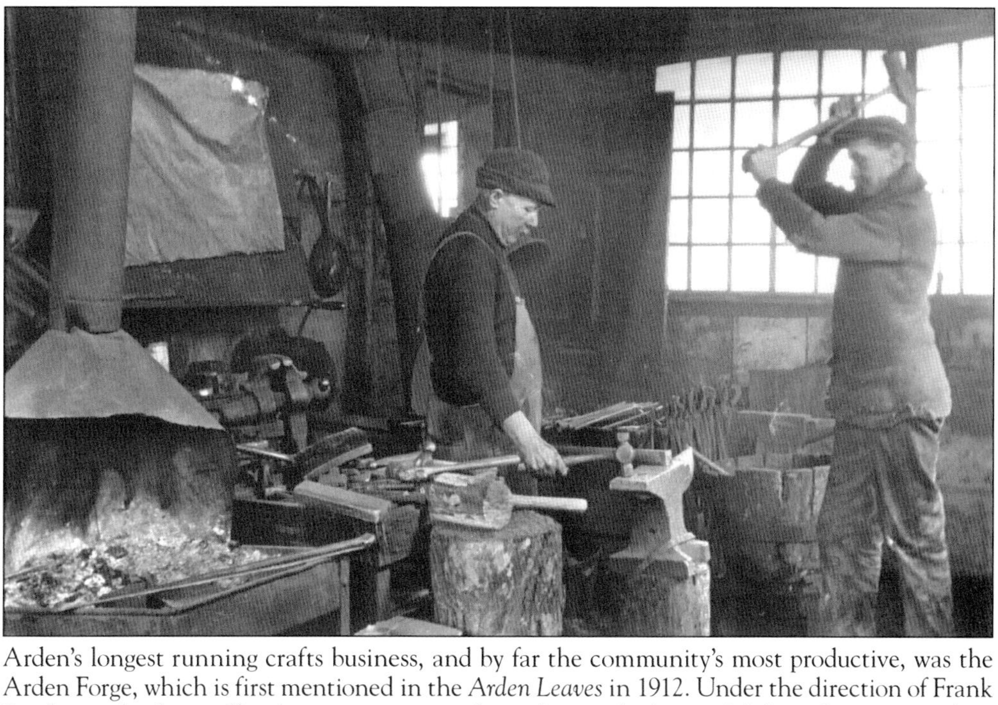

Arden's longest running crafts business, and by far the community's most productive, was the Arden Forge, which is first mentioned in the *Arden Leaves* in 1912. Under the direction of Frank Stephens, the forge offered an extensive catalogue line with the availability of custom work as well. In this photograph, Al Harvey (right) and Al Farmer take turns at the anvil.

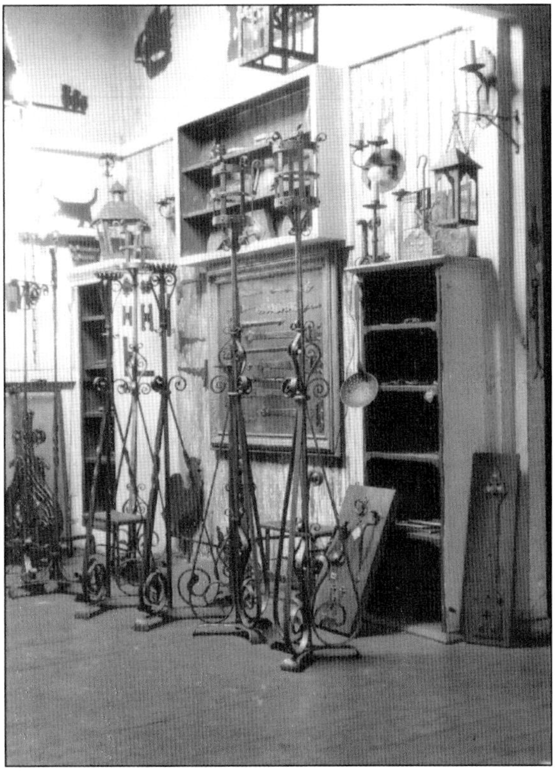

This photograph of the Salesroom from the 1920s gives an indication of the range of products the Arden Forge offered for sale. The lamp in the foreground was the most elaborate floor lamp the shop produced. It retailed for $55.

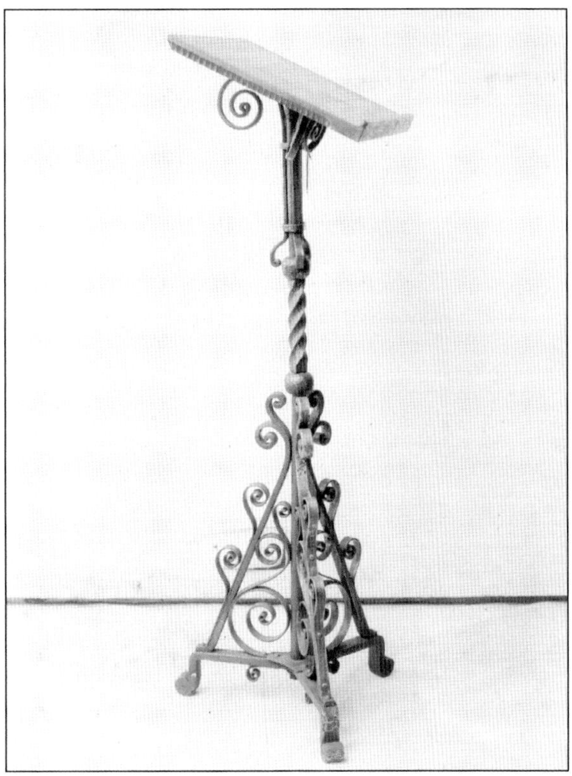

This lectern was the most expensive item offered in the Arden Forge catalogue, and it retailed for $95.

This group of items was known as the $50 Trial Set, and was one of several configurations available to retailers.

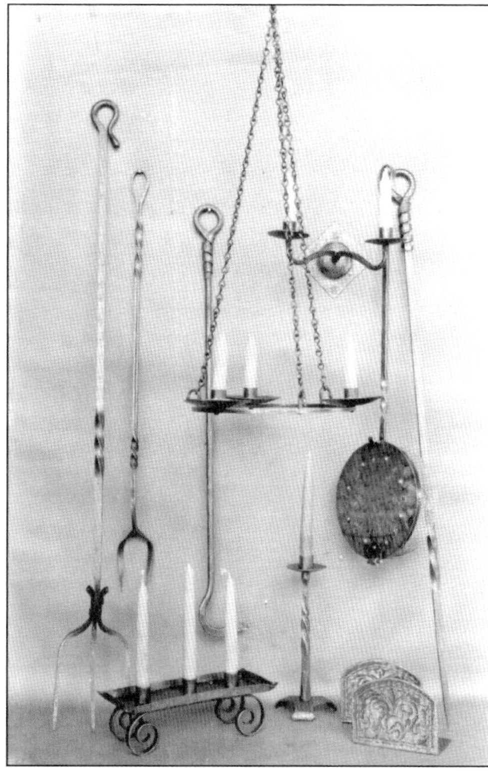

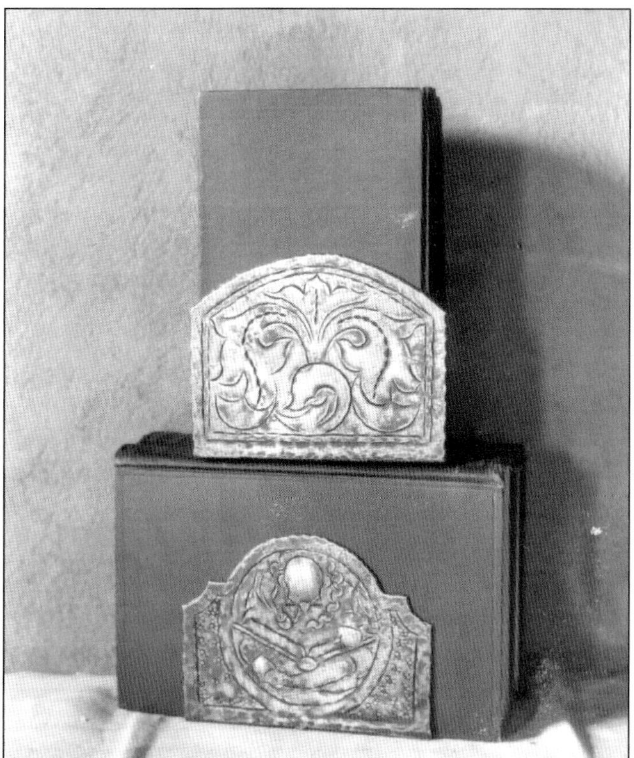

The Arden Forge bookend seen here supporting the horizontal stack of books was known as the Bookworm, and was produced from a design by Buzz Ware. This humorous portrayal of the bald headed scholar with his nose in his book was first incorporated into a stained glass window that originally hung in the Red House library. The bookends retailed for $6 a pair.

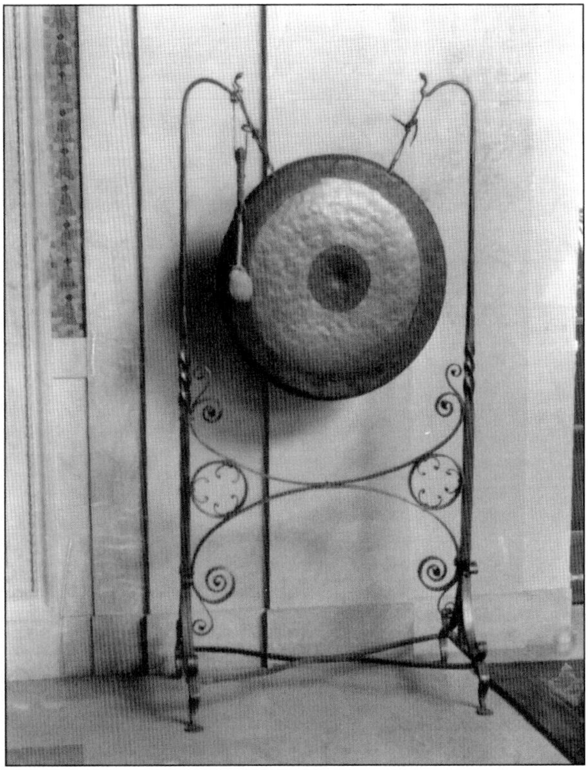

Reminiscent of the Art Nouveau period in its styling, this elaborate dinner gong was almost certainly a special commission.

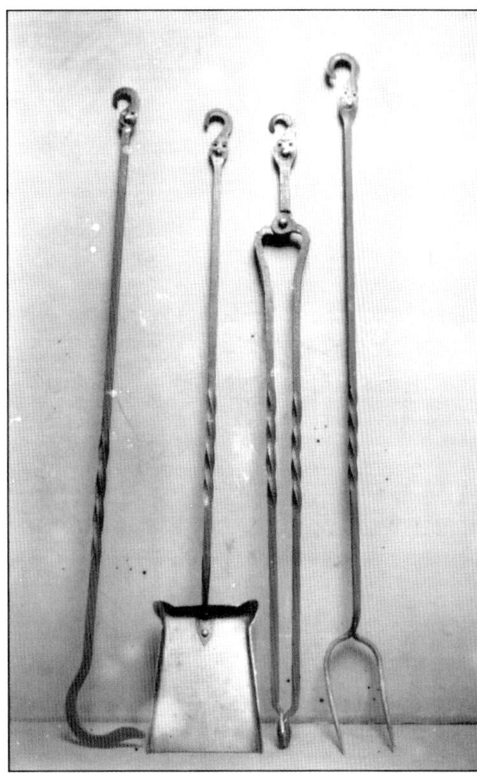

Although it is undocumented, the goblin fireplace set may be a Buzz Ware design as well. The poker retailed for $2, the shovel for $4.50, the tongs for $8, and the fork for $3.50.

While the designs for much of the forge's work harken back to the colonial era, the Five Light Scroll, as it was known, is thoroughly modern in its conception. The retail price was $38.

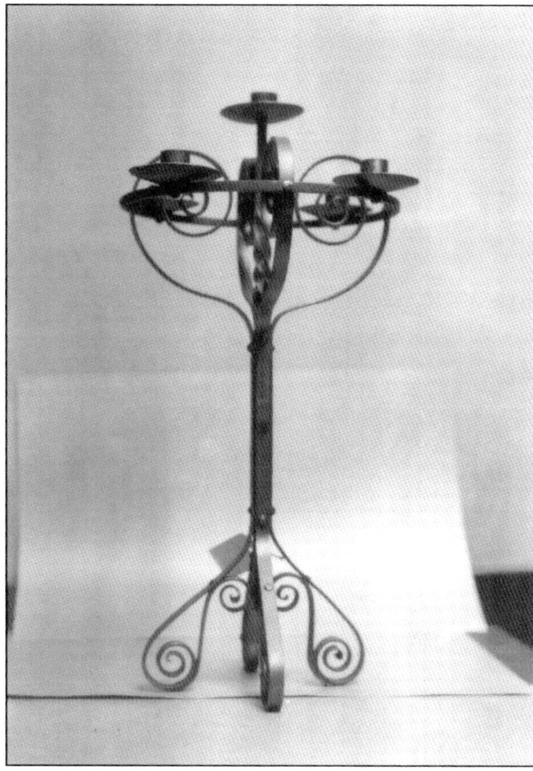

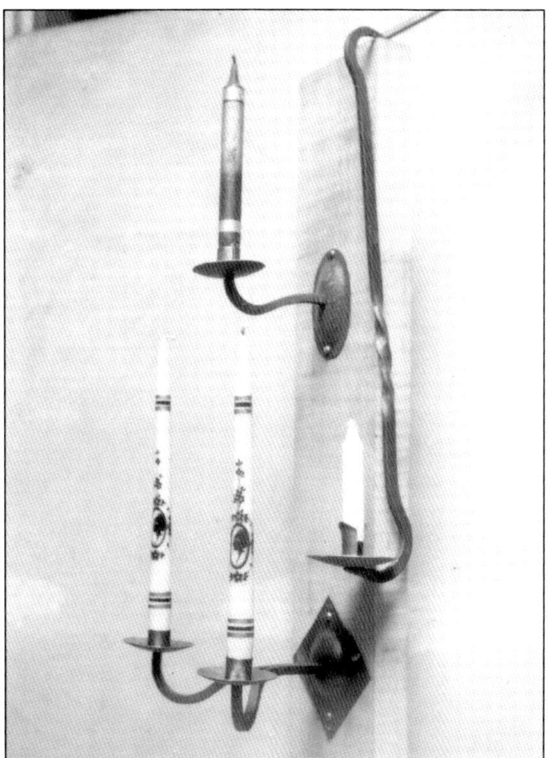

The forge offered a variety of sconces, two of which are pictured here. The one light retailed for $4, the two light for $5.50, and the hanging candlestick for $3.

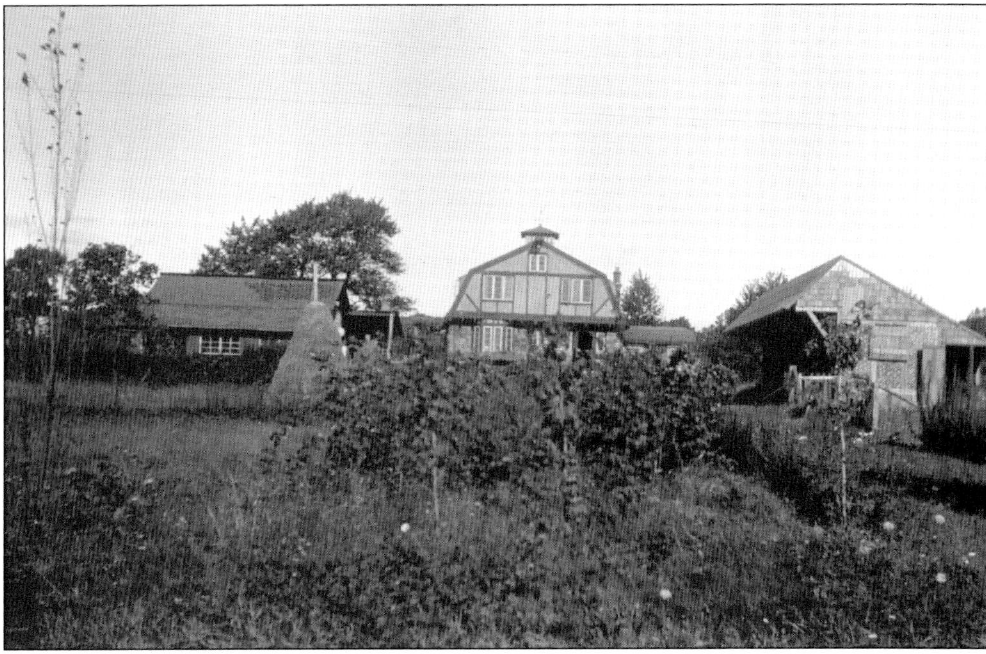

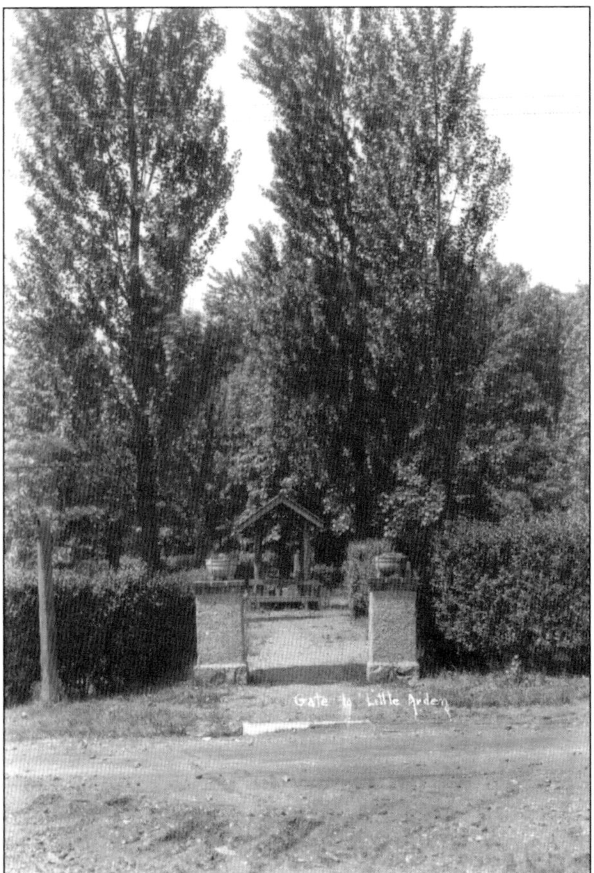

In this *c.* 1914 photograph, the Craft Shop is viewed from Walnut Lane. Visible is a sheepcote used by weaver Maude Rhodes. Of note to the left is a section of the community known as Little Arden, which contained several small cottages designed by Stephens and Price to house workers from the Craft Shop.

The formal entrance to Little Arden, with its hedges and decorative columns, emphasizes the central role Little Arden was designed to play in the village's original land plan. A pump is visible through the gateway.

Little is known about Maude Rhodes, who moved to the community sometime around 1914. According to an undated brochure, she wove scarves, table runners, blankets, and a line of women's sportswear. Woolens were often made using wool from Arden sheep. She is seen here in 1923 working in the Cooler, having vacated the Lone Pine earlier that year.

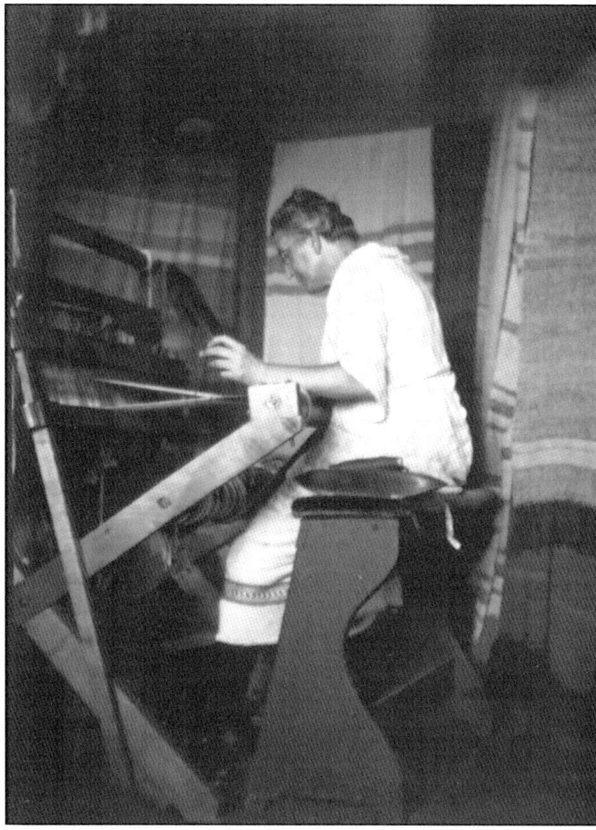

With its open-air porch now enclosed, the Cooler served as Maude Rhodes's weaving studio from 1923 until 1925. One of Miss Rhodes's early students was Anna Hock Riedel, who later took charge of weaving instruction at the Stelton Modern School, the anarchist school in Piscataway, New Jersey.

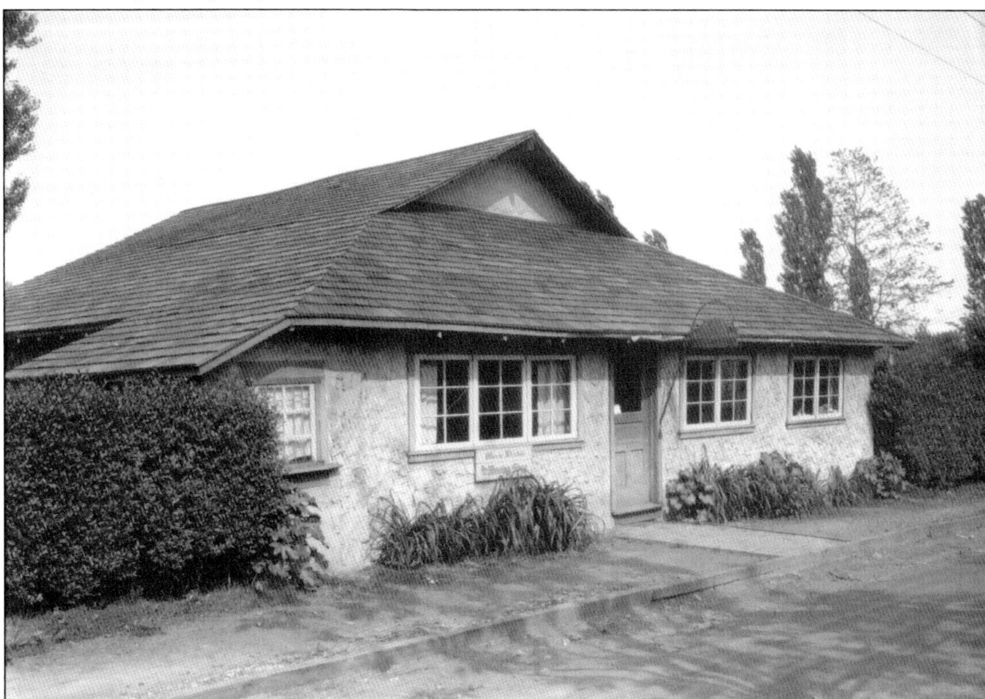

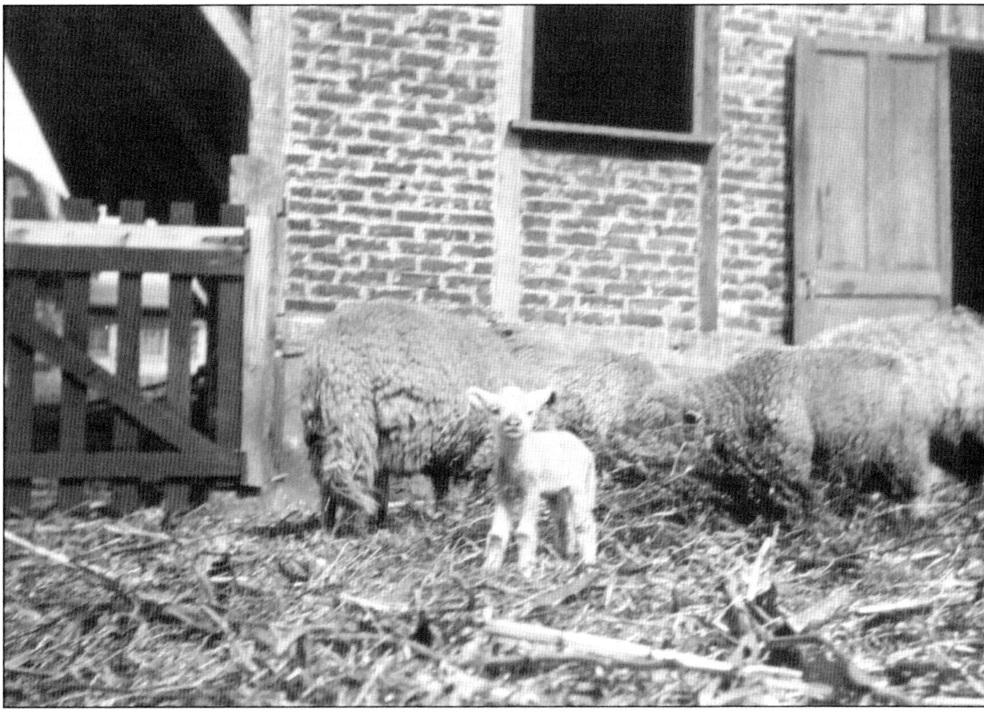

With characteristic humor, Ardenites named this lamb Enoch Arden, after the poem of the same name by Alfred Lord Tennyson. In addition to supplying wool for Maude Rhodes's looms, the sheep served as Arden's first lawn service and were frequently rented out to keep leaseholds trimmed.

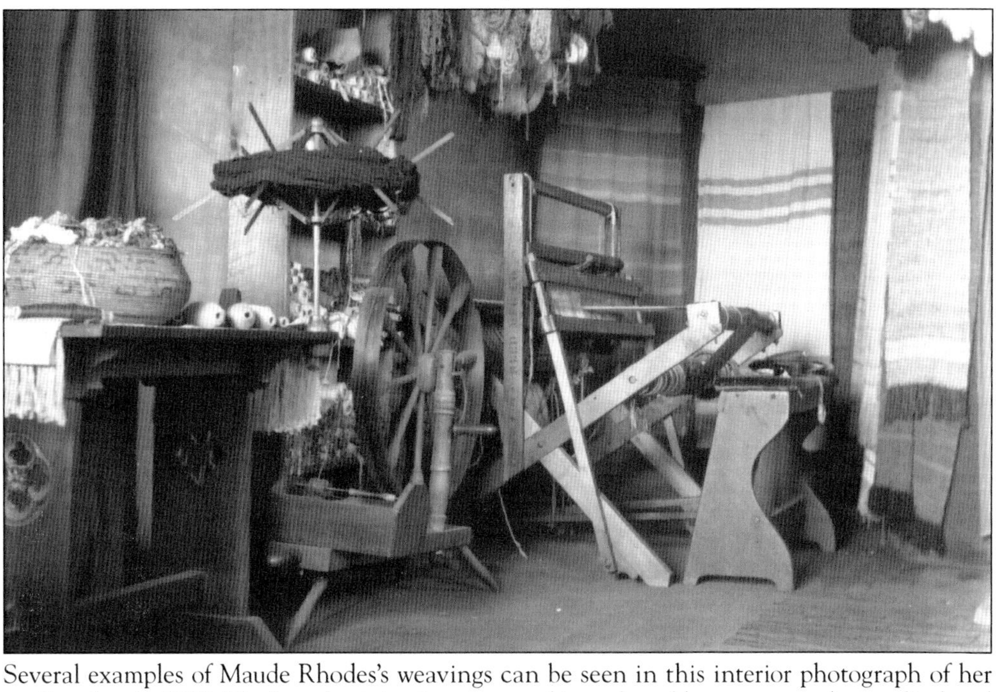

Several examples of Maude Rhodes's weavings can be seen in this interior photograph of her studio taken in 1923. The broad striping incorporated into the table runners or throws displayed on the back wall were characteristic of her work.

Along with economic reform, educational reform, and the revival of handicrafts, Ardenites were interested in bringing change to other areas of society as well. This photograph was taken in France in 1912 by Don Stephens. On the back he has written: "This is how the girls dress here, they all wear dresses modeled more or less on this and look splendid in them. It seems to me here is the solution to the questions of our women as to what to do in dress reform. They allow all the freedom that bloomers do, but are picaresque and pretty, while however laudable bloomers may be, one could hardly say that of them."

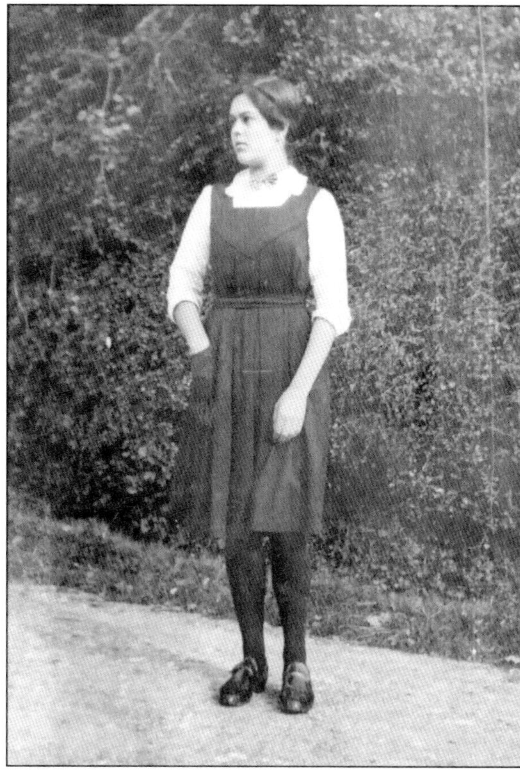

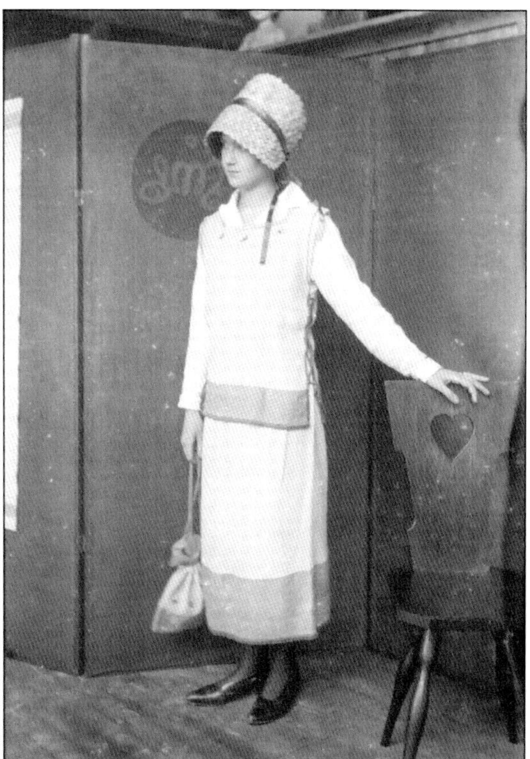

One wonders what Don would have thought of this ensemble woven by Maude Rhodes in 1923. The model is Adelaide Criswell.

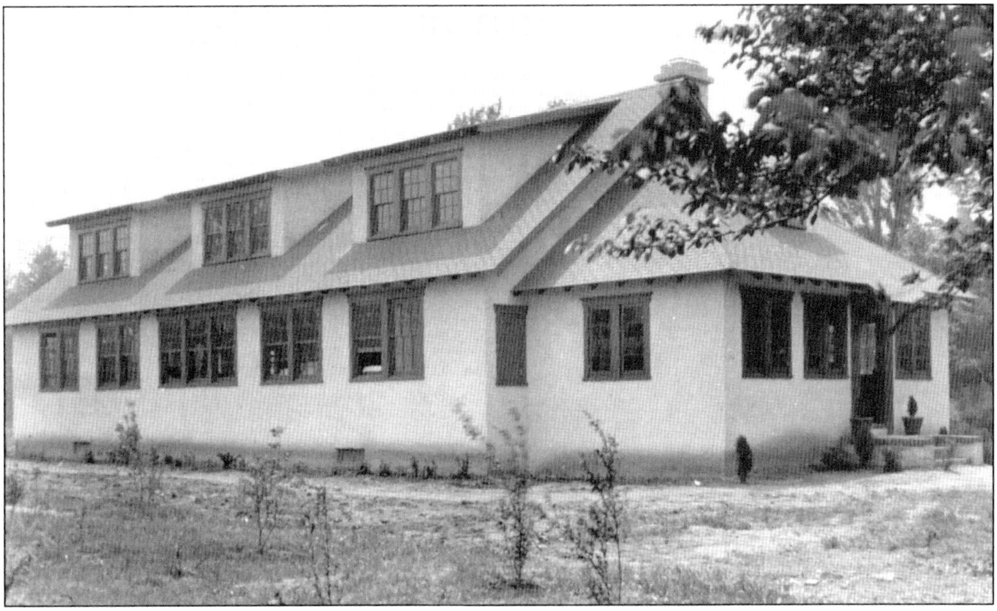

In 1925, Maude Rhodes retired to Jamaica and sold her business to Mildred Noyes, who had moved to Arden the previous year with Herbert Mason, vice president of the S. D. Warren Paper Company in Boston, where Miss Noyes had also been employed. Shortly after purchasing the business, Miss Noyes built this new Weave Shop on Miller's Road at the site of the Arden tennis court.

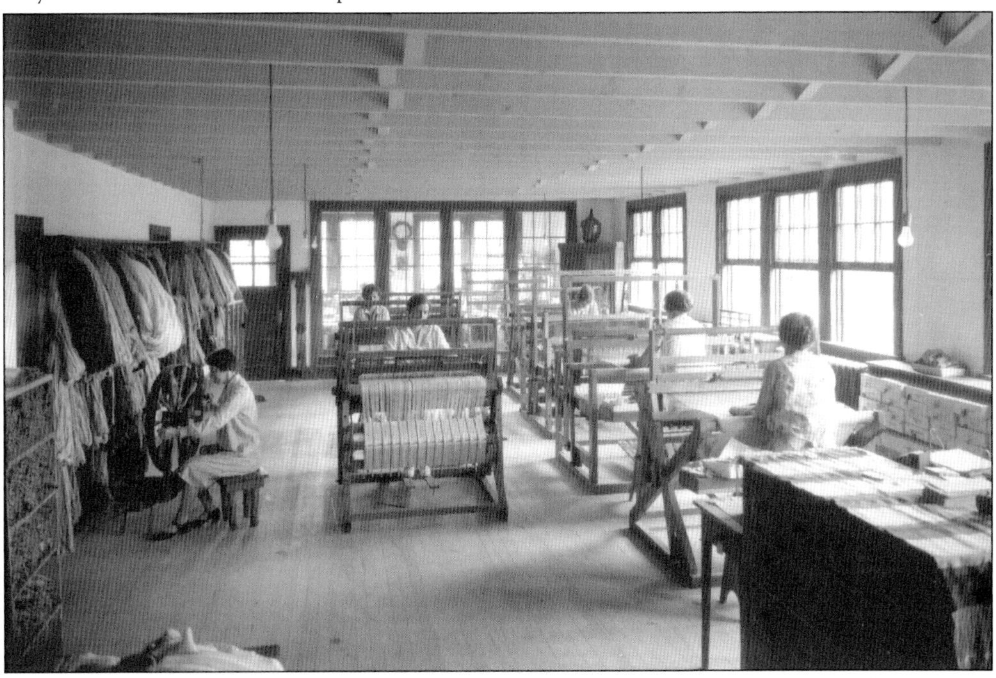

Under Mildred Noyes's ownership, the Arden Weave Shop was greatly expanded to include four or five weavers and a similar number of dressmakers. With few exceptions, employees lived outside the village and were transported to and from work by shuttle. In 1936, Mildred Noyes and Herbert Mason bought the Curtis Paper Company in Newark, Delaware. She closed the Weave Shop shortly thereafter.

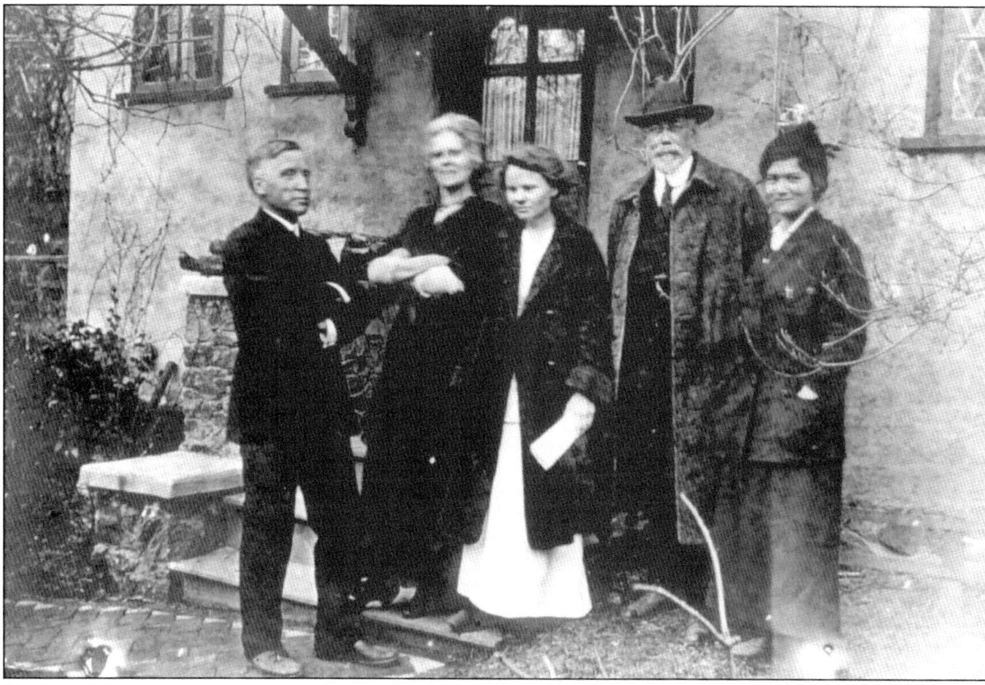

Herbert Mason was introduced to Arden by his cousin Fiske Warren, seen here to the far left in this photograph taken outside the Founder's House around 1915. A prominent single taxer, Fiske was also a practicing nudist and free love advocate. Fiske visited Arden frequently and is known to have led a nude exercise routine on the Village Green on several occasions, the source most likely of Arden's reputation as a nudist colony. Pictured here, from left to right, are Fiske Warren, Eleanor Stephens, Inky Stephens, Will Price, and an unknown woman.

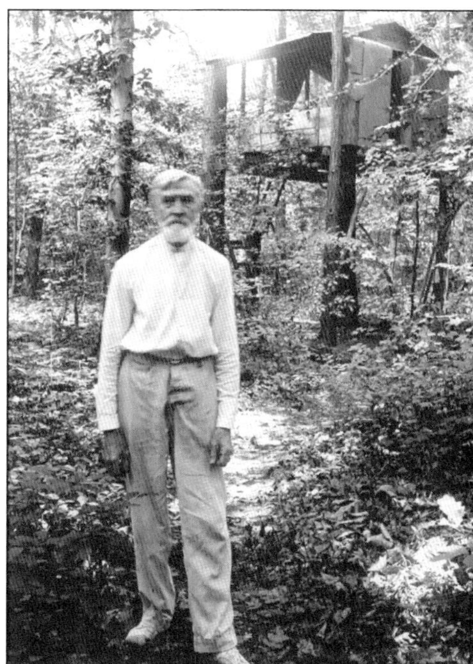

Ardenites were ridiculed frequently in the press, but when the socialist Fred Whiteside built a tree house in 1913, reporters worked overtime. Even Upton Sinclair's name was dragged out for headlines once again since Whiteside had reputedly used Sinclair's tent platform as the base for his new dwelling. While most reporters joked that Ardenites had finally gone the way of their simian ancestry, one writer from the *Philadelphia North American* took a more creative approach. He proposed that the socialists were merely trying to avoid paying their share of Arden's land tax since the "tree top bungalows" literally occupied no land at all.

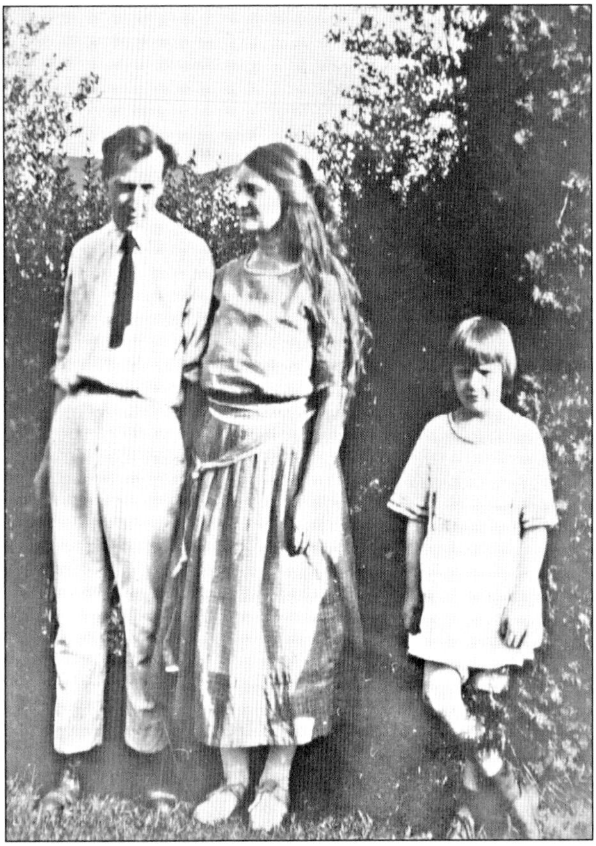

Louise and William Roberts ran the Roberts Press in Rose Valley prior to moving to Arden in January 1917. In both communities, they produced a line of hand-printed greeting cards that are charming examples of the Arts and Crafts aesthetic. Briefly housed at the Lone Pine in Little Arden, the family later moved to Friendly Gables, which had been vacated by the Steinleins. In this photograph they are seen with their daughter Sarah. Son Alex was the photographer.

Located directly behind Friendly Gables, the Roberts Studio was built in 1927 by Bob Austin and Jack Gordon. The tile work visible here on the exterior was made by Henry Chapman Mercer at the Moravian Tile Works in Doylestown, Pennsylvania. The Roberts left Arden in 1933 for the artist community of New Hope, Pennsylvania.

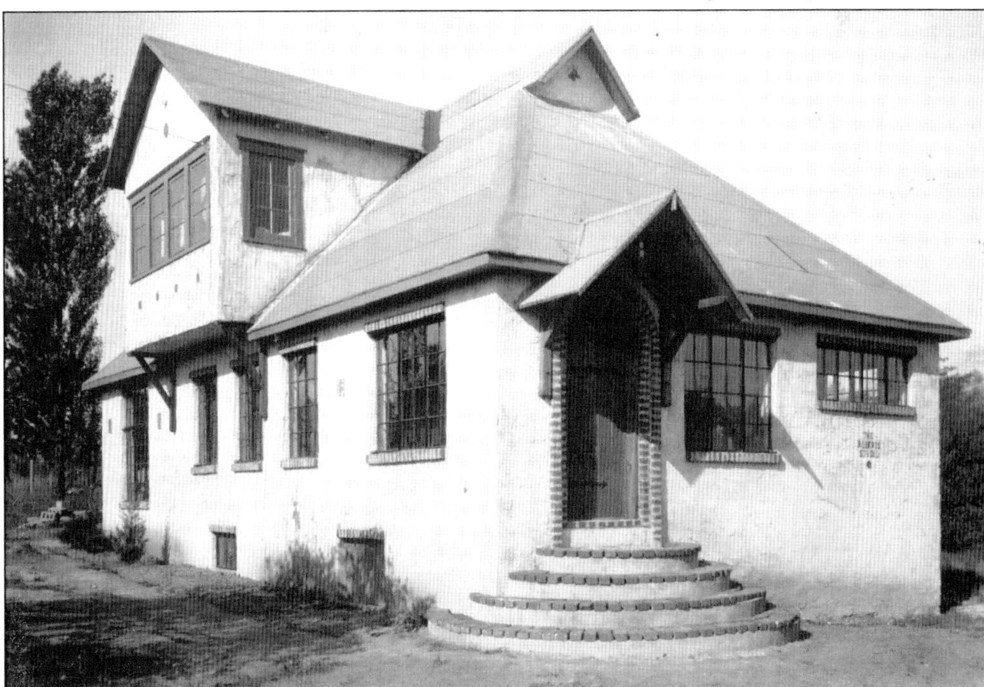

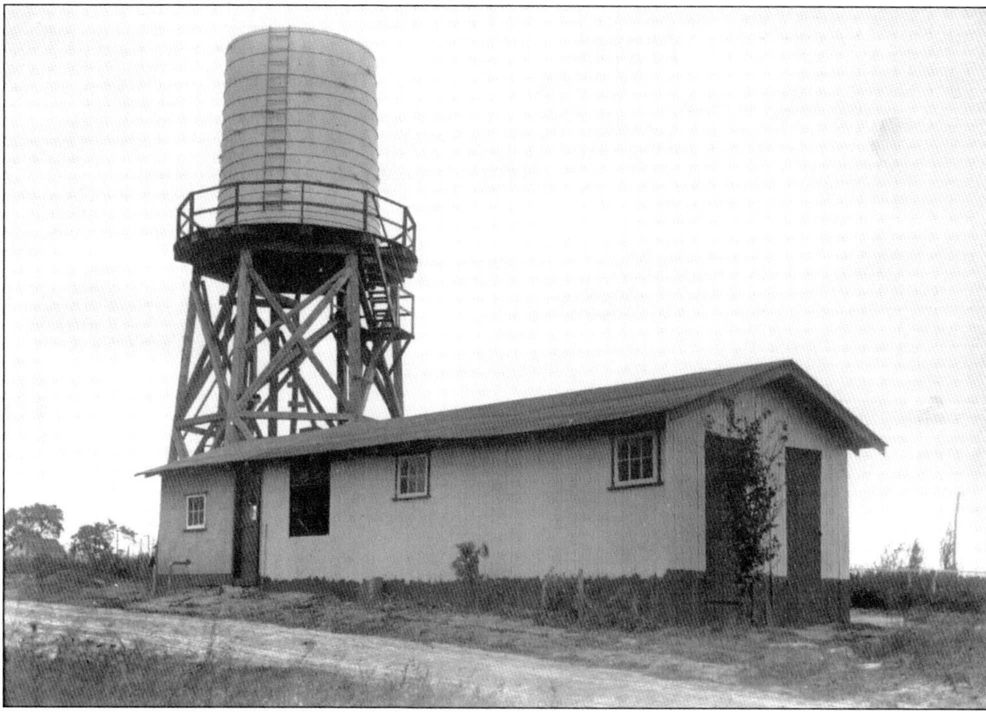

Because even the usually reliable Practical Farmer pump was susceptible to draught, other options for town water were explored. The Hillside water tower with its 14,000-gallon tank was erected in 1913, and it provided service to homes on both the Sherwood and Woodland side of the community. The site at the intersection of Hillside Road and Sherwood Road was chosen because it is the highest elevation in Arden. (Photograph by L. A. MacDonnald of Harvey, Delaware.)

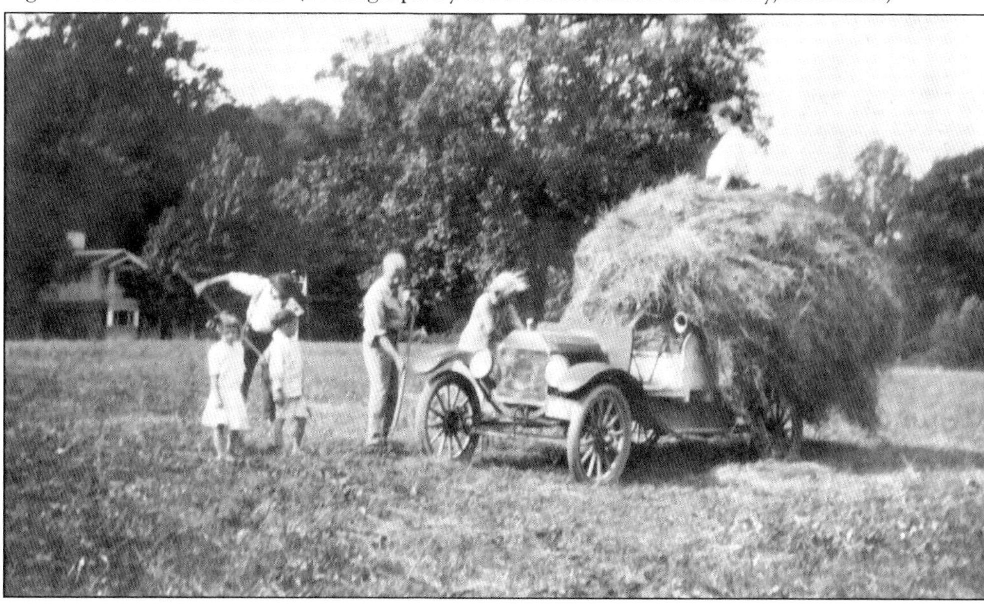

An unidentified group on the Village Green uses their automobile as a hay wagon in this photograph, providing a nice contrast to the bottom image on page 40. The house visible in the background is Upton Sinclair's home, the Jungalow, which has been considerably altered.

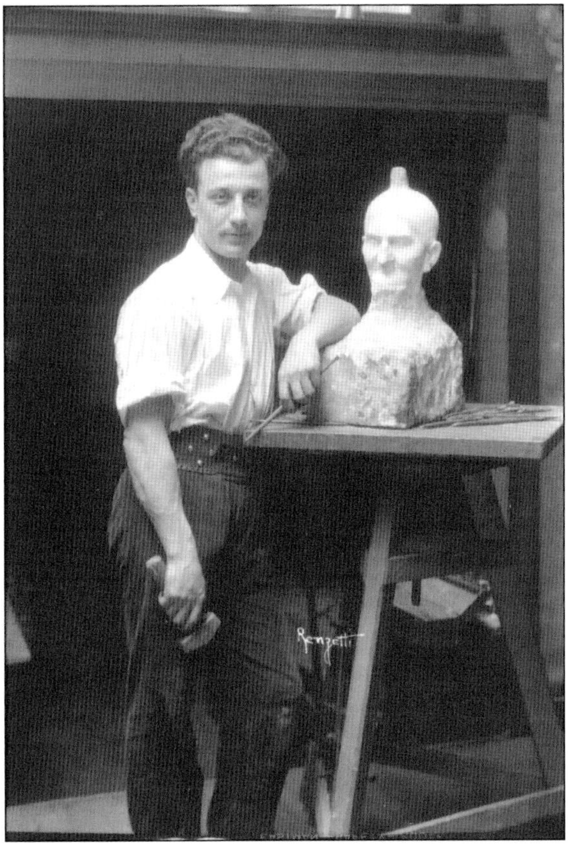

Born in Italy, Marcus Aurelius Renzetti came to Philadelphia with his parents sometime around 1901. A gifted student, he studied at the Pennsylvania Academy of Fine Arts, where he received numerous awards including two Cresson scholarships for travel abroad. He later became an associate professor at the Philadelphia College of Art. A photographer and ceramist as well as a sculptor, he is best remembered for the countless students he inspired during his years of teaching. He is shown here with his sculpture *The Grandmother* around 1925.

Marcus Aurelius Renzetti first began visiting Arden around 1916. His picturesque home on Naaman's Creek was built from the framework of the old Derrickson icehouse.

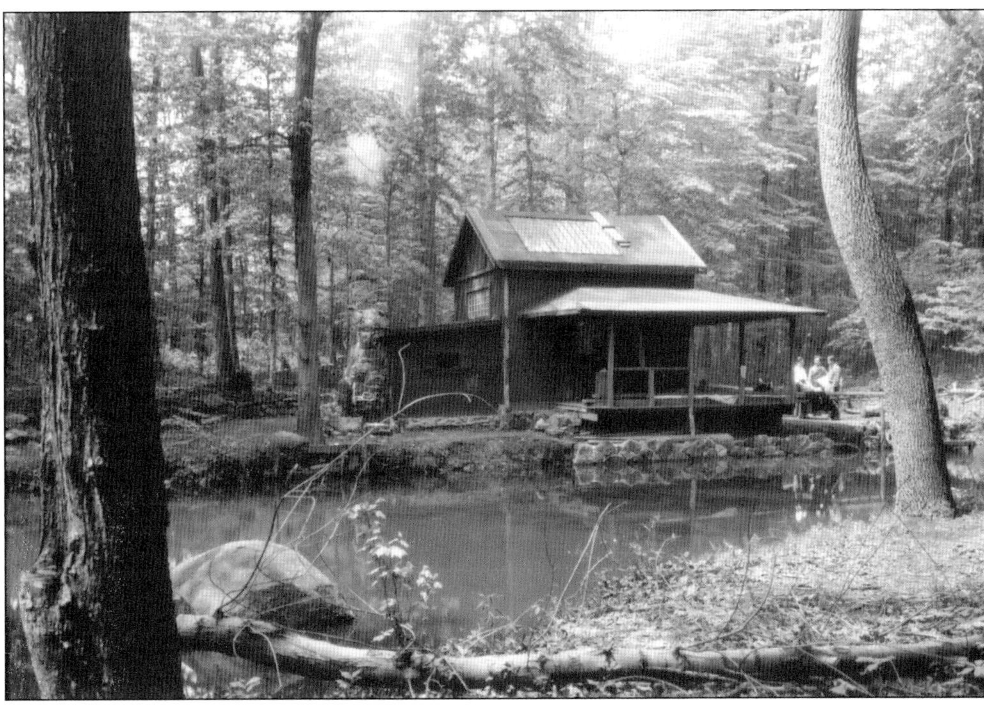

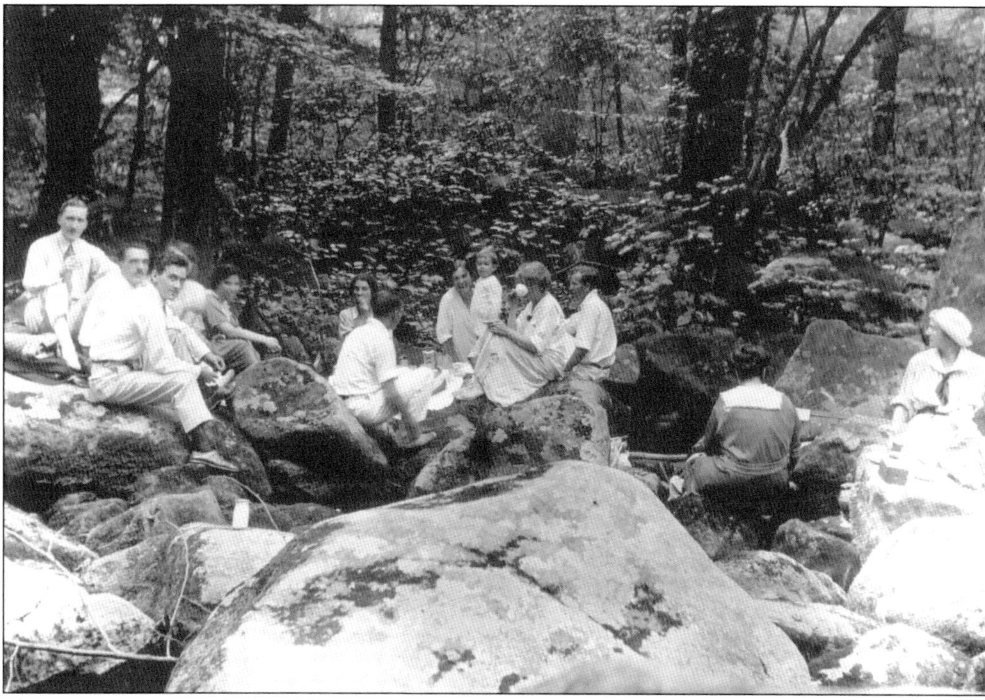

Sharing a picnic on the boulders of Naaman's Creek was a favorite pastime as evidenced by this smartly dressed group in 1915. Inky Stephens can be seen with her teacup in the center of the photograph. Jimmie Ware is at the far right.

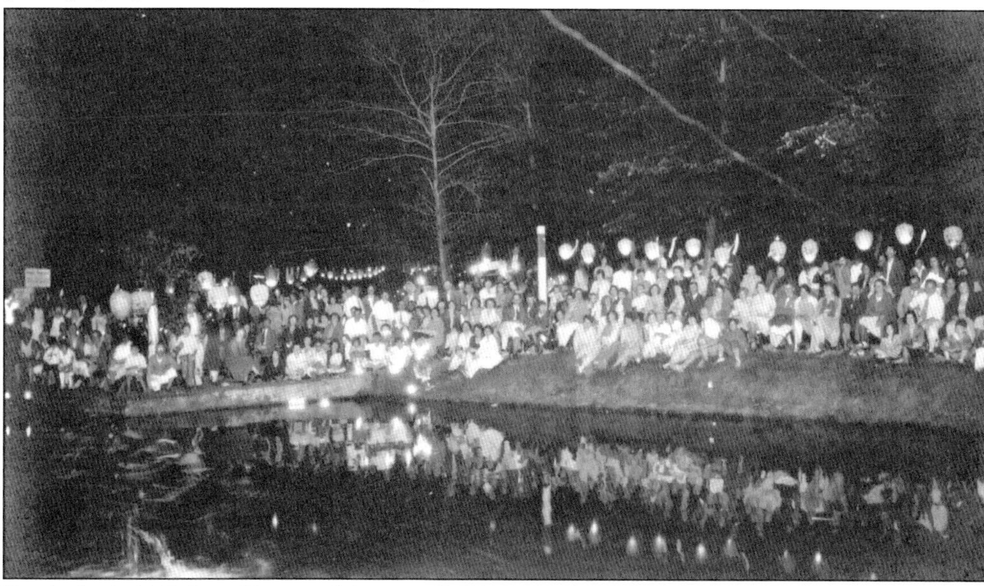

For Arden's *A Night in Venice* celebration, held September 5, 1926, at the Naaman's Creek pool, residents were encouraged to wear the brightest colors in their wardrobe. Participants assembled after dark, and the only illumination came from Chinese lanterns strung along the banks for the occasion. Throughout the evening, residents and their guests were serenaded by strolling accordionists and singing gondoliers, who propelled two small boats festooned with garlands of flowers around the pool.

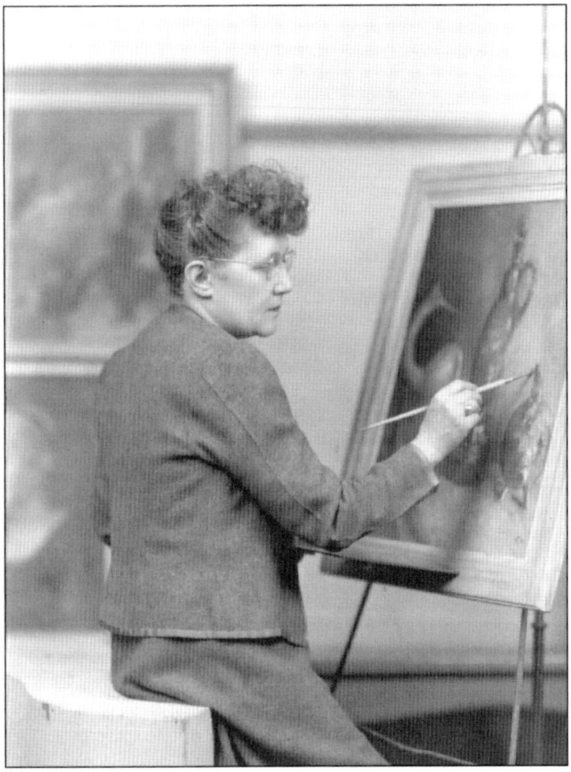

Born in Russia, Clara Finkelstein immigrated to the United States with her parents in 1893, settling first in New York and finally in Wilmington. An active member of the Wilmington Society of the Fine Arts, Clara was also one of the early members of The Studio Group. Clara and her husband I. B. were instrumental in the development of the Brandywine Arts Festival. She is first listed as an Arden leaseholder in 1912 and is pictured here around the 1930s at her home and studio, the Castle.

The Castle was built in 1923 by Don and Jane Marcellus, who were introduced to the community by Cora and Ed Potter. Although the house was considerably altered by the Finklesteins, it nonetheless retains its storybook charm. (Courtesy of Sadie Somerville.)

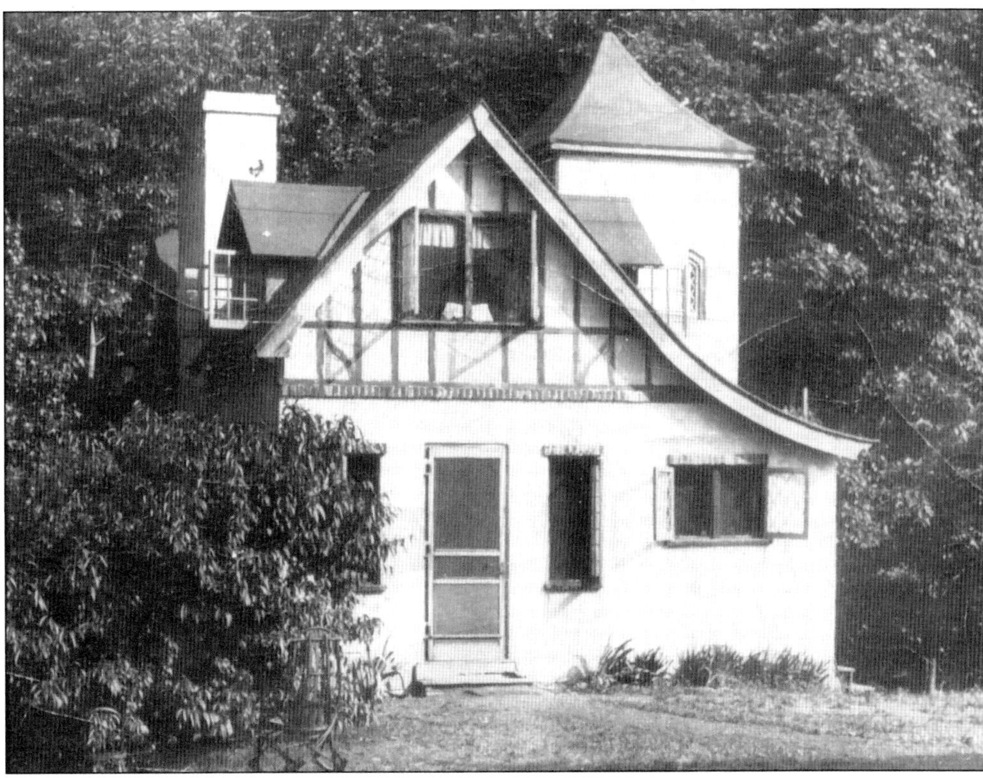

Artist Harry Hoeffler's watercolors have provided important documentation of the architecture and landscape of early Arden. He is pictured here (left) around the 1920s with Tom Farrell, president of the Arden Building and Loan. Founded in 1918, the Arden Building and Loan advertised itself as "a co-operative organization designed primarily to aid members to procure homes." It was one of two loan organizations in town, the other being the Raiffeisen Gild, which was organized in April 1911. (Courtesy of Terry Colgan.)

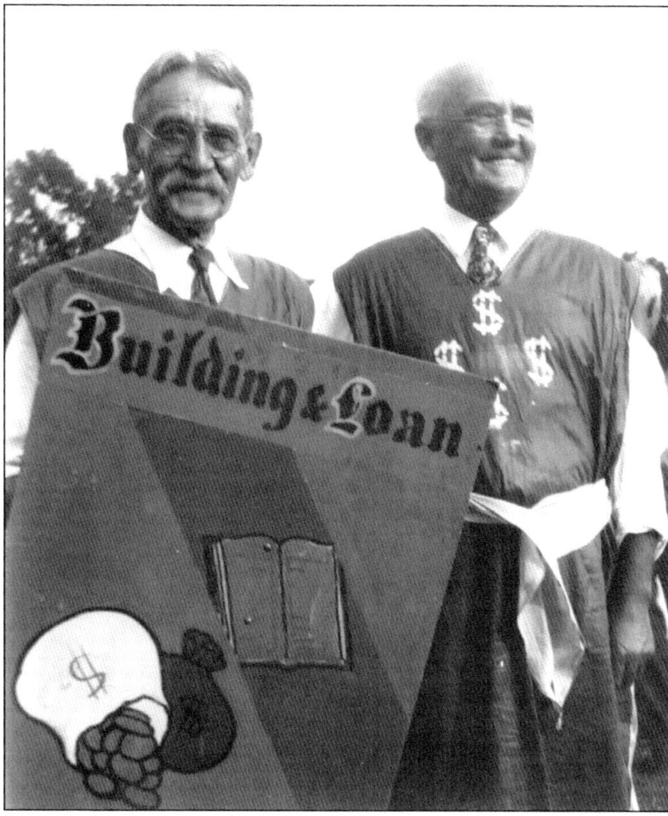

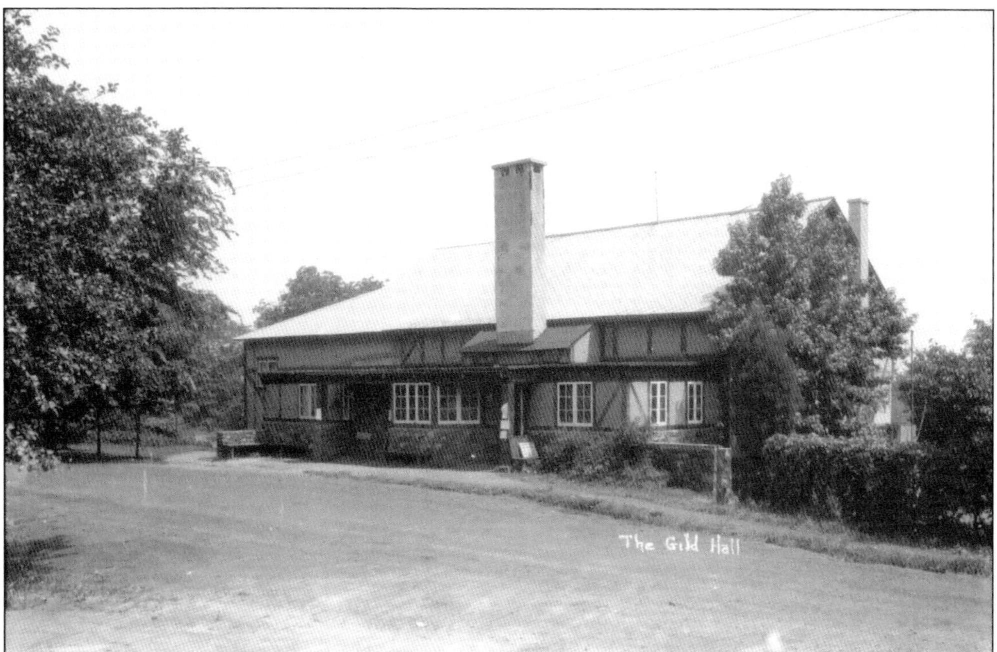

The Arden Gild Hall remains remarkably unchanged from its appearance in this photograph from around 1930.

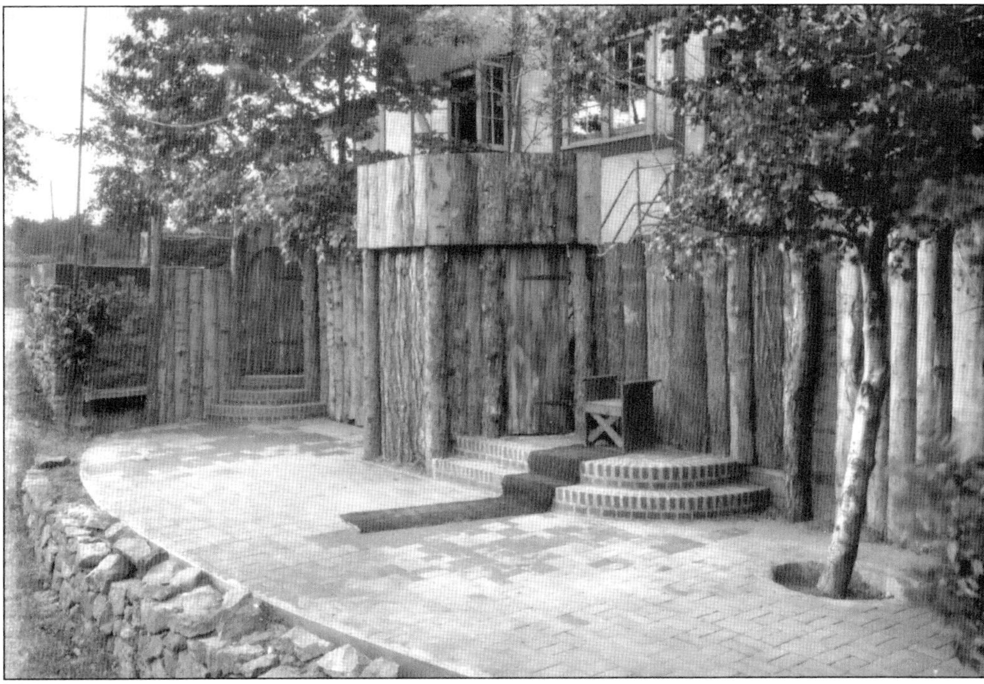

The Moonlight Theater, located on the south side of the Gild Hall, was built during the summer of 1925, with Frank Stephens supervising both the construction and the landscaping. It had originally been designed by the founders in 1910. The stage was the third in the village, and gave Arden's Sherwood side an outdoor performance space to complement the Woodland side's Field Theater.

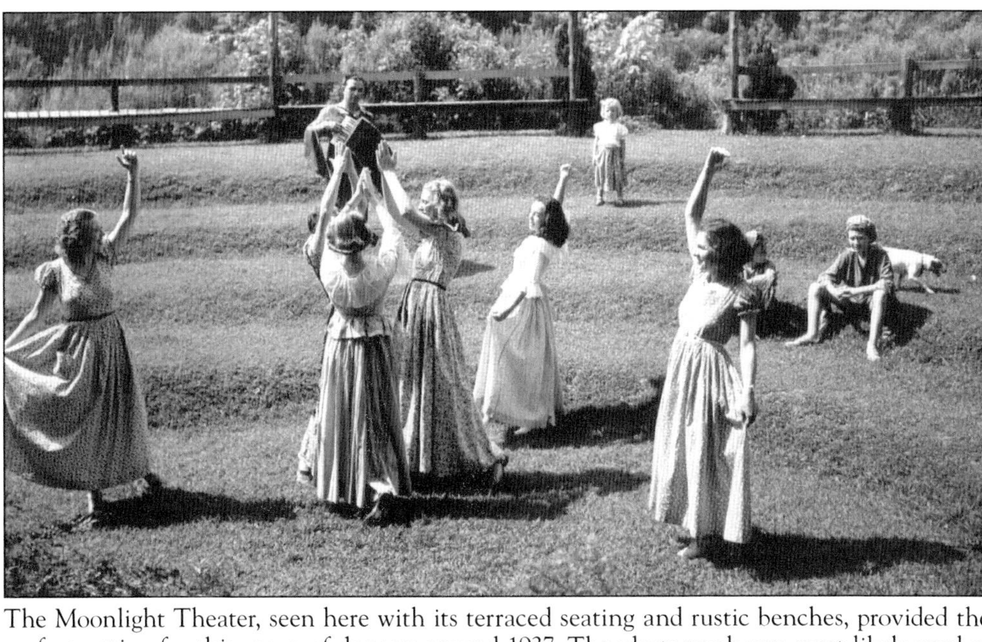

The Moonlight Theater, seen here with its terraced seating and rustic benches, provided the perfect setting for this group of dancers around 1937. The photograph was most likely used as publicity to promote the Arden Fair. The dancer at the center of the photograph in the patterned dress is Pat Liberman.

Like many Arden artists, Leander Leitner (seen here around 1920) and his wife Fidonia were summer residents, keeping a studio in New York City during much of the year and a rustic summer cottage in Arden, near what is now known as Buckingham Heights. They first began coming to Arden sometime around 1915, and moved to the area permanently in the mid 1940s. Both were extremely active in the community.

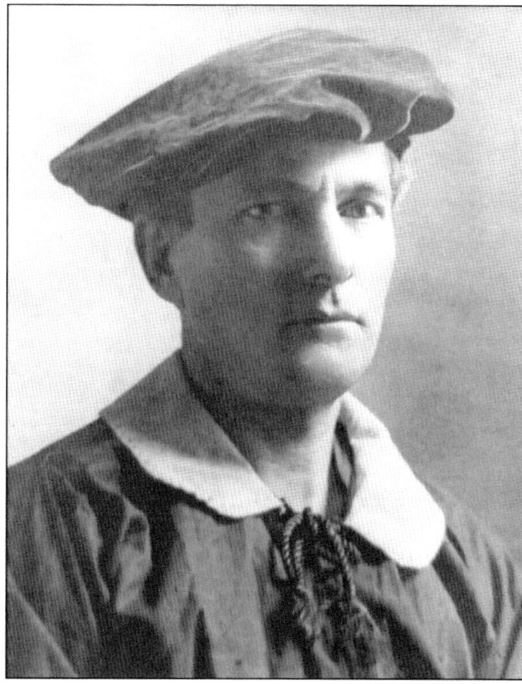

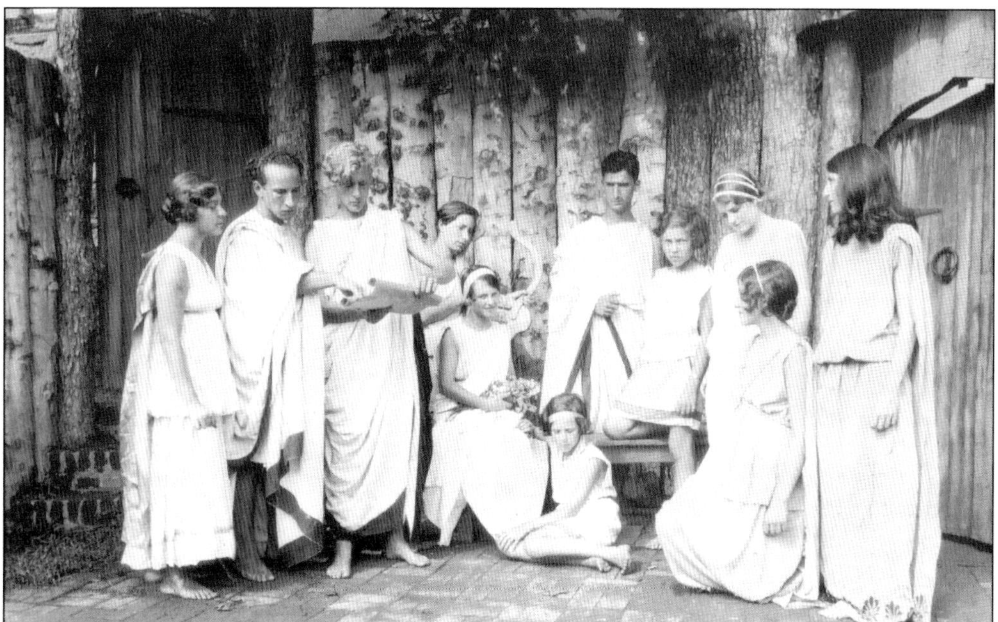

The Pageant of Progress was presented on the stage of the Moonlight Theater in August of 1928. Written by Fidonia Leitner, the pageant was designed as a series of tableaus to illustrate the progress of civilization throughout the ages, beginning with "the Use of Fire" and ending with "the Printing Press." Pictured here are actors representing contributions from ancient Greece and Rome, including Art, Drama, Music, Sculpture, and Literature. Seen on stage from left to right are Charlotte Ross, Ben Sharlip, Edwin Ross, Gertrude Jaffe, Ethel Gordon, Berna Ossler, Harry Pleat, Louise Menkin, Dora Gordon, Elizabeth Bookmyer, and Estella Frankel.

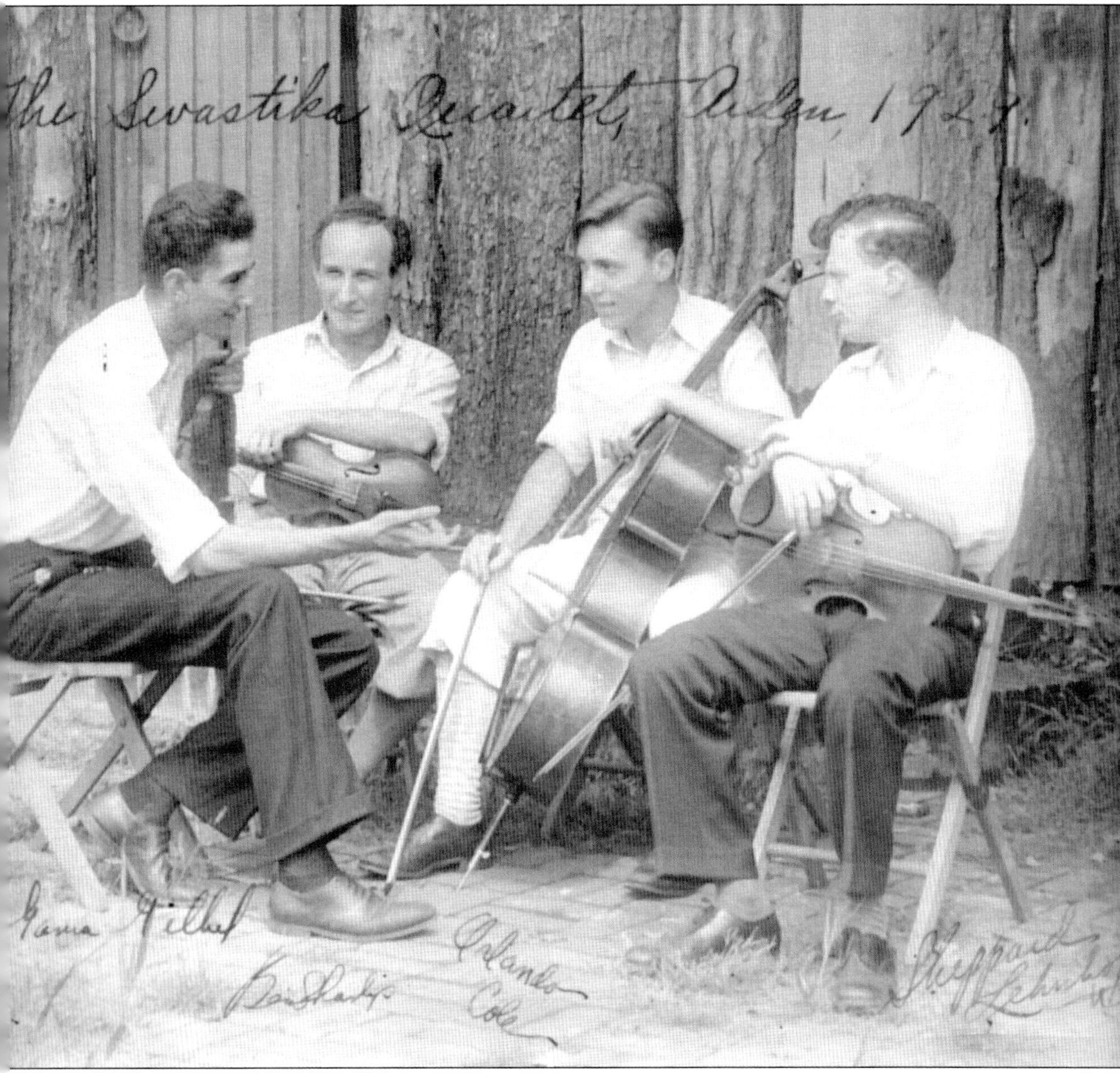

The members of the Swastika Quartet were a group of gifted young students enrolled at the Curtis Institute of Music in Philadelphia. Established in 1927, they spent the summers of 1928 and 1929 in Arden, and were the featured performers at Arden's Sunday afternoon vesper services held in the Gild Hall. The Swastika is an East Indian symbol of good luck, and was the name of their patron Mrs. Edward Boks's estate in Merion, Pennsylvania. Because the German Nazi party later adopted the symbol, the musicians changed their name in 1932 to the Curtis Quartet. From left to right are Gama Gilbert, Ben Sharlip, Orlando Cole, and Sheppard Lehnof.

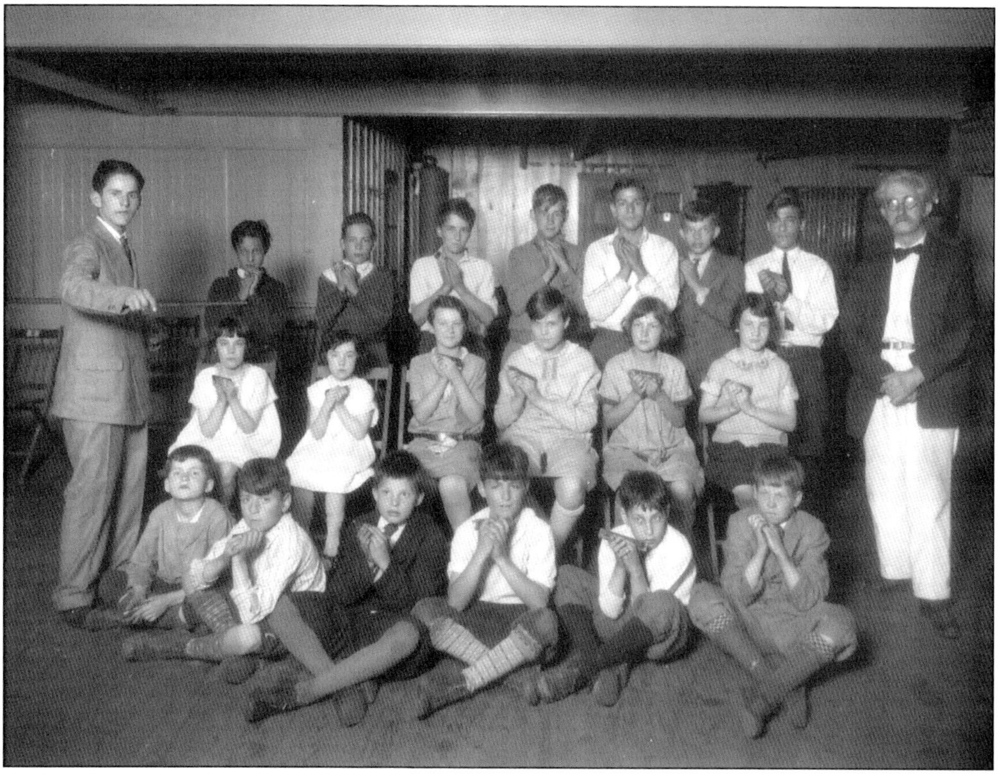

Arden's harmonica band must have seemed quite a contrast to the Swastika Quartet. The band was conducted by George Hay, seen here to the far left with the baton. On the far right is George Newcomb, who served as the band's director. The photograph was taken in the basement of the Gild Hall.

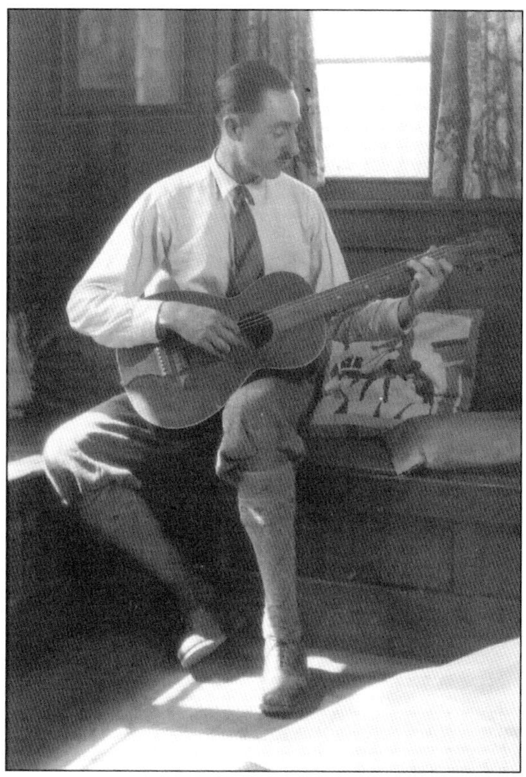

A native of California, Earl Brooks was one of the official photographers of the 1926 Sesquicentennial Exposition in Philadelphia. He moved to Arden shortly thereafter, opening the Brooks Studio in the Arden Craft Shop. He later moved his business to 9th and Market Streets in Wilmington.

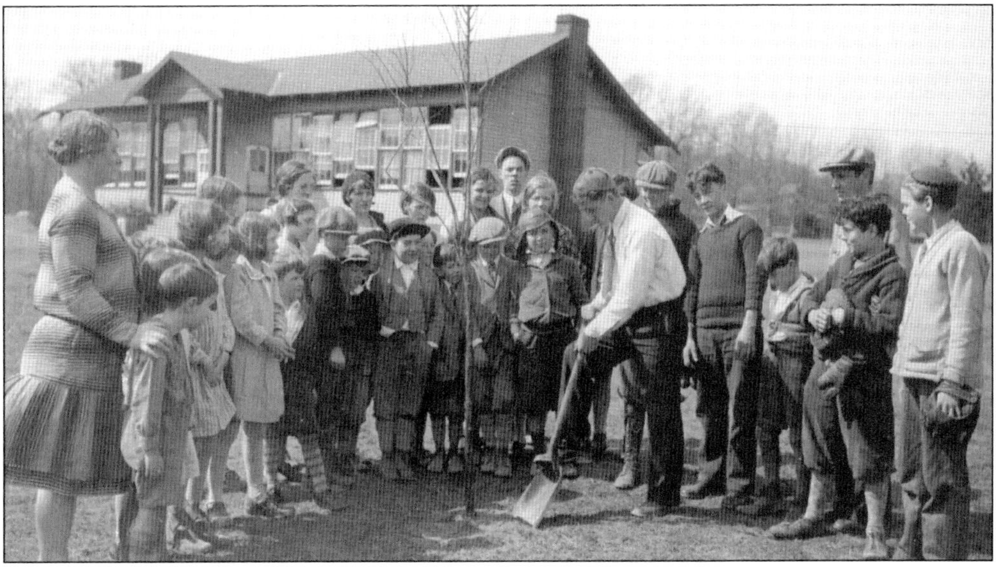

State-sanctioned elementary school first came to Arden in 1920. Classes were held that year at the Red House, but quickly moved to the basement of the Gild Hall. In 1924, the school moved again, this time to a new building on the Sherwood Green. The building burned to the ground in 1945 and students moved back to the Gild Hall once again until a new building was completed in 1947. This photograph was taken on Arbor Day in 1931. The teacher is Mrs. Kerr.

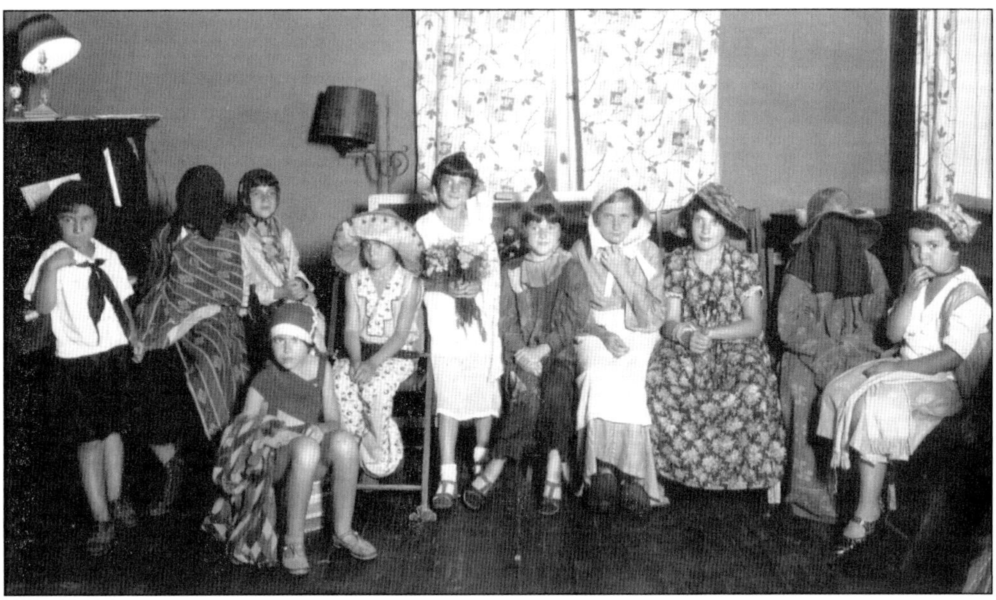

The Hillside Nutrition Camp, located at the corner of Grubb and Hillside Roads, was run as a summer program by Bessie Navro and Mollie Gerstine, Emmanuel Gerstine's sisters. Apparently similar in philosophy to Cora Potter's earlier Playground School, one former student remembers simply "spending all my time at the Arden Pool," much like all the other Arden children. Pictured here from left to right around 1928 are Jenny Levinberg, Milton Gerstine, Katherine Unger, Isabelle Unger, Diana Unger, Lilian Unger, Selma Unger, Eleanor Supple, Phyllis Josephs, Gene Gerstine, and Miriam Gerstine.

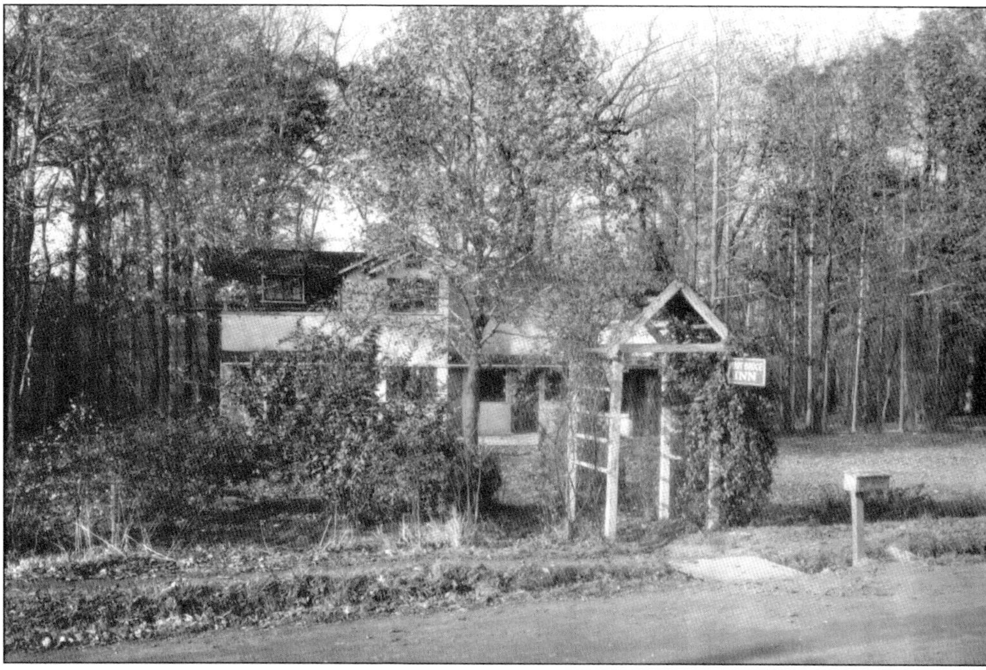

In the 1930s, visitors to Arden could choose between two communist-run guesthouses in town. Canadian Mary Bruce ran the Mary Bruce Inn from 1928 to 1940 in Upton Sinclair's former home the Jungalow, just across the Village Green from George Newcomb's Arden Inn. House rules were apparently few: "Don't disturb the other fellow. Never leave the ice box door open. Be careful of fires. Pay your bills as soon as you can. That is don't let them drift along over too many months."

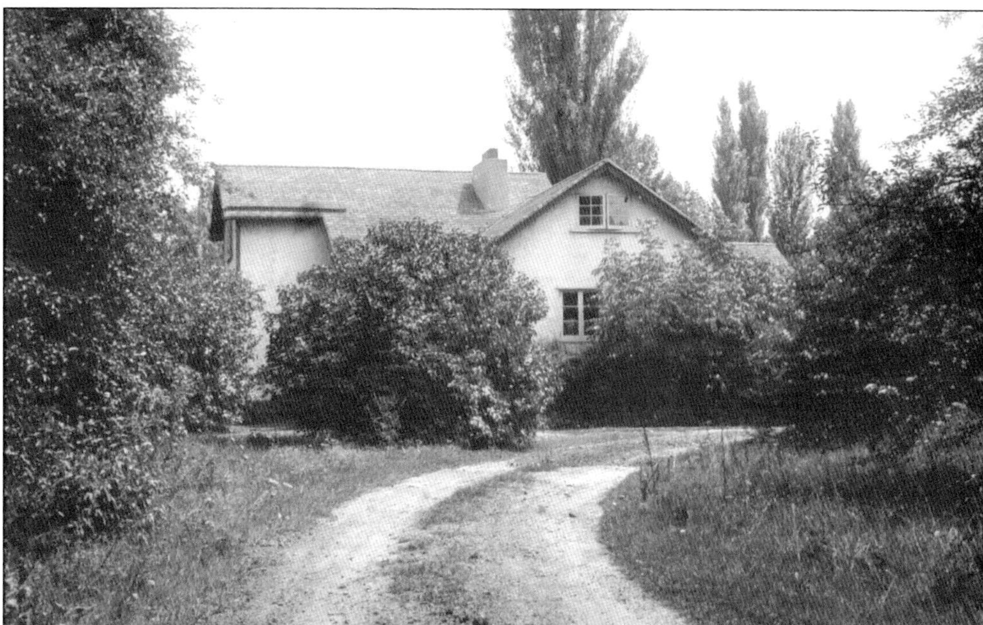

Don Stephens's family home Bide-a-wee was built around 1916 next door to Rest Cottage on Cherry Lane. After his years at the Monastery (page 50), the home must have seemed palatial.

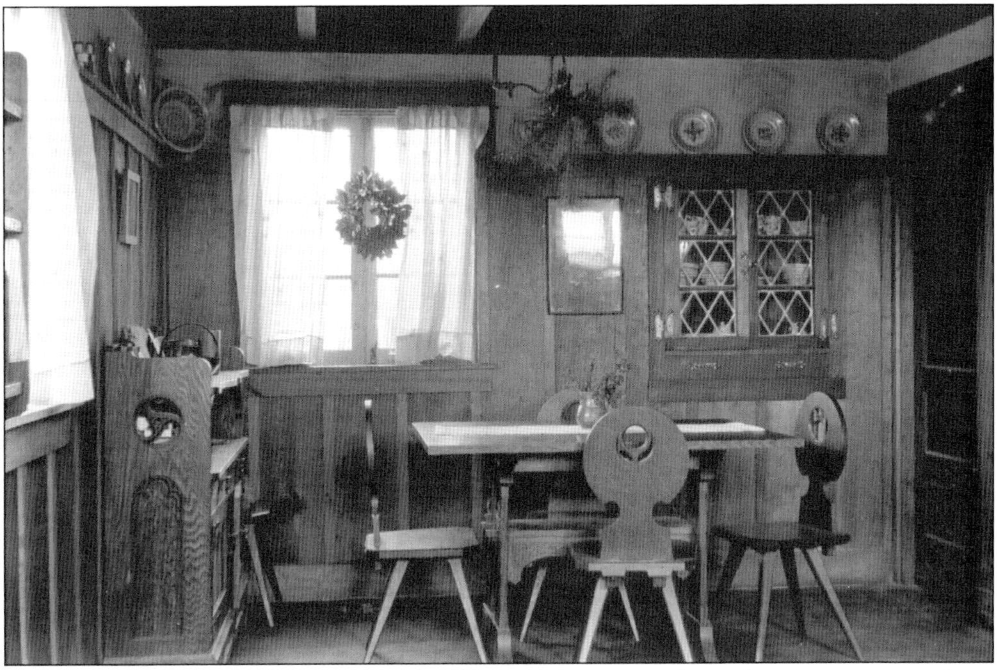

The Bide-a-wee dining room, with its board and batten wainscoting, plate rail, and casement windows, is a textbook example of the arts and crafts interiors popularized by Gustav Stickley and other tastemakers of the era. According to an interview with Don Stephens and his wife that was published in the *Wilmington Morning News*, the dining set was made by Don to Will Price's design.

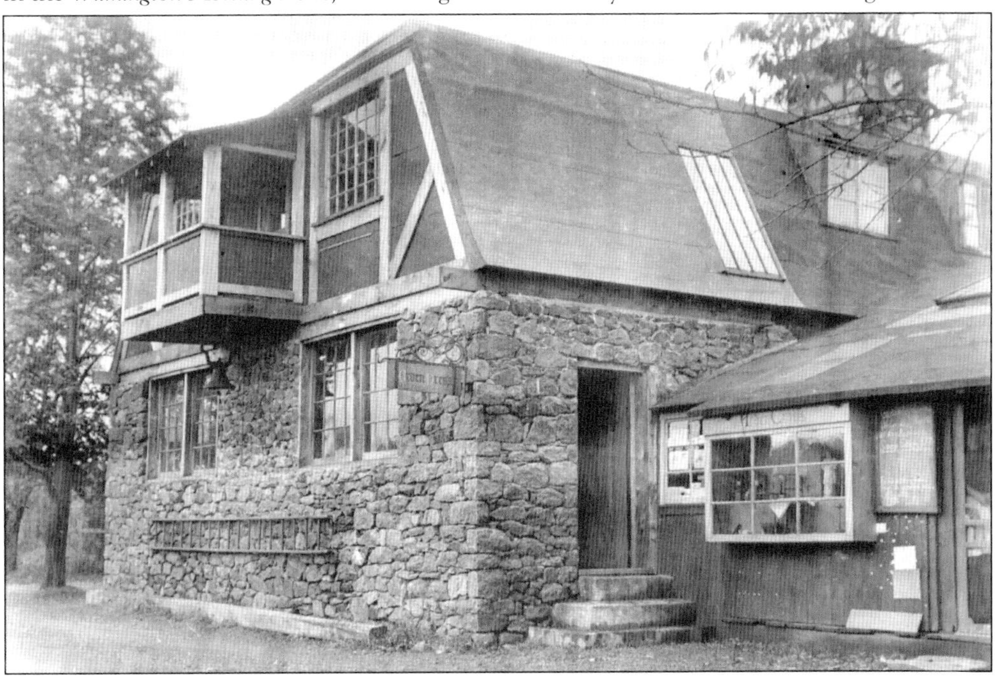

In this photograph of the Craft Shop from the 1920s, the building has been extended to provide additional studio space. A display window for Arden Crafts is visible, as well as a sign for the Arden Press.

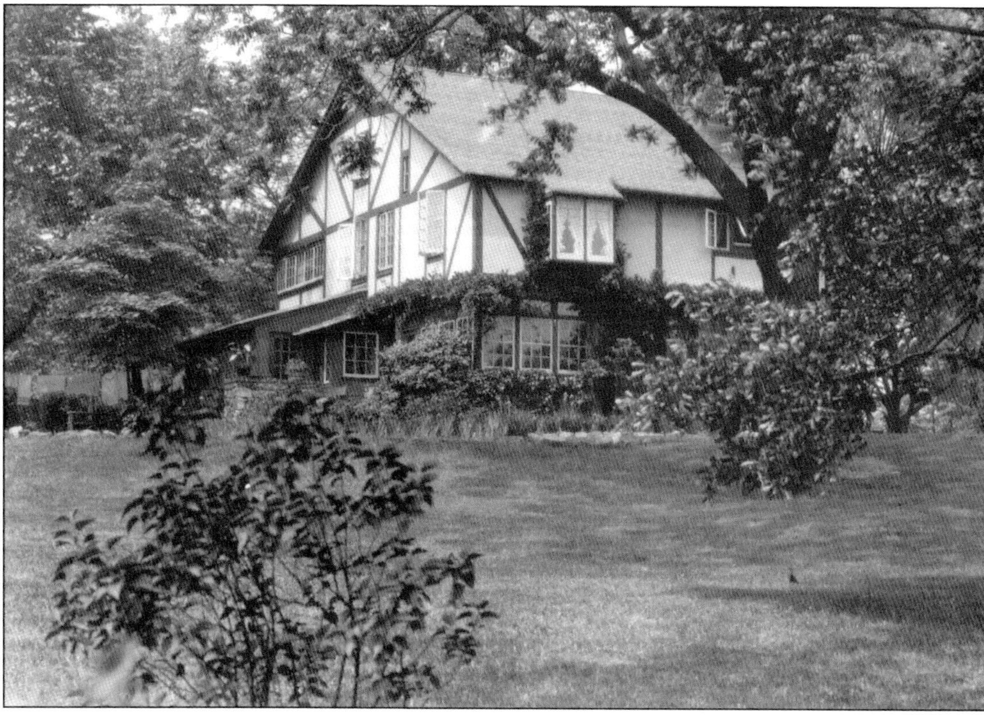

Sometime prior to 1910, the Derrickson Farmhouse, which Frank Stephens once called "the ugliest house in America," underwent extensive renovations. Rechristened the Willows, it is located at 1808 Harvey (formerly Grubb's) Road.

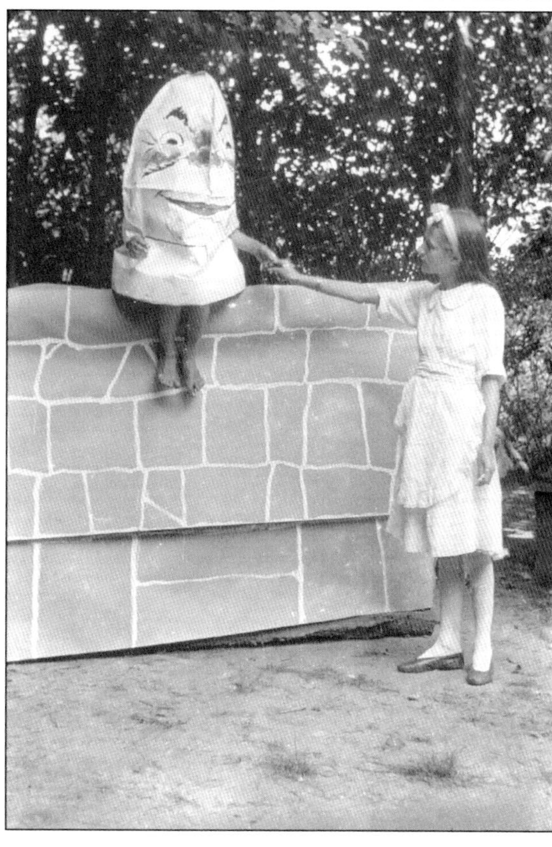

Although the two actors in this 1919 production are unknown, the Humpty Dumpty costume is almost certainly the work of Buzz Ware.

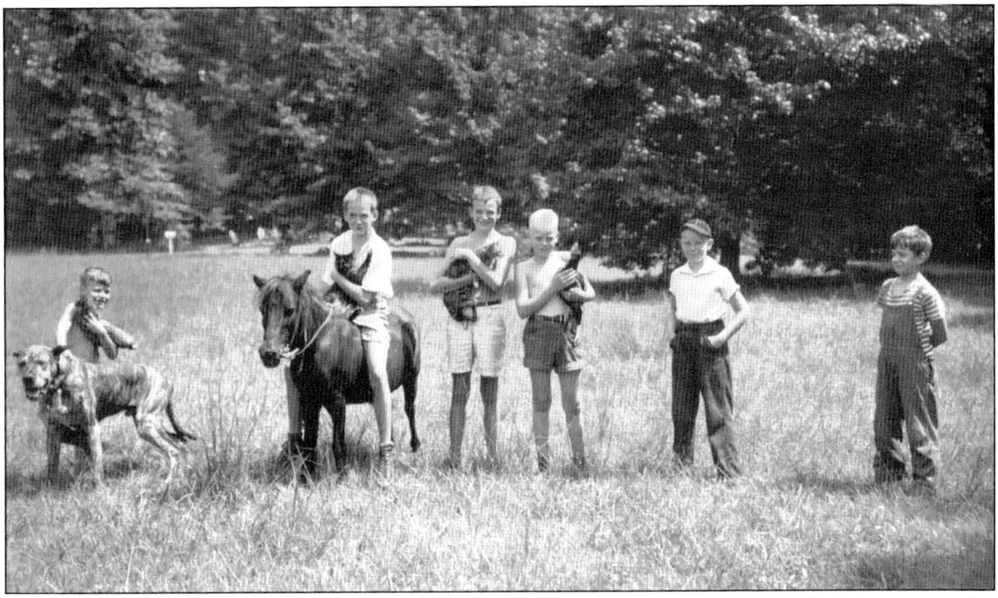

Buzz and Jimmie Ware's twins, John and Jim, and a group of their friends pose with their pets on the Village Green around 1938. Jim sits astride their pony Midgie, who was stabled at the family home, the Barnacle on Green Lane. John stands next to him with his cat. The boy to John's left appears to be holding a chicken, which the cat contemplates intently. (Courtesy of Terry Colgan.)

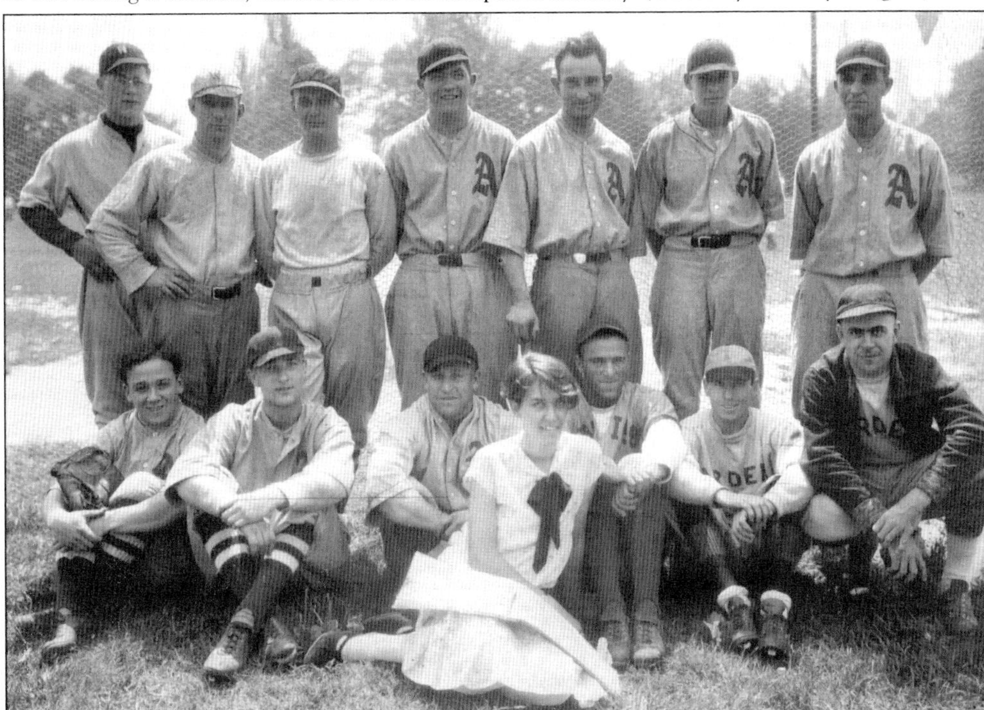

Arden's baseball team poses for a team photograph in the 1920s. The scorekeeper, seated in front, is Peach Worthington. Buzz Ware can be seen standing in the back row, third from left. (Courtesy of Terry Colgan.)

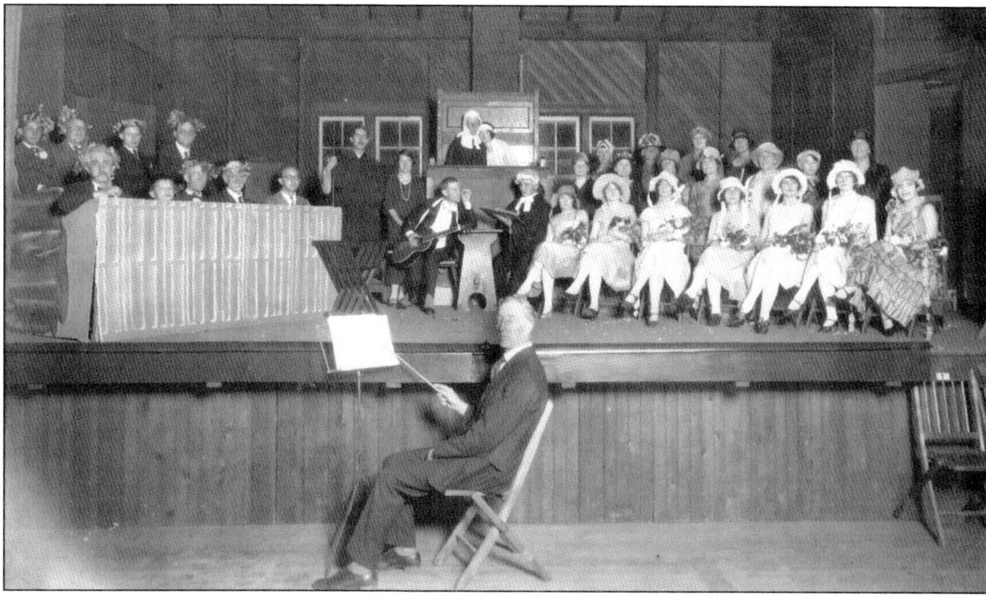

The comic operas of Gilbert and Sullivan have been performed frequently throughout the years in Arden, beginning in 1927 with *Trial by Jury*, a one-act satire of the legal profession. In this Arden Chorus production, Frank Stephens was cast as "The Learned Judge," Edith Hambly Austin as "The Plaintiff," Earl Broadbent as "The Defendant," and Edward Cannon, a local attorney, as "Counsel for the Plaintiff." William Martin directed. The audience at the Gild Hall opening night included many members of the Delaware Bar Association, who had been invited to the performance by Mr. Cannon.

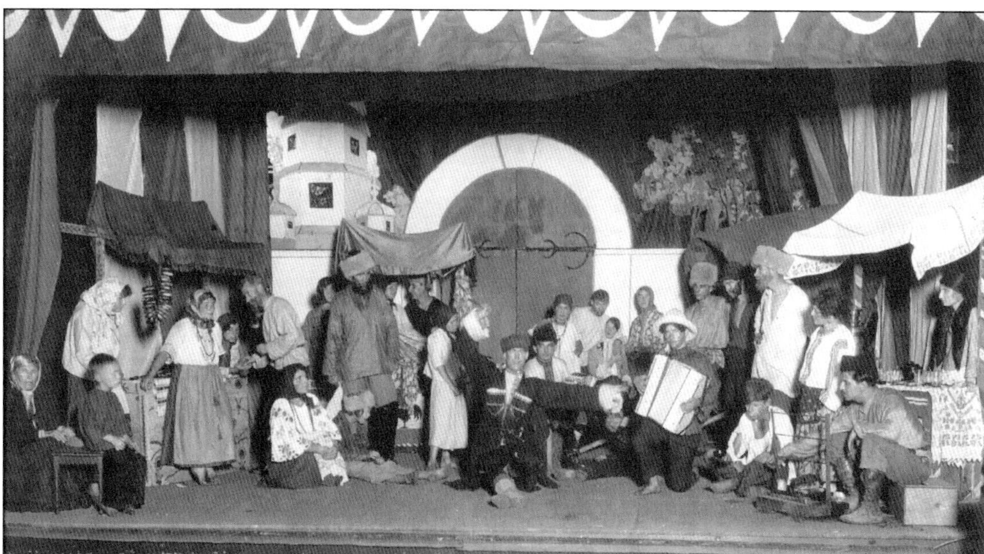

Much like the *Pageant of Progress*, which had been produced the year before, Arden's *Russian Night*, held August 28, 1929, consisted of a series of tableaus highlighted by musical interludes and spoken word. In this scene, entitled *The Weekly Bazaar*, the hustle and bustle of a Russian village marketplace is portrayed. Particularly noteworthy in this scene is Inky Stephens, seen here third from left, who, along with her family, had traveled to Russia in 1925 as part of Hal Ware's Russian Reconstruction Farms.

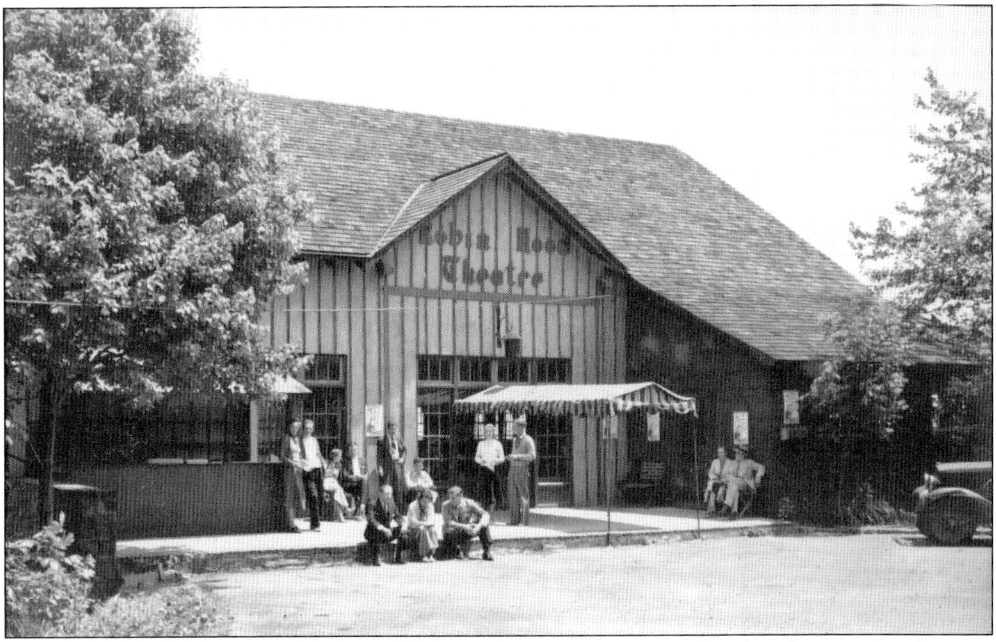

The Robin Hood Theater was established in 1931 by Ebbe Ross and Bob Schnitzer in what was originally the barn for the neighboring Harvey Farm. Although Robin Hood, the outlaw of Sherwood Forest, is referenced in Shakespeare's *As You Like It*, the theater's name is also likely a sly reference to the idiomatic expression "to go around Robin Hood's barn," meaning to take a roundabout or circuitous route.

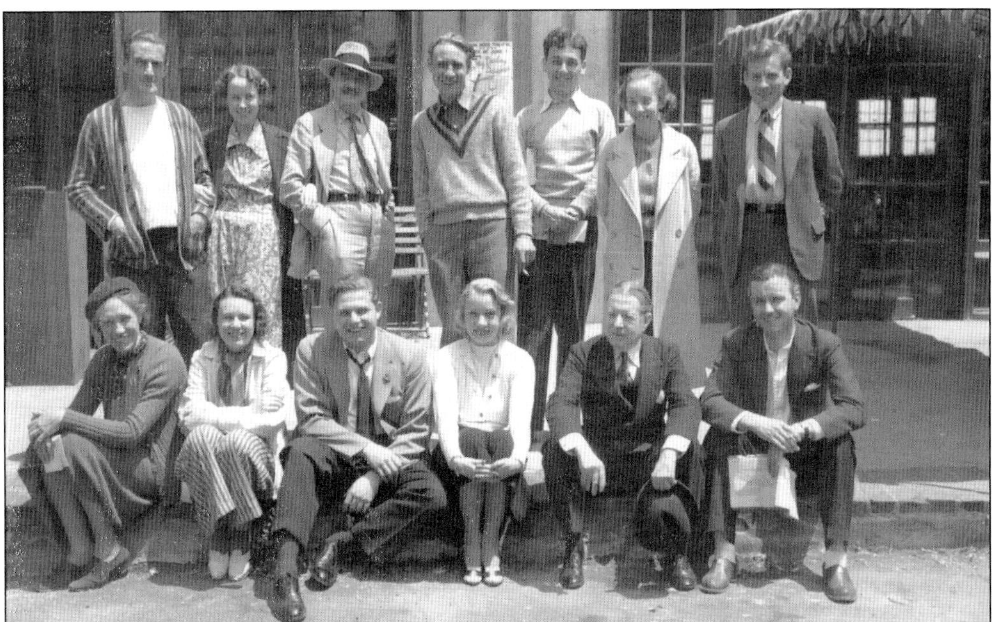

The cast is unknown, but they are all smiles in this photograph taken in June of 1938. The production that week was *My Darling Daughter*.

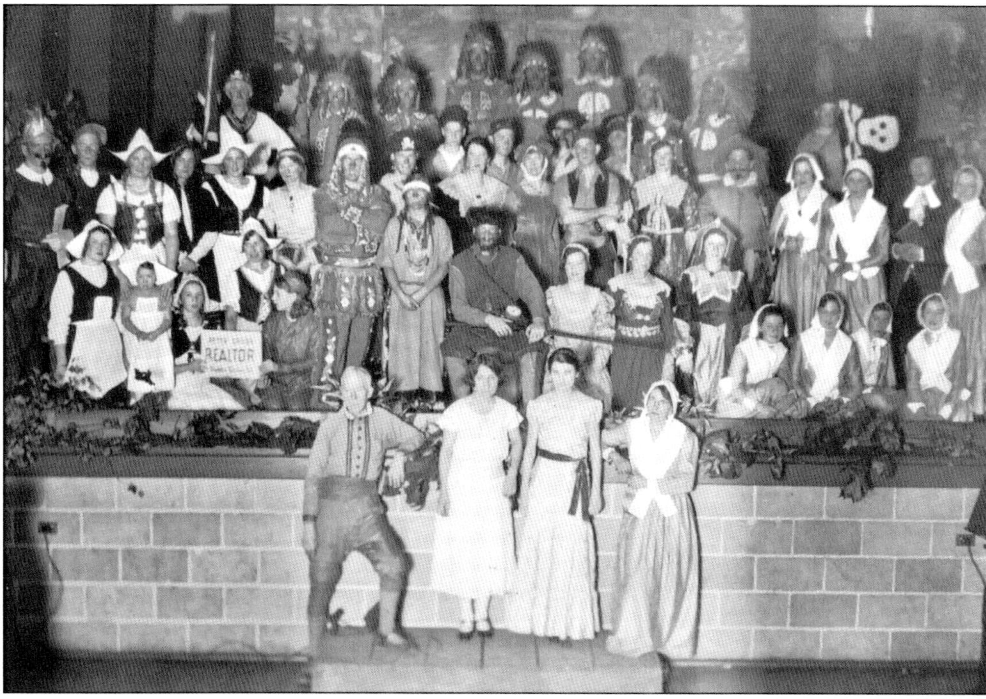

Frank Stephens's comic operetta *Grubb's Corner*, inspired by the works of Gilbert and Sullivan, was first produced at the Arden Gild Hall on October 29, 1932. Set in the 17th century on the banks of Naaman's Creek, the operetta chronicles attempts by Delaware explorers David de Vries, Lord Baltimore, William Penn, and others to steal land for King, Queen, and personal profit, only to be trumped in the end by realtor and land speculator Peter Grubb of Grubb's Corner. Standing on the lower level from left to right are Frank Stephens, author; Margaret Broadbent, pianist; Estella Hillersohn, director; and Jimmie Ware, stage manager.

On April 25, 1935, Eleanor Roosevelt visited Arden to talk with Frank Stephens about subsistence homesteading and the revival of handicrafts. In addition to the residents of Arden, she was met by representatives of Girl Scout Troop 12, who presented her with a bouquet of daffodils. Mrs. Roosevelt consented to pose for a photograph only on the condition that Troop 12 be included. She is seen here with Don Stephens on her right and Frank Stephens on her left.

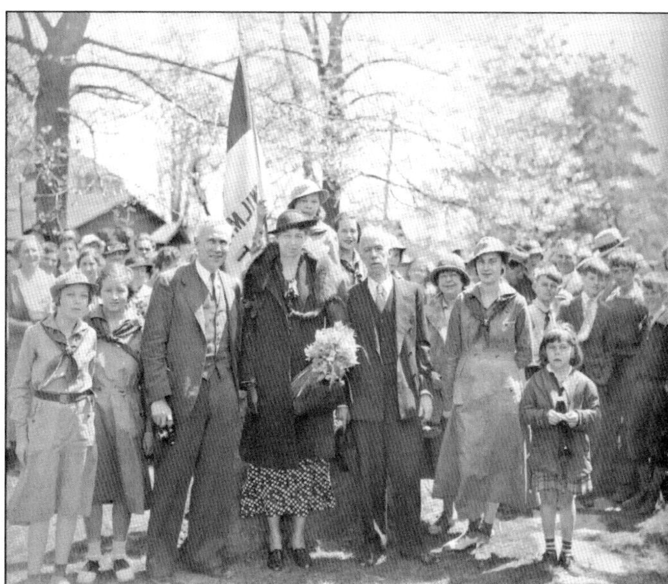

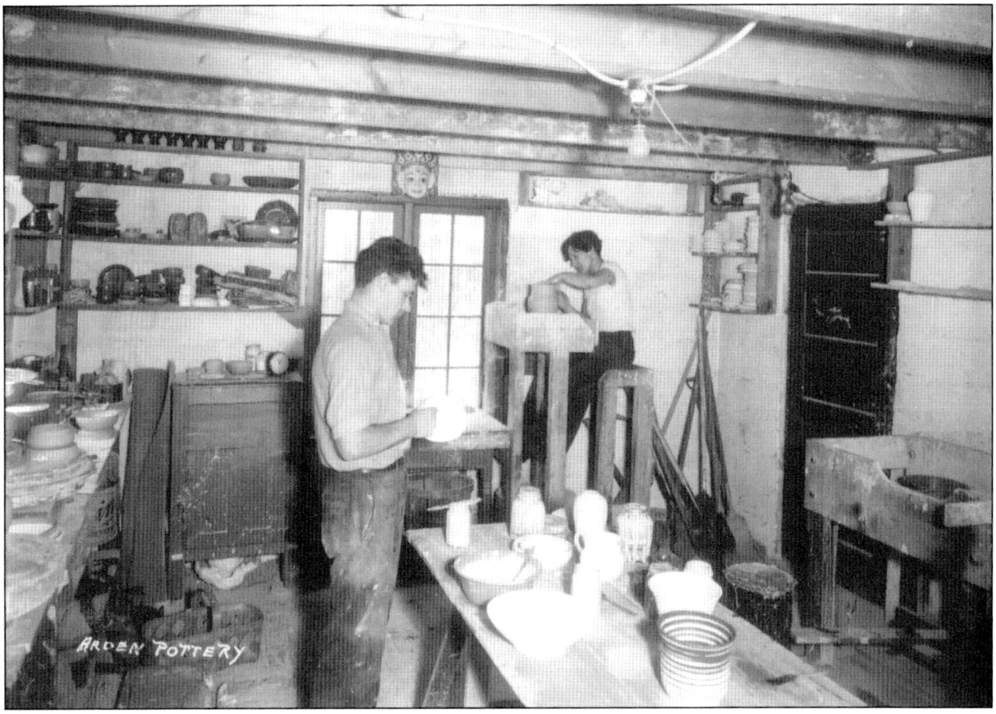

Although her first pottery studio was in the neighboring village of Ardentown, Miriam Hetzel is most associated with the studio she built in 1938 at the corner of Grubb's Road and Meadow Lane in Arden. In this photograph by Earl Brooks, Miriam works at the potter's wheel in the far corner of her studio, while fellow ceramist Don Harding applies glazes to pieces already finished.

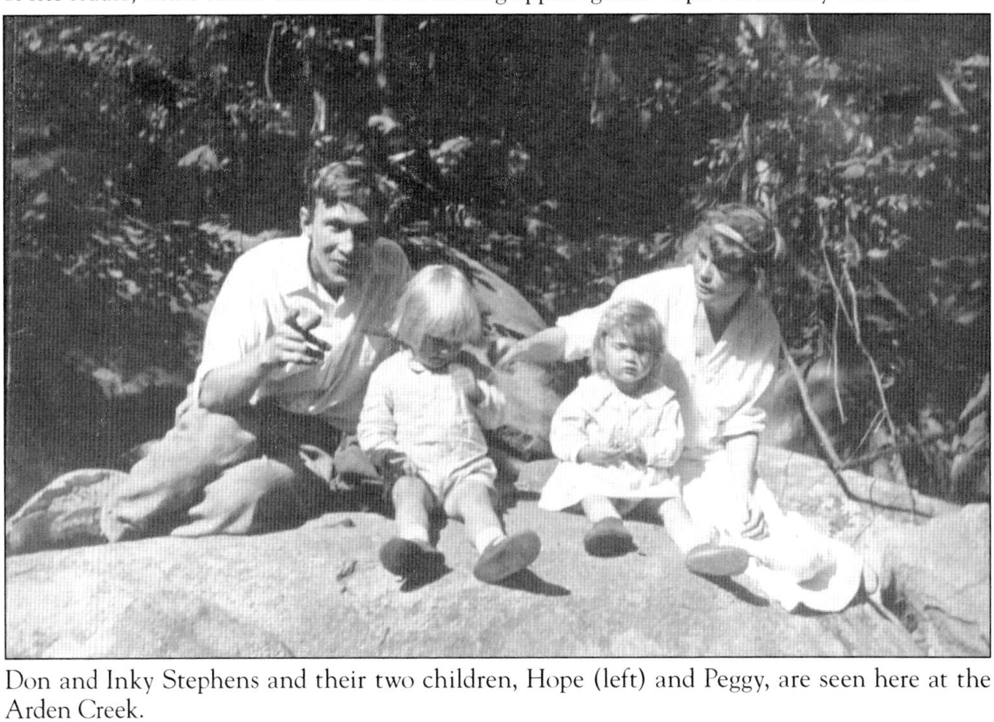

Don and Inky Stephens and their two children, Hope (left) and Peggy, are seen here at the Arden Creek.

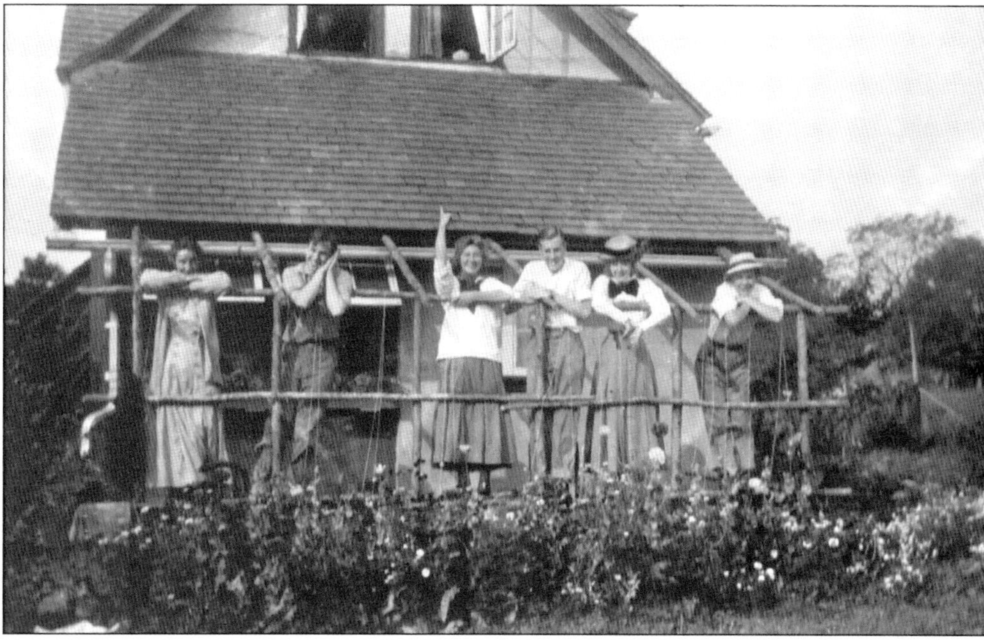

Our journey now at an end, our Arden friends bid us farewell. "If we meet again, why we shall smile." This photograph of the Bunch was taken in 1910.

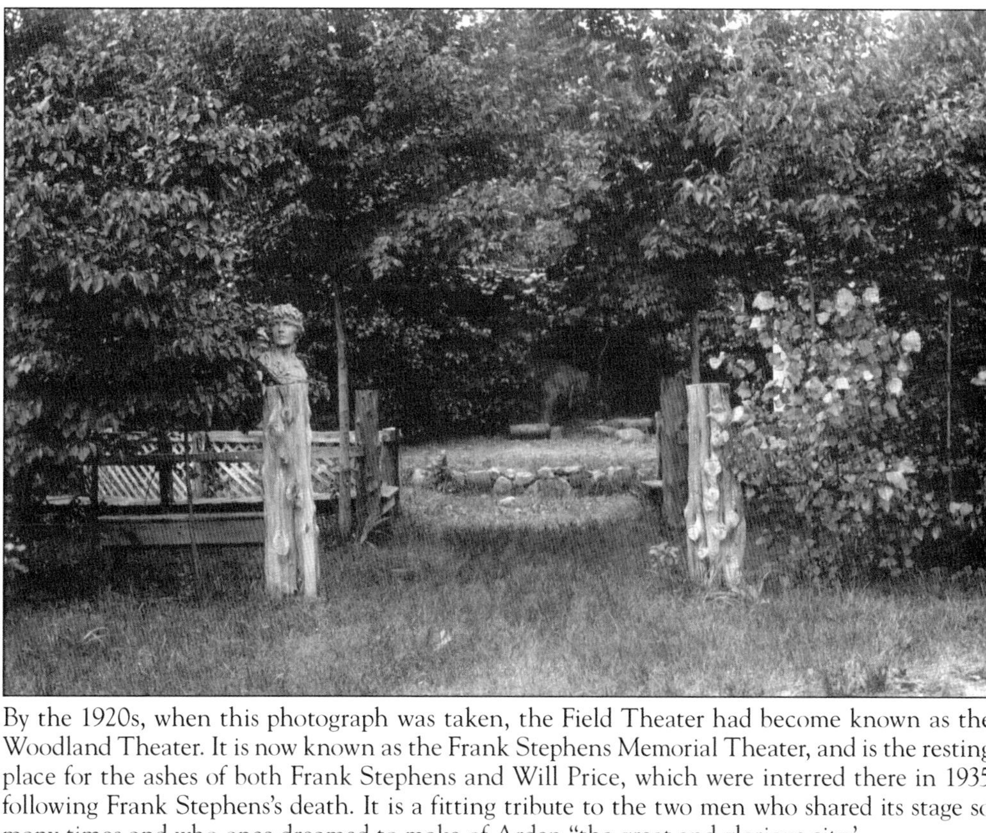

By the 1920s, when this photograph was taken, the Field Theater had become known as the Woodland Theater. It is now known as the Frank Stephens Memorial Theater, and is the resting place for the ashes of both Frank Stephens and Will Price, which were interred there in 1935 following Frank Stephens's death. It is a fitting tribute to the two men who shared its stage so many times and who once dreamed to make of Arden "the great and glorious city.'

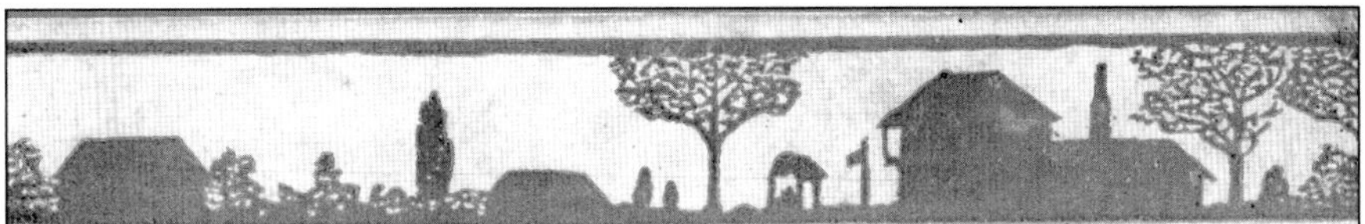

Arden Town.

WHEN Crickets sing and kine are homing,
And lanterned stars come seek the sun,
The village lights aslant the gloaming,
Come twinkling, twinkling, one by one.
O! night and sunset glow and starry splendor,
And cloud-wreathed eve, beneath thy silv'ry crown,
Ye give to me no guide so true and tender
As are the lights of Arden Town.

When wayward winds come back from straying
The wide world o'er, afar and long,
The woodland breezes cease from playing
To catch their rede and steal their song.
O! winds that woo the flowers and roam at pleasure,
Though far ye fared by dale and grassy down,
Ye know no song beside of that sweet measure
Ye taught the leaves by Arden Town

When days are drear and ways are weary,
And sad at heart we wanderers roam,
Light, tiny town thy beacons cheery,
O! whispering woodlands call us home.
For stars will shine again and day will brighten,
And rough roads smooth, that Love shall tread adown,
And evensong ring brave, and sad hearts lighten,
As hope leads home to Arden Town.

Frank Stephens

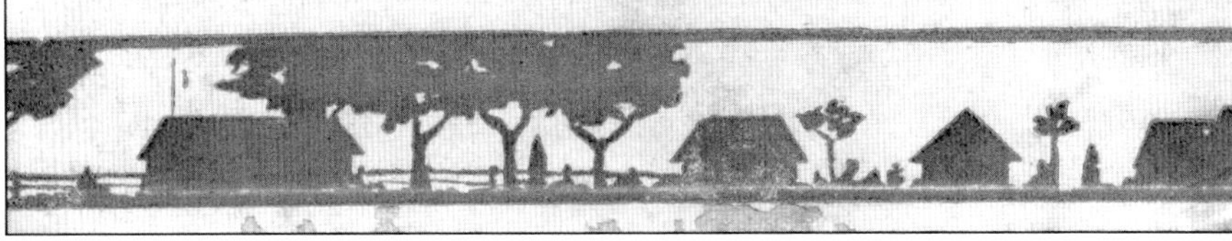

Adapted from a German folk song, the poem "Arden Town" was most likely written by Frank Stephens in 1908, as its first appearance in print is the January 1909 issue of *Arden Club Talk*. The card was printed by Fred Steinlein at the Arden Printery. The woodcut is by Don Stephens and depicts the buildings along Cherry Lane.

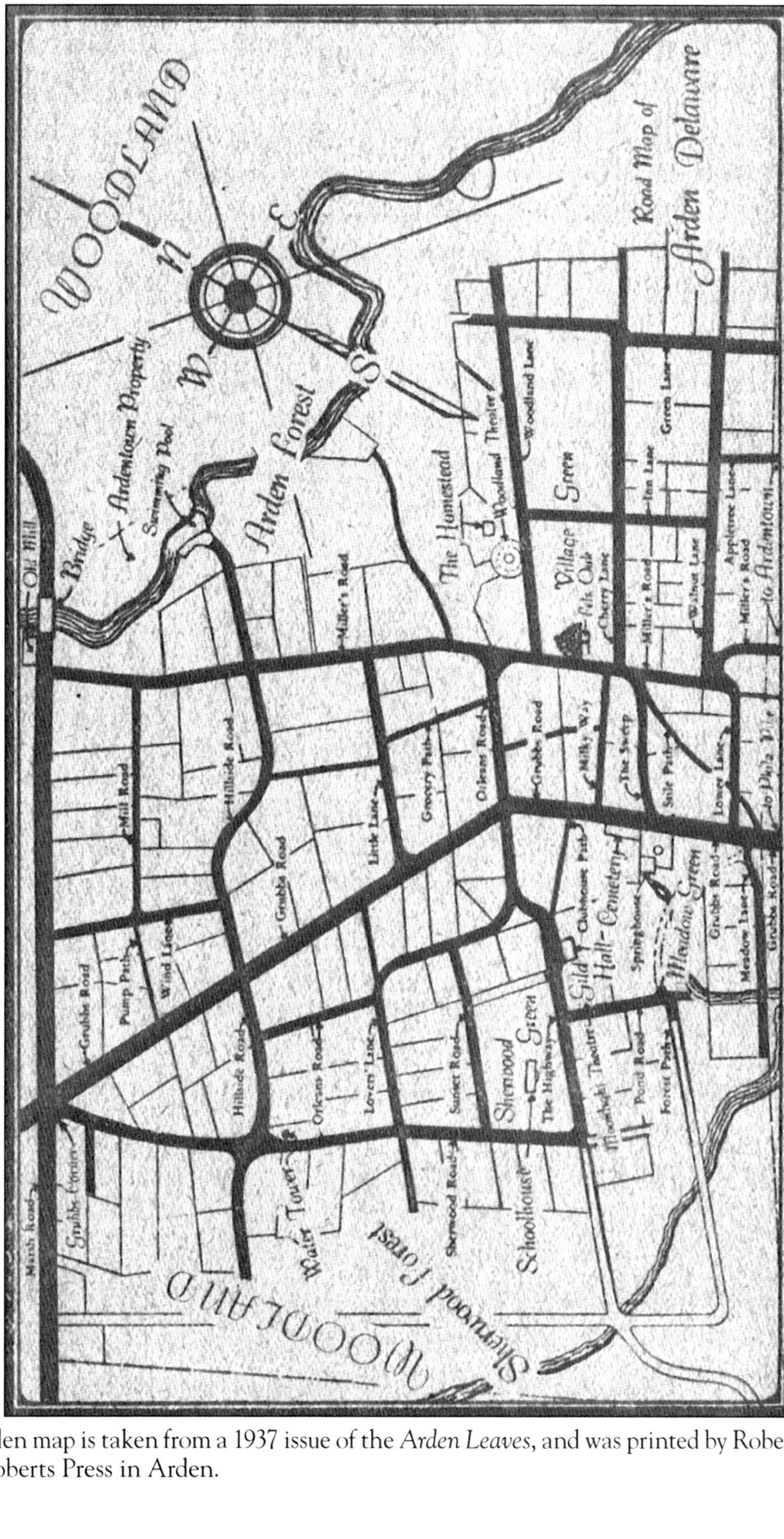

This Arden map is taken from a 1937 issue of the *Arden Leaves*, and was printed by Robert Roberts at the Roberts Press in Arden.